Introduction to Philosophy

HARPERCOLLINS COLLEGE OUTLINE

Introduction to Philosophy

Peter K. McInerney, Ph.D.
Oberlin College

HarperPerennial
A Division of HarperCollins*Publishers*

An American BookWorks Corporation Production

Project Manager: Mary Mooney
Editor: Thomas Quinn

Library of Congress Catalog Card Number: 91-58272
ISBN: 0-06-467124-0

01 00   ABW/RRD   20 19 18 17 16 15 14 13 12

Contents

Preface vii

1 Philosophy 1

2 God 9

3 Reality 23

4 Knowledge 37

5 Science 65

6 Mind 81

7 Persons 100

8 Freedom and Responsibility 114

9 The Good Life 131

10 Moral Theories 144

11 Foundations of Government 158

Glossary 171

Index of Philosophers 181

Selected Readings in Philosophy 183

Aristotle: *Nicomachean Ethics* 185

Plato: *The Republic* 196

Hume: *An Enquiry Concerning Human Understanding* 215

Descartes: *Meditations on First Philosophy* 220

Index 235

Preface

Introduction to Philosophy is designed to help students to understand the major issues and arguments of philosophy. It systematically examines all of the topics that are normally taught in a first course in philosophy at the college level. The book summarizes all of the current theories about each topic and provides all the basic arguments for and against each theory. I have avoided technical jargon and tried to make clear why people are so interested in these issues. In presenting the reasons for and against each position, I hope to encourage students to think for themselves.

The book is intended to serve as a study guide for students, to supplement standard introductory textbooks, and to introduce the general public to contemporary philosophy. It could be assigned by a professor to supplement the main text in a course. It would be a valuable supplement to primary sources or to introductory books of readings, because it outlines the major issues and arguments. It could also be used as a main text in an issue-oriented introductory course. Readers can also consult some original writings of Aristotle, Plato, Hume, and Descartes, in the "Selected Readings in Philosophy" section at the end of the book.

This book draws on ideas that have been developed throughout my entire career of teaching and discussing philosophy. I particularly want to acknowledge the help and support of my wife, my parents and family, and my colleagues, Robert Grimm, Norman Care, and Daniel Merrill.

Peter K. McInerney

1

Philosophy

We all have views about ultimate questions, whether or not we have thought about these views. In everyday life, we operate with conceptions of what it is to be real, how to find out what is true, how the mental is different from the physical, what is morally good or bad, and so on. We assume answers to all these philosophical issues without having to think explicitly about them.

PHILOSOPHICAL THINKING

Philosophy is the activity of thinking about ultimate questions and attempting to develop good, rational reasons for holding one particular position rather than another. There is no simple way to define what an ultimate question is, but in general such questions concern the basic features of our world and worldview. Philosophy investigates issues such as what it is to be real, what knowledge is, whether mind and matter are different, what the best way to live is, and whether God watches over the world. These issues provide the presupposed context for practical activities, for specialized sciences, and for the arts. Philosophy questions our basic assumptions and looks for reasons for that which is taken for granted. Literature, art, and religious teachings may explicitly consider some of these basic issues, but they rarely examine all of the reasons against as well as those for their preferred position.

Rational reasons for a position indicate or show that the position is accurate. They lend support to that position or serve as evidence for it. Evidence in a criminal trial is something that indicates that the accused is innocent or guilty. Evidence concerning claims to knowledge is something that indicates that the claim is true or false. Philosophy seeks objective evidence for the truth of claims about ultimate issues. Such evidence should hold for anyone who can comprehend it and considers it with an open mind. Thus, although some people may be more intellectually capable than others, philosophical positions are in principle available to anyone. No special revelation or social position is necessary to understand them; one need only be able to think and reason about the evidence.

In thinking about ultimate questions, philosophers try to make concepts and positions as clear as possible, in order to understand the exact meaning of the concepts and positions. Probably all of us have had the experience of finding that we actually agreed with someone with whom we had been arguing. The apparent disagreement turns out to be the result of meaning different things by the same words. Being clear about what we mean allows us to understand what the real differences are and what evidence would support one position rather than another. The analysis of concepts and clarification of positions helps to show how they are logically and conceptually connected with each other. Philosophers investigate whether two positions are consistent with each other, whether one presupposes or requires the other, and whether one makes the other more or less probable.

In their attempt to answer ultimate questions with the best supported position, philosophers have to consider all of the reasonable alternatives and provide strong reasons why one position is better than any of its competitors. For this reason, many philosophical discussions are like debates between alternative positions. Defenders of different philosophical positions try to show not only that there is solid evidence for their position, but also that there is more and better evidence for their position than for any of the alternatives.

DISPUTED ISSUES

You will notice that philosophy is different from most other subjects that you study. The study of history, psychology, mathematics, or chemistry involves learning established truths and how the truths were determined. Philosophy focuses on fundamental issues concerning which there is dispute. Philosophical issues cannot be directly settled by sense perception or experimentation, so that it is much more difficult to settle them conclusively.

For this reason, even introductory works in philosophy discuss the reasons for and against alternative positions, rather than teaching established philosophical truths.

However, it would be a serious error to conclude that philosophical positions are just different personal opinions and that any position is as good as any other. There have to be good rational reasons for any philosophical position, so that philosophers argue about only those alternatives for which they can make a reasonable case. Furthermore, at any given time, the evidence for one position may be stronger than that for any of the alternatives. Over a period of time, new distinctions, new arguments, and accumulating empirical evidence make some positions very implausible. This type of progress in philosophy may not be noticed, because once positions lose most of their support, they cease to be included among the reasonable alternatives that are discussed.

ACTIVITY AND RESULTS

Philosophical positions strongly affect how people think, feel, and act. For example, the belief that knowledge is impossible would make a career of pursuing scientific knowledge pointless, and the belief that moral behavior is more important than personal pleasure would affect a person's actions and judgments of other people. Given the importance of philosophical issues and the fact that most previous philosophers thought that they could prove their positions, the results of philosophical activity have been taken to be the most important aspect of philosophy. The value of thinking about philosophy has been thought to be in the knowledge or conclusions to be attained. Even if we cannot prove conclusions or determine, once and for all, what the total truth is, we can discover what the best current evidence indicates. Since we have to live in terms of some position, it is wise to accept the position for which there is currently the most support.

Some philosophers focus on the benefits of the activity of thinking and questioning, without expecting any definite answers. For them the main value of thinking about philosophy is that it makes us consider new possibilities, exercise our intellectual and imaginative abilities, and reflect on ordinary life and customs. The value of thinking about philosophy may lie both in its "deepening" of our ordinary thought and in the knowledge to be attained.

THE AREAS OF PHILOSOPHY

We can think philosophically about practically anything, but there are some traditional divisions of philosophic subject matter. The four traditional areas of philosophy are: logic, metaphysics, theory of knowledge, and ethics. Contemporary philosophy recognizes a large number of subject areas. Some of these are subdivisions of the four traditional areas, but others cut across the traditional divisions. The following are the most important fields of philosophy.

LOGIC

The study of the general structures of sound reasoning and good arguments.

METAPHYSICS (or ONTOLOGY)

The study of the basic categories and structures of what exists, or reality.

THEORY OF KNOWLEDGE (or EPISTEMOLOGY)

The study of the nature of knowledge and of how it can be achieved.

ETHICS (or MORAL PHILOSOPHY)

The study of how to live, of good and evil, of right and wrong, and of the principles of morality.

PHILOSOPHY OF NATURAL SCIENCE

The study of the basic categories of scientific reality (metaphysics) and of the methods for establishing scientific knowledge (epistemology).

PHILOSOPHY OF MIND

The study of the nature of mind, including what it is to be conscious, how we can know about our own and others' thoughts, and what the self and personal identity are.

PHILOSOPHY OF RELIGION

The study of the nature of God, of how we can know about God, and of the significance of religious practices.

SOCIAL AND POLITICAL PHILOSOPHY

The study of the fundamental principles of society and the state, including what the best form of government is.

PHILOSOPHY OF ART (or AESTHETICS)

The study of the basic principles of the appreciation of art, including what makes something a work of art and how we interpret it.

HISTORY OF PHILOSOPHY

The study of the major philosophies of different historical periods and of the influences on and effects of these philosophies.

PHILOSOPHY OF LANGUAGE

The study of the basic structure of language and of how language connects with the world.

PHILOSOPHY OF SOCIAL SCIENCE

The study of the basic categories of social scientific theories and of the methods for establishing social scientific knowledge.

Basic Logic

Philosophy is concerned with providing good reasons for positions. Since logic is the study of the general structures of sound reasoning and good arguments, it is a good idea to start the study of philosophy with some basic logic.

An argument is a sequence of statements, which are called "premises," that leads to a final statement, which is called "the conclusion." The premises are supposed to support the conclusion. They are supposed to be reasons for or evidence for the conclusion. Support is strongest when the conclusion can be deduced from the premises.

Deductive Logic

Deductive logic investigates the form of arguments in which the conclusion must be true if all of the premises are true. The form of an argument is the relationship between the types of statements that make it up. In logic the form of an argument is usually expressed using variables, such as P, Q, and X (see examples, p. 6). Variables are like blanks; each instance of the same variable is to be filled in by the same term. When the variables are filled in, statements result. Variables allow us to isolate the form of the argument without paying attention to the specific content. Regardless of whether we fill in *men, dogs,* or *stars* for each instance of the variable P in the first syllogism below, the form of the argument remains the same.

A valid argument is an argument whose form guarantees that its conclusion is true if its premises are true. An invalid argument is an argument whose form does not guarantee that its conclusion is true if its premises are true. Notice that the validity of a form of argument does not say whether the premises are true or false. Even if the premises are false, the argument can have a valid form. Similarly, an invalid form of argument just does not guarantee that the conclusion is true if the premises are true. It may be that the conclusion is true, but whether it is or is not can not be deduced from the truth of the premises.

The most familiar types of valid deductive arguments are called *syl-logisms*. Some examples of valid deductive arguments along with their forms are as follows:

(1) All *P*'s are *Q*'s.   All men are immortal.

    X is a *P*.   Woody Allen is a man.

    Therefore, *X* is a *Q*.   Therefore, Woody Allen is immortal.

(2) If *P*, then *Q*.   If the rock hits the window,
                             the window breaks.

    P.   The rock hits the window.

    Therefore, *Q*.   Therefore, the window breaks.

(3) If *P*, then *Q*.   If the rock hits the window,
                             the window breaks.

    Not *Q*.   The window does not break.

    Therefore, not *P*.   Therefore, the rock does not
                             hit the window.

Valid arguments "pass on" the truth of their premises to their conclusion. An argument that both has a valid form and has true premises is called a "sound" argument. The conclusion of a sound argument is true, because its form guarantees that the conclusion is true if the premises are true (validity), and its premises are true. The argument that is an instance of deductive argument 1 (above) has a valid form, but people would disagree as to whether it is sound or not, because they would disagree about the truth of its first premise.

Fallacies are invalid arguments that are easily mistaken for valid arguments because their forms are somewhat similar. Here are two fallacies whose forms are easily mistaken for arguments 2 and 3 above.

(1) If *P*, then *Q*.   If the rock hits the window,
                             the window breaks.

    Q.   The window breaks.

    Therefore, *P*.   Therefore, the rock hits the window.

(2) If *P*, then *Q*.   If the rock hits the window,
                             the window breaks.

    Not *P*.   The rock does not hit the window.

    Therefore, not *Q*.   Therefore, the window does not break.

As you can see from the arguments next to the forms of the fallacies, the conclusions of these fallacies are not by themselves always false. The point is that the truth of the premises does not guarantee the truth of the conclusion. In the case of the example of (1), we know one way that the window can break (according to the first premise, the rock's hitting it can break the window). We also know that the window breaks (second premise). However, there are other ways that the window can break. Hence, from the fact that the window breaks, it is not absolutely necessary that the rock hits it.

Inductive Logic

Inductive arguments have two features: true premises provide support for the conclusion but do not guarantee it; and the conclusion contains information that is not in the premises. Drawing a general conclusion from a number of individual cases is the most common form of inductive argument. For example, from our observation that every dog we have seen has four legs, we may form the generalization that all dogs have four legs. This generalization contains the new information that all dogs, not just the ones we have seen, have four legs. Our observations do provide support for this conclusion, but they do not guarantee its truth, because there is new information (all dogs) in the conclusion that is not in the premises.

Inductive arguments are the most important way of forming views about the world. Their conclusions are not absolutely necessitated by their premises even if all the premises are true, but true premises can provide strong support for the conclusion. Deductive arguments either prove their conclusions or do not. Inductive arguments can provide stronger or weaker support for their conclusions. In forming general conclusions from individual cases, it is important to work from a relatively large number of individual cases that are as varied as possible—a random sample. More cases and more varied cases provide stronger support for a conclusion about all cases. It is also important to limit the conclusion as much as possible. From the observation that every dog that you have seen has four legs, it is better to draw a conclusion about "all dogs" than to draw a conclusion about "all pets." After an inductive conclusion is drawn, it is a good idea to treat it as an "hypothesis" that can be tested by further sampling. (See chapter 4.)

***P**hilosophy is the activity of thinking about ultimate questions and attempting to develop good, rational reasons for holding one particular position rather than another. Philosophy seeks objective evidence for the truth of claims about ultimate issues. Philosophers try to make concepts and positions as clear as possible in order to understand exactly what is meant by them. The analysis of concepts and clarification of positions helps to show how they are logically and conceptually connected with each other. Many philosophical discussions are like debates between alternative positions.*

Philosophy discusses the reasons for and against alternative positions on fundamental issues that cannot be directly settled by sense perception or experimentation. The value of thinking about philosophy may lie both in the knowledge to be attained and in the expanded use of our minds.

The most important areas of philosophy are logic, metaphysics, theory of knowledge, ethics, philosophy of natural science, philosophy of mind, philosophy of religion, social and political philosophy, philosophy of art, history of philosophy, philosophy of language, and philosophy of social science.

Logic is the study of the general structures of sound reasoning and good arguments. An argument is a sequence of statements that leads to a conclusion. Deductive logic investigates the form of arguments in which the conclusion must be true if all of the premises are true. A valid argument has a form that guarantees that its conclusion is true if its premises are true. A sound argument has a valid form and true premises. Fallacies are invalid arguments that are easily mistaken for valid arguments because their forms are somewhat similar.

Inductive arguments have two features: True premises provide support for the conclusion but do not guarantee it; and the conclusion contains information that is not in the premises. In forming general conclusions from individual cases, it is important to work from a large and varied sample and to limit the conclusion.

Selected Readings

Edwards, Paul (ed.). *The Encyclopedia of Philosophy* (8 volumes). New York: Macmillan & Free Press, 1967.

Fogelin, Robert. *Understanding Arguments, 2nd Edition*. New York: Harcourt Brace Jovanovich, 1982.

Salmon, Merrillee. *Introduction to Logic and Critical Thinking*. New York: Harcourt Brace Jovanovich, 1984.

Woodhouse, Mark. *A Preface to Philosophy, 2nd Edition*. Belmont, CA: Wadsworth, 1980.

2

God

God provides the meaning of life for religious people. Everything has a purpose because of God. God is the source of morality and of the order of the physical world. There have been many different ideas about gods and goddesses throughout history. The major Western religions—Judaism, Christianity, and Islam—share the conception that there is only one God who is self-existent, personal, all-powerful, all-knowing, and all-good. Is there any reason to believe that such a God exists? This chapter examines the major arguments for and against the existence of this God, as well as the claim that faith in God without proof is the best that humans can do.

GOD'S NATURE

What do we mean when we think or talk about God? Although God's complete nature may not be fully knowable by limited intellects, there are characteristics that distinguish God from other things. These characteristics allow people to think of God in some way. Without some characterization of God, there would be no way for people to conceive of God. The main traditions of Judaism, Christianity, and Islam conceive of God in the following way.

SINGULAR

Judaism, Christianity, and Islam all maintain that there is only one God (monotheism), in contrast with the multiple gods (polytheism) of many religions; for example, early Egyptian, Greek, and Roman religions. All of the powers and features of the divine are unified in one God, rather than being distributed among several gods.

SELF-EXISTENT

The one God is not dependent upon anything else for existence. God is not caused or sustained in existence by anything else. God is his (or her) own source of existence or is self-caused.

ETERNAL

God is either totally outside time (timeless), or always has been and always will be. God cannot come into or go out of existence.

CREATOR

God creates and preserves all things. Matter, minds, and any other type of thing that exists all depend upon God for their existence. God brings everything into existence and keeps the created world in existence.

TRANSCENDENT

God is distinct from creation. The created world is not all there is to God. Although God is present in some way throughout the universe, God also exists beyond the universe.

ALL-POWERFUL (OMNIPOTENT)

As the creator and preserver of the universe, God is able to do anything that can be done. God has the power to do anything that is not self-contradictory. Not being able to do self-contradictory tasks is no limitation on God's power, because these self-contradictory "things" are not really coherent things that could be done.

ALL-KNOWING (OMNISCIENT)

God knows everything that ever has or will happen in any part of the universe, including what goes on in our minds. God knows our most secret thoughts. God even knows what, to us, is in the future.

PERSONAL

God is like a human being in having an intellect and a will. Rather than being a totally detached force, God is concerned about what happens in the world, particularly about what happens to humans. God watches over human events. God is beyond biological categories and, therefore, officially neither male nor female, although the human trait of maleness has frequently been projected onto God.

ALL-GOOD

God is perfectly good and is the source of morality. Humans cannot fully understand all of God's purposes, but God always does what is right.

HOLY

God is holy and sacred; therefore, God deserves our worship. God inspires awe in humans.

The major non-Western religions—Hinduism, Buddhism, Taoism, and Confucianism—conceive of God differently or do not include a supreme being at all.

ARGUMENTS FOR THE EXISTENCE OF GOD

There are many reasons that have led people to believe that the God of this nature exists. Because God's characteristics are different from those of ordinary physical objects, God cannot be perceived or detected in ordinary ways. For example, God normally cannot be seen, touched, or found on radar. For this reason philosophers and theologians have attempted to prove the existence of God from his (or her) effect on the universe or from his nature. The three main arguments are the argument from design, the first-cause argument, and the ontological argument. Some religious thinkers believe that the combination of these arguments, along with other evidence, such as the occurrence of miracles and religious experience, show conclusively that God exists.

The Argument from Design (Teleological Argument)

The basic idea of the argument from design relies on analogy. The complex order of the universe requires a designer and creator just as a watch, for instance, requires a watchmaker. The complex order of the universe is taken to be highly unlikely or improbable; so that the universe could not exist without an intelligent and beneficent creator of this order. There are different versions of the argument that emphasize different features of the order of the universe. The most common version, such as the "fifth way" that Saint Thomas Aquinas (1225–1274) proved God's existence, relies on the common observation that many things in nature operate so as to accomplish a goal (*telos* in Greek) even though they do not have such a goal in mind. For example, some insects lay their eggs in a location which does not have food for the young at that time, but which will have food at the time the eggs hatch. Another popular illustration of this goal-directedness (teleology) is the way natural resources, plants, insects, and animals are interdependent in an ecosystem. The activity of each part affects the others, and each part can operate properly only if the other parts operate properly. Each seems to be contributing to the common goal, but clearly none of them has this goal in mind.

Some versions of the argument from design emphasize the basic physical order that is necessary for life, and particularly human life, to be possible on earth. If the earth were much closer or farther from the sun, or if the physical constants of the universe were significantly different, human life could not have arisen at all. The conditions that are necessary for living things to exist and to develop might, according to scientific laws, never have existed. According to scientific laws, many other conditions that would not have allowed life to develop might have occurred instead. The extreme improbability of the conditions that support life indicates that a beneficent power must have created the universe to be favorable to life.

Objections and Replies

The usual counterargument to the first version of the argument from design is that evolution has shaped organisms to operate so as to accomplish goals which they do not have in mind. According to evolutionary theory, genetic changes occur in random members of the population of a type of organism. Some of these genetic changes produce behavior—such as feeding more effectively, being able to attract more mating partners, or providing better care for offspring—that, in their environment, allows these organisms to produce more offspring that are themselves more likely to survive and reproduce. Over long periods of time, the organisms with this revised set of genes become the dominant population. Through natural selection, organisms acquire ways of operating that promote their "reproductive success," even though they do not understand what they are doing. Evolution, not God, produces the apparent design.

A second common objection to the argument from design is that the complex order of the universe is as much like the order within an organism as it is like that of a watch or clock. Organisms are born from parents, not designed and created by someone. Hence, as David Hume (1711–1776) argued, there is at least as much reason to think that the current order of the universe was "born out of" some previous order (or "parent universes") as there is to think that it was designed and created by God. Even if this order were designed and created by an intelligent being, that being need not be all-powerful, all-good, and so on. In myths and science-fiction stories, an inferior god, who is one amongst many, or a very powerful but finite being designs and creates the universe that we know.

The second version of the argument from design, that a beneficent power must have designed the universe to be favorable to life, has proven to be more difficult to refute conclusively. The main counterargument is that chains of explanation must stop somewhere, so that some original facts do not have any further reason for being as they are. Something has to explain other things without itself being explained. For theists, the unexplained explainer is God. For others the unexplained explainers are the basic physical features of the universe or the primeval explosion, the "big bang," at the beginning of the universe that formed the physical features. There is no further explanation why these are the way they are, rather than some other way that would not support life. From our perspective, it may appear that there was a "grand plan" leading up to human life, but this is just a case of inflating our own importance. We may be inclined to think that the basic physical features of the universe exist for our sake, but in reality we are just one type of being in the universe without any special significance for its origin or nature. Our thinking that the physical features of the universe exist for our sake is like the grand winner of a state lottery thinking that everything was somehow arranged so that their number would be picked.

Supporters of the argument from design respond that this objection leaves too much unexplained. They claim that God is a self-explainer, rather than an unexplained explainer (see the second version of the first-cause argument). In the case of random numbers, we know why they occur randomly. However, in the case of the basic physical features of the universe, we do not know why any of them occurs. God is an explanation for this.

The First Cause Argument (Cosmological Argument)

There are really *two* distinct types of argument that involve different senses of "first cause." One concerns antecedent causation and argues for a first cause of the universe in time. The second concerns the dependent existence of the whole complex series of causes and effects composing the universe, and argues for a necessary, self-existent, and independent being to account for this.

FIRST ANTECEDENT CAUSE

The argument that God is the first cause of the universe in time relies on two notions: (a) The passage of time is an intrinsic part of causation. Present events are caused by earlier states of the universe that were just present, and these were caused by even earlier states of the universe that were once present, and so on; (b) An infinite series cannot be completed. Each member cannot be "run through" up to a final member. For example, if we start counting "1, 2, 3, 4 . . . ," we cannot reach a final member of the natural numbers. The series of natural numbers is an infinite series.

Combining these two notions, the first antecedent cause argument claims that because of the passage of time in causation, there could not have been an infinite series of causes preceding the present. There must have been a first cause to start the *finite* series of causes that leads up to the present. Otherwise, the present could never be reached, because to do so would be to complete an infinite series (this would be like reaching zero by counting the negative integers). God is this first cause of the universe.

This argument attempts to prove that there must have been a first cause because the assumption that there was no first cause produces a contradiction, as shown below.

(1) There was no first cause.

(2) If there were no first cause, the series of antecedent causes would be infinite.

(3) The series of antecedent causes is infinite (from 1 and 2).

(4) Causation proceeds from earlier states to later states (from notion (a) above).

(5) There was an infinite series of antecedent causes proceeding up to the present (from statements 3 and 4).

(6) This infinite series of antecedent causes has been completed. Each member has been passed through in order to reach the present (from statement 5 and notion (a)).

(7) An infinite series cannot be completed, from notion (b).

(8) Statements 6 and 7 contradict each other.

FIRST EXPLAINING CAUSE

This argument claims that the universe requires a necessary and self-existent being, God, to explain its existence. The argument relies on the principle that the existence of any thing or positive fact must have an explanation or source. This is called the Principle of Sufficient Reason. According to this principle, nothing exists just arbitrarily or "by chance"; there is a sufficient reason why anything exists.

The basic structure of the first explaining cause argument is as follows.

(1) Ordinary things and facts are dependent beings that need not have existed; they are contingent—non-necessary—beings.

(2) An ultimate explanation or source of the existence of these contingent beings is required.

(3) This ultimate source must be a necessary and self-existent being.

(4) God is the only necessary and self-existent being.

There have been many somewhat different forms of this argument that a necessary and self-existent being explains the existence of the universe. The versions of the argument that have been most frequently used since the eighteenth century hold, not that there cannot be an infinite regress of dependent beings, but that the totality of dependent beings needs a source or cause. The existence of dependent beings itself needs an explanation. The source or cause of the totality of dependent beings—even if there is an infinite number of these, each causing another—must be a nondependent being that is its own source or cause. This self-existent being exists necessarily because its existence is accounted for by its own nature. This is God, who is his (or her) own sufficient reason.

Objections and Replies

The major objection to both types of the first-cause argument is that a physical state or occurrence, rather than God, could be the "first cause." Since the arguments involve only the "first cause" of the universe, and do not involve all of God's characteristics, such as being personal and holy, something other than God (as earlier defined) could be this first cause. The first cause of the universe in time might be the original existence of or, according to the "big bang" theory, the explosion of matter. The necessary and self-existent being might be matter-energy, which cannot be created or destroyed, or, in classical atomic theory, indestructible atoms. Whatever the specifics of the scientific explanation, the "first cause" would not be the traditional God.

Defenders of both types of the first-cause argument reply that these physical states and occurrences are too similar to other physical facts to be the first cause. Defenders claim that the same issues should arise about these supposed scientific first causes. Did something precede and cause the "big bang"? Why does matter-energy exist? The first cause, according to the defenders, must be different in type from the facts that it explains.

The first antecedent cause argument claims that, because of the passage of time in causation, there could not have been an infinite series of causes preceding the present. There must have been a first cause to start the series of causes that leads up to the present. Objections to this argument, other than the one mentioned above, attack the notions that the passage of time is an intrinsic part of causation and that an infinite series cannot be completed. Critics claim that the passage of time is not an intrinsic part of causation, so that the series of causes does not "move toward" the present. The series of causes exists statically, in a time that is like space. This objection depends upon time being unchanging. Time does not pass in this conception (although it may seem to us that it passes). In opposition to the claim that an infinite series cannot be completed, critics claim that an infinite series can be completed in an infinite time. An infinite task can be performed in an infinite amount of time.

Another objection to the argument that the universe requires a necessary and self-existent being (God) to explain it resembles one of the objections to the argument from design. Some critics deny the Principle of Sufficient Reason. They claim that chains of explanation must stop somewhere, so that some original facts do not have any further reason for being as they are. These original facts are not necessary and self-caused; they just are. Thus, God is not necessary.

The Ontological Argument

The basic idea of the ontological argument is that existence is part of the nature of the greatest or most perfect being (God). Therefore, it follows from God's nature that God exists. Existence is one of the features that makes God the most perfect being. Saint Anselm (1033–1109) was the first to develop a version of the ontological argument:

(1) God is that than which nothing greater can be thought.

(2) If God did not exist, we could think of something greater than God, namely, a being with all the same characteristics who did exist.

(3) Therefore, God must exist.

Descartes's (1596–1650) formulation of the ontological argument makes explicit some features that are part of the background for Anselm's argument:

(1) Everyone, even the atheist, has the idea of the most perfect being (God).

(2) The most perfect being must have all perfections.

(3) To exist in reality is greater than to exist merely as an idea in the mind.

(4) Therefore, the most perfect being (God) must exist in reality, as well as exist as an idea in the mind.

Objections and Replies

Most philosophers reject the ontological argument on the grounds that a mere definition or a concept cannot establish that there is any instance of that definition or concept. Even if it is the most perfect being's (God's) nature to exist, the question remains whether there is anything that is the most perfect being.

Immanuel Kant's (1724–1804) famous objection to the ontological argument was that existence is not a predicate. He claimed that the ontological argument treats existence as a quality or predicate of a thing, whereas the qualities that compose something's nature are different from whether or not something of that nature exists. Having four legs is a quality of dogs. Existing is not a quality of dogs. That dogs exist is a fact, but their existence is something different from the qualities that define what it is to be a dog. Defenders of the ontological argument respond that this distinction is not clear.

A contemporary of Anselm's, Gaunilo, tried to show that Anselm's argument was absurd because it could be modified to show that any "most perfect thing" (such as "the island than which none greater can be thought") exists. Anselm responded that his argument applied only to "the most perfect being" (in all respects), not to specific types of being, such as island, human, or carrot.

Another objection to the ontological argument is that it is not obvious that existence is a perfection. In the case of horrible, evil, painful, or ugly things, it seems that to exist in reality is not greater than existing merely as an idea in the mind. Defenders of the ontological argument respond that, at least in the case of good things, existence is a perfection.

ARGUMENTS AGAINST THE EXISTENCE OF GOD

The Problem of Evil

The traditional and most common argument against the existence of God is that an all-powerful and all-good God could not permit so much suffering and hardship in the world. People die horribly from starvation, fires, and diseases. Innocent children suffer through no fault of their own. That there is such evil in the world seems to be inconsistent with the existence of the traditional all-powerful and all-good God. The problem of evil is stated in the following argument:

(1) There is evil in the world.

(2) If God has the power to prevent this evil but chooses not to, God is not all-good.

(3) If God wants to prevent this evil but cannot, God is not all-powerful.

(4) Therefore, an all-powerful and all-good God does not exist.

Objections and Replies

The standard objection to the problem of evil is that evil does not really exist, or if it does exist, it is necessary for a greater good. What appears to us to be evil is really something that makes the world a better place. If we view the apparent evil from a broad perspective, we can frequently appreciate how it really contributes to a better world. We can divide the apparent evil into that portion caused by human action and that portion caused by nature—natural catastrophes, diseases, limited resources, and so on. The portion of apparent evil that is caused by human action is a necessary price for humans' free will. Free will is a good thing, but it means that humans can choose to harm other people or may harm them unintentionally. It is better that humans have free will and be free to act so as to produce evil result, than that they not have free will and be constrained to act so as to produce only good results. The price of the greater good, free will, is that some evil acts and evil consequences occur.

The evil that is caused by nature also contributes to a better world. This apparent evil provides an environment in which humans can use their free will to face up to hardships, to be charitable to others, and to be moral. If we lived in an earthly paradise with no natural evil, there would be no temptations to do wrong and no occasions to develop our moral character. The apparent evil of the natural world forces us to make these difficult choices. From a larger perspective, the apparent evil of the natural environment can be seen to help humans to develop. Even in this life we are ultimately better off because of this "evil." Religious thinkers argue that we are infinitely better off if "natural evil" promotes eternal salvation.

The critical reply to this objection is that there need not be so much evil in the world. An all-powerful and all-good God would limit evil to the absolute minimum. God could allow people to choose freely to do evil and then intervene to prevent the evil. God could provide other, less painful, occasions for humans to use their free will. That God does not minimize pain and hardship shows that the traditional God does not exist.

God as a Human Creation

Many atheists argue that there is good reason to think that God is nothing but a human creation. Humans have created the idea of God, but usually do not realize that what they think of as God is a figment of human imagination. Ludwig Feuerbach (1804–1872) and Karl Marx (1818–1883) claimed that, in response to the deficiencies of their lives in this world, humans unconsciously project an idealized form of human nature into another world. The idea of God comes from our idea of humans, but it makes up for all our limitations, frustrations, and imperfect ways of living with each other (alienation). Like the reading of romance novels and works of fantasy, belief in God is an escape from reality, "the opiate of the people." Marx claimed that if humans improve their material and social conditions, they will have no more use for the idea of God.

The theory that humans create the idea of God, and that this idea serves various purposes in this world, is an alternative explanation of the origin and continuation of the widespread human belief in some type of higher being. Humans, not God, are the source of our idea of God. This theory does not attempt to prove that God cannot exist. Rather, it tries to explain why people believe in higher beings, even though such beings do not exist. To support the human creation theory, defenders point out that it explains why different cultures and historical periods have had different conceptions of God, gods, goddesses, demons, and spirits. For example, Friedrich Nietzsche (1844–1900) claimed that we can see how the Hebrews' idea of God changed according to their material and social conditions. When the Hebrews were conquerors of Israel, they had a strong warrior god, but when they were enslaved by the Assyrians and the Romans, they developed a more peace-loving and otherworldly God, which eventually gave rise to the Christian "God of love" (and weakness).

Objections and Replies

Opponents of the human creation theory generally admit that conceptions of God have been influenced by the material, social, and historical conditions of the people who have had those conceptions. This is why ideas of God have been different. Nevertheless, they claim that all these different ideas are directed toward the one true God, who is inaccurately portrayed by most, perhaps all, of them. Some conceptions are more accurate than others because they better reveal the independently existing God. Humans can make progress in their understanding of this real God, just as they can make progress in other areas of knowledge. Humans can develop better, though always imperfect, conceptions of God. Critics reply that there is no objective evidence for the accuracy of any of these conceptions of God.

RELIGIOUS EXPERIENCE AND FAITH

Some religious thinkers claim that to consider God's existence in terms of intellectual proofs is an overly detached and "objective" approach. Such thinkers emphasize a more personal approach that utilizes our whole being, including our emotions and special intuitive abilities.

Religious Experience

Throughout history, there have been many people who have had religious and mystical experiences. Many of them consider their experiences to be a direct revelation of God. Although God cannot normally be perceived through sight, hearing, smell, taste, or touch, people who have had religious experiences claim that they have been aware of God's presence through a special intuition or perception. Mystical experiences are a communion with God. This "merging" with God is something totally different from our everyday interactions with physical objects. For this reason, communion with God cannot be easily described in everyday language, but it nevertheless happens. An all-powerful God should certainly be able to reveal his (or her) divine nature to humans, despite their limitations.

Critics do not deny that people have these experiences, but they argue that they are hallucinations. Critics claim that mystical experiences are delusions that are psychologically influenced by the person's antecedent beliefs and religious background. Using the human creation theory, critics point to the differences between people's supposed revelations of the one God and to the impossibility of checking these "perceptions" by other evidence.

Faith

One meaning of "faith" is "confident belief." With respect to God, faith is frequently contrasted with knowing, so that faith means "confident belief without the ordinary types of evidence." Through such faith people commit themselves to God without any of the objective reasons they might have for believing in everyday facts.

Religious thinkers have attempted to justify this faith in several different ways. Some claim that in the face of uncertainty about God's existence, even a slight chance of eternal reward or punishment should outweigh the benefits in this life of disobeying God's commands. Because it would be eternal, reward or punishment in an afterlife should be given more importance than temporary benefits in this life. According to Blaise Pascal's (1623–1662) Wager, it is in people's rational self-interest to do whatever they can to get themselves to believe sincerely in God. This is because an infinite reward or punishment multiplied by the finite probability that one will receive that reward or punishment is greater than the finite benefits of an irreligious life multiplied by the much higher probability that one will receive those benefits. A weighing of the risks and rewards shows that it is prudent to believe, so that people should try to get themselves to believe. Critics reply that one cannot know the probability of receiving any reward or punishment after death.

Another defense of faith is that people live better in this life with faith rather than without it. Faith brings emotional rewards, such as a sense of contentment, security, and joy. The absence of faith, on the other hand, is likely to produce a sense of meaninglessness and insignificance (see The Meaning of Life, below).

A third type of justification is the claim that God is basically mysterious. Because God is so different from humans and the natural world, people should not expect to know God by rational means. As Sören Kierkegaard (1813–1855) emphasized, all humans can do is commit themselves to the mysterious God; humans must take the blind "leap of faith." Critics reply that if God were so mysterious, humans could have no idea about God's nature and would have no way to determine what God wants humans to do.

THE MEANING OF LIFE

Even for the nondevout religious believer, God provides the answer to all ultimate questions. God has designed an order into the universe. God has decreed objective values, so that there are objectively right and wrong ways to live. God cares about humanity in general, so that history is significant. God cares about each of us individually, so that our lives are significant.

The loss of belief in God, or its absence in the first place, can produce a sense that life is meaningless. Existential philosophers have explored this crisis of meaninglessness. Without God, the universe may seem to have no ultimate order or rational unifying principle. Without God, there may seem to be no objective values, so that any action or way of living is as good as any other. Without God, human history and our own individual lives are of no significance for the universe at large. Nothing we do will have any impact on the immense and everlasting universe. The individual feels alone and adrift.

For religious existentialists, such as Kierkegaard, this experience can lead us back to faith in God. According to Kierkegaard's "existential dialectic," there are problems that cannot be solved in any value system that does not rely on God. Problems such as the meaninglessness of life and the uncertainty about the correct values cannot force us to believe, but we can find ultimate answers to such problems only through faith in God.

Atheistic existentialists, such as Nietzsche, Albert Camus (1913–1960), and Jean-Paul Sartre (1905–1980), have offered a different solution. They claim that humans can recover from the "death of God" or the "absurd" by creating their own values and significance. Humans must have the courage to accept their place as a mere part of the natural world. By accepting the fact that this earthly life is all there is, humans can go on to make earthly life important and valuable. By developing their personal strength, humans can lead fulfilled and even joyous lives without God.

*T*he main traditions of Judaism, Christianity, and Islam share the conception that there is only one God, who is self-existent, eternal, the creator of all things, transcendent, all-powerful, all-knowing, personal, all-good, and holy.

Because God's characteristics cannot be perceived or detected in ordinary ways, philosophers and theologians have attempted to prove the existence of God. The argument from design claims that the complex order of the universe is highly unlikely and could not exist without an intelligent and beneficent creator. Critics respond that something other than God could be the source of this order, or that the order may have no source.

There are two distinct types of the first-cause argument. One claims that because of the passage of time in causation, there could not have been an infinite series of causes preceding the present. There must have been a first cause (God) to start the finite series of causes that leads up to the present. The other first-cause argument claims that a necessary and self-existent being (God) is necessary to explain the existence of the universe, because the universe need not have existed. Critics respond that something other than God could be the first cause, or that there might be an infinite regress of causes.

The ontological argument claims that existence is part of the nature of the greatest or most perfect being (God), so that it follows from God's nature that God exists. Critics respond that a mere definition or concept cannot establish that there is any instance of that definition or concept.

The existence of evil in the world has been taken to show that the traditional God does not exist. If God has the power to prevent this evil but chooses not to, God is not all-good. If God wants to prevent this evil but cannot, God is not all-powerful. Theists respond that the apparent evil is really a necessary part of a greater good.

Another argument against the existence of God is that humans create the idea of God and that this idea varies according to material, social, and historical conditions. A real God is not the source of the different conceptions of a higher being. Theists respond that all these conceptions aim at the one God.

Some religious thinkers emphasize a more personal approach to God, either through special religious awareness of God, or through faith. In faith people commit themselves to God without any of the objective reasons they might have for believing in everyday facts. Attempts to justify such faith include Pascal's Wager and pointing to the meaninglessness of individual lives without a belief in God.

Selected Readings

Cahn, S., and D. Shatz, (eds.). *Contemporary Philosophy of Religion*. New York: Oxford, 1982.

Hick, John. *Philosophy of Religion*. Englewood Cliffs, NJ: Prentice-Hall, 1973.

Mackie, John. *The Miracle of Theism*. New York: Oxford, 1982.

Nietzsche, Friedrich. *The Antichrist*. R. Hollingdale (Tr.). New York: Penguin, 1968.

Pojman, Louis (ed.). *Philosophy of Religion: An Anthology*. Belmont, CA: Wadsworth, 1987.

Rowe, William. *Philosophy of Religion*. Belmont, CA: Wadsworth, 1978.

Smith, Huston. *The Religions of Man*. New York: Harper & Row, 1958.

3

Reality

In everyday life, we operate with a conception of what it is to be real. We understand that what we seem to perceive and to do in dreams is not real, and that what happens in works of fiction is not real. Many philosophies and religions question whether the things that we ordinarily consider to be real are truly real. Is there some deeper reality behind the everyday world? Is the everyday world only a false picture, in our minds, of the ultimate reality? Does anything exist independently of our thoughts, or is everything in the mind?

ORDINARY REALITY

What we mean by "reality," both in everyday life and in philosophical thought, is that which exists on its own, independently of what anyone thinks. Reality is there whether or not anyone perceives or understands it. We try to portray this independent reality accurately in our perceptions and thoughts, but it is possible for a group of people to be mistaken. Reality is distinct from mere appearance and from the imaginary and the fictitious. Perceptual illusions—such as water appearing to be on the road ahead, or sticks in water appearing to be bent—are appearances that are different from reality. In hallucinations and dreams, we may experience whole episodes that do not correspond to reality. This is evident from the fact that if you wake up from a dream in which you were stabbed in a swordfight, you have no wound and no sword. Works of fiction, such as movies and books, do not attempt to give a fully accurate picture of reality. In reading or viewing them, we may temporarily enjoy the "make–believe" episodes, but we know that the episodes are not happening in reality. This is why we do not act to change what is happening.

The major reason that people distinguish mere appearance and fiction from reality is that we have to act in reality. Action that is based on an appreciation of what is real will be more successful than action that is based on false conceptions or "wishful thinking." This is because in acting we really affect things and things really affect us, whether our conception of what is happening is accurate or not. Someone who hallucinates that he can fly may have the (illusory) experience of flying when he jumps out the window, but he will fall and hit the ground and probably be injured.

Characteristics of Reality

In ordinary life, we consider the things that we perceive and use to be real. These "tangible" (touchable) things have certain characteristics that make up their independent existence or reality. The "real-making" characteristics of ordinary things are: (1) continuous existence, even when they are not being perceived or used; (2) the capacity to be experienced by other people who have the same faculties that we have; and (3) the ability to have causal effects upon other things, even when the occurrence of the causation is not perceived by anyone. If we are unsure whether something is real, we generally check to determine if it has these characteristics. For example, a real pond in a desert will continue to be there while we approach it, will be visible to our companions who are not blind or near-sighted, and will water plants and bushes, even if no one is there.

Substance

Things that endure through time are the prime cases of real things. Some features of these things may change while they continue to exist. For example, a continuing tree grows leaves in the spring and loses them in the fall. A special terminology to describe this situation was developed Aristotle (384–322 B.C.) and has continued throughout Western philosophy. Metaphysics, the branch of philosophy that explores the basic categories and structures of reality, calls the continuing thing a "substance" (in Latin, "that which stands under"); and its features, "properties" or "attributes" or "qualities." Properties (or attributes or qualities) are dependent upon substances for their existence. They cannot exist independently of substances but always have to exist in—"inhere" in—a substance. For example, greenness always exists in the physical world as the green color of some thing, such as a green plant or a green car. A substance may continue to be the same thing even though many of its properties change. For instance, a green car will remain a car if it is repainted blue.

Ordinary enduring things can also come into or go out of existence; for example, a tree may burn in a fire or a new tree may grow from a seed. As understood by Aristotle, and others, substances have essences or sets of "essential properties" that make them what they are. The loss of essential properties destroys a substance. Whereas a tree can change color or grow leaves while remaining the same thing, the tree ceases to exist if essential properties, such as the organization of roots, trunk, and branches, are removed; cutting a tree into lumber destroys it. A substance is the essence, or "essential nature," existing in matter.

Universals

There are many different general types or classifications that apply to any individual substance or property. For example, this book is an instance of the general type "book," as well as of the general types "physical object," "human artifact," "rectangular," and "black and white." These general types, or ways in which things are the same, are called "universals" and are distinguished from individual instances, which are called "particulars." There are universals for substances, properties, happenings, relationships, numbers, and practically anything else. One of the classic questions of metaphysics is whether universals exist over and above their instances (see Plato's Forms, p.31), or whether our minds create universals by abstracting from the real particulars, which are all that exist (nominalism). Aristotle claimed that neither of these is correct. He claimed that universals are real, but that they exist only in their instances. The only real things are substances of various types with their properties, numbers, relationships, and so on.

Matter

Material things are made of matter. We ordinarily think of matter as some type of substance—like putty—that can be shaped into different forms. This substance can take on many different properties, including the essential properties that define a substance. Hence, the same matter may be part of the soil at one time, part of a plant at another time, and part of a human body at another time. Existing in matter is how many universals have instances. The particulars of material things, properties, and events have to exist in matter. Two material things whose properties are exactly alike, such as two television sets of the same model, are distinct from each other—two particulars, not one—because they are made of different matter.

Our ordinary conception of matter is not very precise, so that there are many puzzles about what exactly matter is. Philosophers and scientists have tried to figure out how matter is related to space and time; whether matter is just a general term for materials like gold and wood; and whether there are basic "pieces" of matter, such as fundamental particles. Since matter underlies properties and endures through changes of properties, philosophers have also wondered whether matter is itself a basic substance.

Cause and Effect

Substances causally act upon each other. One thing makes another thing change its properties, or come into or go out of existence. The cause is that which makes something have some property or go through some change, while the effect is the outcome of the causal process. We ordinarily think that a cause has some power or force which it exerts to bring about the effect. The effect has to occur because of the cause. For example, your moving foot has a force, or momentum, which produces the movement of a ball when you kick it. Such "push-pull" causal relations, in which the causing thing (your foot) spatially contacts the caused thing (the ball, which is caused to move), are very familiar from everyday life. However, there are also cases of causation in which the cause at least seems to be spatially separate from the effect. For example, the gravitational attraction between the Earth and Moon causes the Moon's orbit and the tides on Earth.

Although cause and effect is a very familiar and basic relation between things, there are many philosophical questions about it. Does every change require a cause, or do some things happen "by chance"? If we knew that there is always some cause, or set of causes, we would know that we could not fully understand an event until we found its cause. There are other questions about the nature of causation itself. Is power a necessary part of causation, or can causation be defined in terms of one type of thing regularly occurring after another type of thing (constant conjunction)? If the power to create an effect is not part of causation, how are cases of causation different from cases of things simply regularly occurring together? Must a cause precede its effect, or can cause and effect be simultaneous (for example, the air currents cause a piece of paper to remain suspended in the air)?

Space and Time

All ordinary particulars exist in space and time. We frequently think of space and time as types of "containers" within which matter, substances, properties, events, and everything of "this world" exist. Location in space and time make different parts of matter different from each other. Spatial-temporal location can also individualize mental things. Although there are special issues about minds and thoughts, in everyday life, we consider two thoughts whose properties are exactly alike to be distinct from each other if they occur at different locations in space and time.

Space and time consist of different parts, or locations, that are surrounded by other spatial or temporal parts. Space is thought to have three dimensions—length, width, and height—and to have the structure described by Euclidean geometry. Time is different from space in that time is intrinsically dynamic. Space remains the same, but time passes. What is future becomes present, and what is present becomes past.

Many metaphysical questions have been raised about space and time. Are they distinct from each other, or are they only parts of one space-time? Are they unlimited in all directions, or is some type of boundary possible? Are they really distinct from what exists within them, or are they only relations between things? Does time really pass, or is it static like space? (To see what difference some of these issues make, see the discussion of the first antecedent cause argument in chapter 2.) Attempts to answer these questions become very complicated and are beyond the scope of an introductory work.

Metaphysics of the Ordinary World

At least within our culture, we can agree that things such as chairs, buildings, trees, and animals are material things with properties in space and time; that they can causally affect each other; and that there are many kinds, or universals, of such things. The notions of substance, properties, essential properties, universals, particulars, matter, causation, space, and time are familiar in that we make such distinctions in everyday life, even if we do not always use these words in making the distinctions. There is a general, although largely unstated, agreement that these are real.

However, philosophers want to make concepts and positions as clear as possible. The basic features of the ordinary world, which most people agree on, are not exact philosophic positions. Many metaphysical theories concern the exact ways to understand these features of our ordinary world. In attempting to clarify the basic categories of the ordinary world and to make them consistent with their ideas about what exists, philosophers have proposed different accounts. For example, there are many different metaphysical accounts of what an enduring thing is, such as Aristotle's claim that a substance is the essential properties in matter; John Locke's (1632–1704) claim that a substance is a featureless supporter of properties; and the contemporary view that an enduring thing is an extended event. As with universals, matter, causation, space, and time, there are also general metaphysical issues about the nature of possibility and necessity.

In addition to these general metaphysical issues about the basic categories of the ordinary world, there are also many metaphysical issues about the specific types of ordinary things. Philosophers investigate how mental things are different from material things (see chapter 6), how the self exists through time (see chapter 7), and whether minds can make decisions that are not completely caused by antecedent factors (see chapter 8). Consideration of the metaphysical issues about the ordinary world has led some philosophers to believe in another, ultimate reality. However, some philosophers consider our ordinary world to be the only reality that there is, and some philosophers believe in a multi-featured reality (see Alternative Realities, p. 31).

ULTIMATE REALITY

Many philosophies and religions maintain that our ordinary world is not the true reality. They claim that there is an ultimate reality that "lies behind" the ordinary world and is qualitatively different from it. The reasons for thinking that the ordinary world is not the most real are different in the different theories. The major types of ultimate reality and the reasons for contrasting each type with the ordinary world are surveyed below.

Life After Death

There are many different conceptions of life after death, including rebirth into our familiar world. Many philosophies and religions have claimed that after death a person, or his or her soul, enters another realm of existence that is distinct from the ordinary world. The existence of an afterlife is usually accepted on religious grounds. The philosophical arguments for it rely on the notion that the soul or mind is distinct from the body and should survive the death of the body (see chapters 6 and 7).

The new realm itself may not be more real than the ordinary world, but, insofar as the afterlife is conceived to be permanent, our afterlife may be thought to be more important than this life. Many philosophers have equated permanence with ultimate reality. According to this view, a permanent afterlife would be more real than our temporary existence in ordinary reality, even if the ordinary world itself is permanent.

Plato's Forms

Plato claimed that there are degrees of reality. What is most real is eternal, unchanging, and perfect. Anything that is eternal, unchanging, and perfect is real in the fullest sense, whereas whatever can change through time or is imperfect is only partially real. An imperfect circle, for example, is only partly a circle, because it does not fit exactly the definition of a circle. It is a sort of mixture of a circle and something else. Only a perfect circle would be a fully real circle. Whatever can change through time is not fully real because it is never simply identical with what it is currently. Furthermore, any thing that can come into or go out of existence is not fully real, because it has this element of nonexistence, non-reality, within it. As able to be or not to be, it also is a sort of mixture of the real and the unreal.

No ordinary thing is eternal, unchanging, and perfect. Everything in the ordinary world occurs in time, is subject to change, and has imperfections. However, there is another realm of fully real things, which Plato called "Forms" (sometimes translated as "Ideas"), that exists behind and supports the ordinary world. Forms are the universals for substances, properties, mathematical characteristics, and moral notions. Forms are the essences of these things, that which defines them as what they are. While no individual tree in the ordinary world is eternal, unchanging, and perfect, what it is to be a tree—the Form of tree—is eternal, unchanging, and perfect. Similarly, the Form of circle is the perfect, eternal, and unchanging standard to which all circles in the ordinary world only partially measure up.

Forms are not only the ultimate reality, but they also transcend the ordinary world. Ordinary things exist only because they "participate in," or share in, the Forms. In order to be a definite something, a particular must be an instance of a universal. Plato's universals, the Forms, exist separately from their particulars and are most fully real. Plato's particulars depend on the Forms for their existence and are never more than approximations of them. Notice the contrast between this theory about universals and particulars and Aristotle's theory that universals exist only in their instances (see Universals, p. 25).

The human soul is immortal, according to Plato, and capable of coming into direct contact with the Forms. Through long training, a lover of wisdom, a philosopher, can ascend from taking worldly things to be real to direct knowledge of the Forms themselves. Plato describes this progression in the famous "Myth of the Cave," in *The Republic*.

God or Oneness

Some religions and philosophies claim that the ordinary world is largely a product of our own minds. It is not that there is another, more real realm that is separate from the ordinary world, but rather that this world is not what we ordinarily consider it to be. What we ordinarily consider to be independently existing things are really not distinct from one another. The room in which you sit is really not a separate thing or a different part of matter from the trees outside or the stars above. Furthermore, our minds are not distinct from these things or from other minds. Your conception that you are a separate soul, mind, or person is mistaken. All ultimate separation and distinctness are but an illusion. Everything is really one.

There are many different versions of this theory that all is one in Indian, Buddhist, and Western thought. Some versions claim that this oneness is God, who is present in all things (pantheism). The reasons for thinking that all is one range from special religious experience and mystic insight to Benedict Spinoza's (1632–1677) deduction of oneness from definitions of substance and causation.

The Unknowable

In contrast with the view that all is one, some philosophies claim that there is an ultimate reality that is independent of our minds, but that it is intrinsically unknowable. According to this view, the ordinary world is the result of an interaction between the unknowable and the structures of our minds. Ordinary substances, properties, universals, space, and time do not exist independently of our minds. These appear in our experience because our minds impose certain structures and basic categories. Just as things will appear reddish if we wear red-tinted glasses, so independent reality appears to have the features that our minds impose. Independent reality can appear only through these "filters."

According to this theory, we do not create our entire experience of the world. What we perceive is partly given to us, so that we have to perceive specific data whether we want to or not. While looking at this book, you have to see the book, not a sunny beach in Hawaii. Our minds cannot control the raw facts that appear. That data are given to us is the major reason for thinking that something exists independently of the mind.

Since our minds structure everything that we experience or think, we can never know ultimate reality. We can take off red-tinted lenses, but we cannot take off the structures of our minds. According to Immanuel Kant (1724–1804), we can never know the "thing-in-itself." The source of the data given to us is unknowable but real. See chapter 4 for an evaluation of the theory that the structures of our minds prevent us from knowing independent reality.

Scientific Entities

Natural science agrees with our everyday conception of the world on many issues. Science extends the range of our knowledge in many ways that do not challenge ordinary conceptions. For example, geology investigates the types of rock and soil and how they were formed in ancient ages; and biology investigates the types of plants, animals, insects, and microorganisms in a natural environment. These investigations may reveal some surprising things, but they accept the existence of ordinary material things with properties in space and time. Even the discovery of material things and properties that we can detect with instruments but cannot perceive with the five senses does not challenge our ordinary world. These new things and properties exist together with the familiar things and properties. They are additions to the ordinary world, not replacements for it. If we had more powerful senses or some additional senses, such as being able "to feel" magnetic fields, we could perceive these new things and properties along with the more familiar ones.

Scientific entities would be an ultimate reality that "lies behind" our ordinary world only if they were replacements for ordinary things. Some philosophers and scientists think that scientific entities, such as neutrons, protons, electrons, and quarks, are the only things that actually exist. The "only" here is important. It distinguishes between two positions, both of which claim that scientific entities are real. One position claims that ordinary things and properties are real but dependent on the scientific entities of which they are made. Both the scientific entities and the things and properties that they compose are real, according to this view. The second position claims that only the scientific entities are real, and that ordinary things and properties are our mistaken conceptions of what exists. According to this position, our ordinary world is not the real world. Chapter 5 examines these issues more fully.

ALTERNATIVE REALITIES

Some thinkers have proposed that there may be alternative realities, rather than one reality for everyone. Different types of things might be real for different people or cultures. Scientific entities might be ultimately real for scientists or members of a scientific culture, while the "spirits of things" might be ultimately real for members of an animistic culture. According to this view, reality is relative to people, cultures, or forms of thought.

The notion that "reality is relative" may mean different things. The first response of philosophers to such an idea is to find out exactly what it means. There are at least three different positions that may be meant by claiming that there are alternative realities: (1) All of the different types of things and properties are real. They all exist together, and all of them exist independently of what anyone thinks. However, different people or cultures are sensitive to different features of this complex reality. Different people or cultures "tune into" or understand different features; (2) None of the different types of things and properties are real. Whatever exists independently is unknowable, because our minds, language, or culture necessarily structure everything that we experience and think. However, there are different ways of structuring experience and thought. Different minds, different languages, or different cultures structure experience and thought in fundamentally different ways. Hence, the "everyday realities" of different people, linguistic groups, or cultures are different, even though the ultimate reality is the same for all, but unknowable; (3) None of the different types of things and properties is real, because nothing is real. Everything exists only as some type of idea or conception in people's minds (idealism). Different minds, different linguistic groups, or different cultures have different conceptions. Since there is nothing that exists independently of these conceptions, these different "everyday realities" are all that exists.

Position (1) claims that reality consists of many different types of things and properties. Many philosophers think that both scientific entities and ordinary things, with ordinary properties, exist, so that the notion of a multi-featured reality is a philosophically defensible position. Reality may include both ordinary things and other types of things, of which most of us are unaware. The two major challenges to this position are whether all of these different types of things and properties can exist together, and whether there is adequate evidence for each of them. Some sets of features seem to contradict one another. Philosophers, who generally accept the basic principles of logic, including the Law of Non-Contradiction, generally deny that reality can have contradictory features. If two types of things or properties can be shown to be inconsistent with each other, an argument is made against both being features of reality.

Positions 2 and 3 claim only that the "everyday realities" of different people, linguistic groups, or cultures are different. An "everyday reality" is the world as experienced and capable of being experienced by people. It is what they find and can find in their world. Both positions 2 and 3 make interesting claims, but they do not really involve alternative realities. Position 2 is a form of relativism concerning knowledge; this topic is addressed in chapter 4. Position 3 is idealism.

IDEALISM

Idealism is the position that only minds and their thoughts, or "ideas," exist. Ordinary substances, properties, events, matter, space, and time do not exist independently of minds, nor does any ultimate reality exist independently of minds. Nothing is real other than experience and the mind or soul to which it belongs. In ordinary life, we consider the things that we perceive and use to be real, but this is just a natural illusion. Our experiences of seeing, touching, hearing, smelling, tasting, acting on, and struggling against things do occur, but the things do not have any existence beyond the experiences. What we ordinarily take to be real things are like the things we experience in dreams. At the time they may seem to be real, but they are actually nothing more than a part of the experience.

There are different forms of idealism that make different claims about which minds exist. Solipsism is the view that only one's own mind exists. This is a strange idea, but if you think that you can never know anything other than your own thoughts, you may start to think that nothing exists other than you and your thoughts. Individual, or subjective, idealism claims that other minds exist as well as yours, but that everything else is just an idea in someone's mind. Social idealism claims that everything other than the features of a society is dependent upon the conceptions of that society. A society, culture, or linguistic group is considered to be a sort of overarching mind. The conceptions that occur in that society, its ideas, are all that exist. Finally, divine idealism claims that everything exists as an idea in God's mind. Those who think that God created the universe and sustains it in existence sometimes believe in divine idealism. They reason that God creates and sustains things simply by thinking of them, so that matter must be only an idea in God's mind. As Bishop George Berkeley (1685–1753) noted, God thinks of things even when no individual person is thinking of them. Our ordinary belief that things continue to exist when we are not thinking of them is correct. They exist, not as material objects, but as ideas in God's mind.

Religious belief about God creating and sustaining the universe is one reason that people have been idealists. The most common reason for idealism is the claim that we can know only our own thoughts (chapter 4 examines this thesis in detail). If we think of experience as occurring entirely in the mind, or in the brain, we might conclude that there is no direct mental contact with external things. The conception of perception as an awareness of images or pictures (ideas) in the mind leads toward idealism. If we have direct access only to images or pictures in the mind, we have no way of knowing whether these images represent external reality. We would have no way of knowing whether there was anything over and above the images. In this case, there seems to be no need for an external reality. Our experience would be the same whether or not there was an independent reality. Many idealists go so far as to claim that we do not even know what is meant by the term "external reality." It is not just that we cannot know whether it exists. We cannot even think of it. To be is to be conceived, as Berkeley claimed. In his formulation "to be is to be perceived," "perceiving" includes all conception, not just sense perception. Everything that we think of is part of our thoughts, so that the whole idea of a reality independent of our thoughts is meaningless.

Arguments Against Idealism

There are several types of arguments against idealism. These arguments try to show that an external reality is necessary for the existence of thoughts and minds. They argue that something must exist over and above minds and their thoughts, because minds and thoughts cannot exist without this something else.

One type of argument concerns the nature of sense perception. If sense perception involves any type of contact with independently existing things, then the nature of sense perception would show that idealism was false. That there is some type of contact with external things is indicated by the fact that sensory data appear to come from outside our minds. Most of what we perceive is not under our control and much of it is surprising to us. If someone is playing loud, obnoxious music right next to you, you have to hear it. It seems to be forced on you. The music itself may also be unlike anything you have ever heard before. There is much novelty in what we perceive. These new and surprising things do not seem to come from our minds. Since we do not control most of what we perceive, and much of it is new to us, there seems to be something else which makes us perceive what we perceive. The source of our sensory data must be something outside of the mind.

A second type of argument concerns the nature of bodily action. In acting to bring about what we want, we confront the resistance of the world. Things in the world, and even our own bodies, may prevent our actions from being successful. Even in a simple action such as hammering a nail into a wall, the wall may be too hard, or the nail may be too thin and so bend, or we may hit it badly and bend it. The world may resist the success of our actions in innumerable ways. This resistance, frequently manifested in ways we had not even considered beforehand, indicates that there is something other than our thoughts involved. There is something else that resists what we are trying so hard to accomplish. This "something else" is independent reality. Our actions have to take account of the independent reality in order to be successful.

A third type of argument concerns the way our experiencing and thinking seem to be dependent upon the proper functioning of our brain and nervous system. When the brain and nervous system are damaged or interfered with, people's experiences become very different. Destruction of brain tissue, tumors, drugs, chemical imbalances of neurotransmitters, and neurosurgery affect a person's abilities to perceive, remember, have emotions, and think rationally (see chapter 6 for more details). These effects occur even when the person himself does not know anything about his brain or how it works. Hence, all of our conscious experiences and mental abilities seem to depend upon something other than our thoughts and minds. They seem to depend upon a real brain and nervous system.

A fourth type of argument is that the understanding of language is essentially social in character. The meaning of words depends upon how they are used by the group of people that speak a language. As Ludwig Wittgenstein (1889–1951) argued, the meaning of a word is not just what you think it means. The meaning depends upon its use by other people, who can correct us if we use it improperly. For example, you might think that cannibalism means "an outdoor barbeque." You might think that you want to engage in cannibalism with your friends this evening. It would then be true that you wanted to have an outdoor barbeque, but not true that you wanted to engage in cannibalism. The point of this type of argument is that something other than any individual person's thoughts affects the meaning of language. The meaning of some of your thoughts, those that use language, depends upon other people. If this is so, solipsism and individual idealism cannot be true. Social idealism might still be true, but the first three types of arguments contend against it.

Reality *is that which exists on its own, independently of what anyone thinks. Ordinary things are real in that they exist continuously, even when they are not being perceived or used; they can be experienced by other people who have the same faculties that we have; and they have causal effects upon other things, even when the occurrence of the causation is not perceived by anyone.*

Substances endure through time and can change many of their properties. The essence of a substance defines what it is. A substance goes out of existence if it loses any part of its essence or essential properties. Universals are general types of substances, properties, happenings, relationships, numbers, and practically anything else. Particulars are the individual instances of universals. Existing in matter is how many universals have instances. Matter is some type of substance that can be shaped into different forms and can take on many different properties. Cause and effect is the relation in which one thing makes another thing have some property or go through some change. Space and time are frequently thought to be "containers" within which matter, substances, properties, events, and everything of "this world" exist. Location in space and time can distinguish parts of matter from one another and thoughts from one another.

Metaphysics is the branch of philosophy that explores the basic categories and structures of reality. Many metaphysical theories concern the exact ways to understand the basic features of our ordinary world and the types of things that exist within it. Other metaphysical theories concern an ultimate reality that "lies behind" the ordinary world and is qualitatively different from it.

Heaven or an afterlife is one type of ultimate reality. If there is a permanent afterlife outside of this world, it would be more important and perhaps more real than our temporary existence in this world. Plato's Forms are another type of ultimate reality. Forms are the universals for substances, properties, mathematical characteristics, and moral notions. Forms are eternal, unchanging, and perfect and so exist to the highest degree. Ordinary things are less real and exist only because they "participate in" the Forms.

That "all is oneness" is a type of ultimate reality that denies the separateness of the things in our ordinary world. The unknowable is a type of ultimate reality that cannot be known because our minds impose structures and basic categories on everything that we can experience and think. Our ordinary world is the result of the ultimate reality appearing through these distorting lenses. If scientific entities, such as electrons and quarks, are all that there is, they are another type of ultimate reality. According to this view, ordinary things and properties are only our mistaken understanding of these scientific entities.

Some thinkers have proposed that, rather than one reality existing for everyone, different types of things might be real for different people or cultures. This claim that reality is relative may mean three different things: (1) all of the different types of things and properties are real, but different people or cultures are aware of only some of them; (2) the "everyday realities" of different people or cultures are different, even though the ultimate reality is the same for all, but unknowable; (3) none of the different types of things and properties is real, because everything is ideal.

Idealism is the position that only minds and their thoughts exist. Our ordinary belief in the independent existence of the things that we perceive and use is a natural illusion. Solipsism, individual or subjective idealism, social idealism, and divine idealism make different claims about which minds exist. The most common argument in favor of idealism is that we can know only our own thoughts. We have no reason to think that there is anything over and above the images and ideas in our minds.

Arguments against idealism are of four types. One type argues that sense perception includes contact with independent things because we do not control most of what we perceive and much of it is new to us. A second type argues that the resistance of the world to our action shows that there is an independent reality. A third type argues that thought and experience are dependent upon a real brain and nervous system. A fourth type argues that the meaning of our thoughts, which use language is dependent upon other people, not just on our minds.

Selected Readings

Aristotle. *Categories*. (Several good translations.)

Berkeley, George. *Three Dialogues Between Hylas & Philonous*. Indianapolis: Hackett, 1979.

Carr, Brian. *Metaphysics: An Introduction*. Atlantic Highlands, NJ: Humanities Press, 1987.

Hamlyn, D.W. *Metaphysics*. New York: Cambridge, 1984.

Plato. *The Republic*. (Several good translations.)

4

Knowledge

*N*obody wants to be ignorant. All people think that some knowledge is a good thing. Knowledge gives you power in the world. It is interesting on its own, and it tells you how to act. There are some subjects about which people would like to know more, and they generally think there are ways to find out about these subjects. Is it possible to acquire more knowledge? What do you do to attain knowledge? Do you really know anything at all? From ancient times philosophers have raised questions about what knowledge is and whether we can really know anything. Many have attempted to refute the skeptical claim that knowledge cannot be attained. This chapter examines the major views concerning what knowledge is, whether and how we can acquire knowledge, and what things we can know.

COMMON SENSE CONCEPTIONS

In everyday life, we take ourselves to have knowledge of some things and not to know others. What we mean by "knowledge" is some accurate account of the facts for which we have good reasons, and that we can explain to other people. Starting as far back as Plato's *Theaetetus*, philosophers have summarized our notion of knowledge in the formula "knowledge is justified true belief." This basically means "believing what is true and having sufficient reasons for it." There are three features to the definition of knowledge—belief, truth, and justification—and each of them covers a lot of ground.

Belief

In the formula for knowledge, there are two important features of belief, or believing: belief portrays the world to be a certain way, and we accept this or "believe in" it. The first feature is something very remarkable that we ordinarily take for granted. Believing is about the world and it portrays specific facts in the world. In believing, you believe that there are some facts in the world. This is remarkable because very few things are intrinsically about other things (rocks and trees, and even sharp twinges of pain in your foot, are not about something else). Belief portrays the world to be one way rather than another. "What we believe" is how the world is supposed to be according to our belief. "What we believe" is usually expressed in the form "that p," where "p" is a statement of a fact, for example, the belief that summer is hotter than winter.

Philosophers and psychologists have proposed many different theories of how beliefs are able to portray the world. One traditional theory is that a belief contains something like a picture or an image of what it is about. This picture is usually called either an "idea" or a "representation." In being directly aware of the idea or representation, we indirectly think of what it "pictures." There are many problems with this theory—for example, why does not "direct awareness" of the idea itself include a picture of the idea and so produce a regress?—and there are many alternative theories. The "picture" theory of belief is important because many previous philosophers have presupposed it in thinking about questions of truth, knowledge, and reality.

Other types of consciousness are also about the world. Sense perception, memory, thought, theoretical reason, emotion, and even some types of desire take the world to be one way rather than another. In order to simplify things, philosophers have tried to separate out that feature of our consciousness that portrays the world. They use the term "belief" for this. Hence, emotions that portray the world, such as being afraid of the large, snarling dog, are considered to include beliefs, such as the belief that there is a large, snarling dog. It is such beliefs that might be true or false.

The second feature of belief is that we accept the account of the facts. We take what we believe—for example, that summer is hotter than winter—to be an accurate account of the world. This is in contrast with other states of consciousness in which we are less sure or are undecided. You might consider, hypothesize, or suspect that spring is hotter than fall, without believing it. You may even have some evidence for it, but not enough to believe it. Ordinarily we believe what we perceive, but there are special circumstances in which a person may discount what he or she perceives. If you think that the water on the road ahead is just an illusion, you continue to see the water, but you do not believe it is there.

There are various degrees of belief. Our certainty of the facts that we believe can vary, from barely accepting them to being totally convinced of them. You may believe two things, but be willing to bet your life, or bank account, on only one of them and not the other. In this case, you believe more strongly in one than in the other. Philosophers have disagreed on how strongly you must believe in something for it to count as knowledge. Descartes and others have claimed that you must be absolutely certain of something in order to know it. Anything less than absolutely certain belief is not really knowledge. Locke (1632–1704) and others have claimed that strong belief is sufficient for knowledge. The strength of belief is closely connected with the strength of the justification for the truth of the belief.

Truth

Beliefs are true when they depict things as they are. Truth is the accuracy of an account of the world. Beliefs are false when they depict things inaccurately, that is, when they portray facts that do not exist as existing. All philosophical theories of truth share this much. They all must admit that there is a difference between true beliefs and false beliefs. They differ about what makes true beliefs true and false beliefs false. They differ about the status of "facts" and the nature of "portraying the world accurately."

CORRESPONDENCE THEORY

People ordinarily accept the notion of reality. Almost everyone assumes that some facts exist independently of our thoughts (see chapter 3). Our ordinary notion of truth assumes that there are things and states of affairs that are real. These real things are the basis of truth. In order to be true, our beliefs have to portray real things as they are. Truth is a real agreement between what is believed and an independent reality. This position is called "the correspondence theory of truth." Notice that the correspondence theory of truth does not say how we find out whether beliefs are true or false. It is an account of what truth is, not a procedure for developing true beliefs. How we find out whether or not our account of reality is accurate is a further issue (see the discussion of justification, p. 41).

That beliefs are about the world is the basis for truth and falsity (in all theories of truth, not just the correspondence theory). Beliefs can be true or false because they portray the world to be a specific way and the world may either be or not be that way. According to the "picture" theory of belief, beliefs portray facts by means of ideas or representations. According to the correspondence theory of truth, beliefs are true because they correspond to an independent reality. Putting these two theories together, the truth of a belief is a matter of the idea or the representation corresponding to reality. There are actually two things—a mental picture (representation or idea) and the real facts in the world—that correspond with each other. Just as a painting of a person may look like that person, so a representation or an idea may be just like some independent fact and so be true.

COHERENCE THEORY

The ordinary notion of truth, correspondence to reality, might lead you to think that idealists could not have any notion of truth, since they deny that there is an independent reality. However, idealists have developed an alternative account of truth: truth is the coherence of our beliefs with each other. This is usually called the "coherence theory of truth." The notion of coherence is not precisely defined, but the basic idea is that beliefs cohere when they fit together well. Coherence is like the relationship of the parts of a jigsaw puzzle. Our beliefs are like pieces of different jigsaw puzzles that are all mixed together. Some of them fit together with others, but some pieces cannot be fitted with those that do fit together. The objective is to assemble the largest possible picture. To do that you have to throw out some pieces—beliefs—that do not fit and acquire some new pieces. What we ordinarily think of as reality is the largest possible number of such consistent beliefs. These form a coherent conception of the world, even though there is no independent world, and so are true. For example, the belief that a room has walls seems to be true because it coheres with what you see, what you can touch, what you know about other rooms, and many other things that you believe. If you thought that the walls of the room are flexible, that belief would be false because it would be inconsistent with all of your other beliefs and perceptions (you cannot stretch the walls; if you press on them, they will not bend, and so on).

Coherence of what we believe is a major part of justifying beliefs. Defenders of the correspondence theory of truth accept coherence as an important way of determining which beliefs are true or false. However, they deny that truth is just the coherence of beliefs. Rather, they claim that the coherence of beliefs is an important way of finding out whether what we believe corresponds to an independent reality.

PRAGMATIC THEORY

There is a third notion of truth that is usually called the "pragmatic theory of truth." The pragmatic theory maintains that the truth of beliefs, or theories, is just a matter of the usefulness of the beliefs. We consider beliefs to be true if using those beliefs allows us to accomplish our objectives in the world and to get what we want. For example, beliefs about the existence and nature of electricity are true, insofar as they allow us to build electrically powered machines, like lights, clocks, and televisions. Even the basic principles of deductive and inductive logic are true only because they work for us! False beliefs are those which are ultimately not useful. Using false beliefs does not help us accomplish our objectives in the world. For example, beliefs about magic spells are false, insofar as using magic spells does not work.

Defenders of the correspondence theory treat the pragmatic theory in the same way they treat the coherence theory. They accept the pragmatic usefulness of beliefs or theories as an important indication of their truth. In determining whether or not beliefs are true, people do pay careful attention to whether the beliefs work practically. However, this does not show that truth is equivalent to pragmatic usefulness. Some beliefs which later turn out to be false can be useful for a while. Other beliefs can be true but have no apparent use, for example, many past beliefs about past history and about the far reaches of the universe.

Justification

True belief is not sufficient for knowledge. We can have beliefs that are true, yet still not have knowledge. Something more—a justification for what is believed—is needed. The most obvious reason for this is that the believer needs some way to recognize that his beliefs are true. In your own case, you always need some way to tell whether what you believe is true. A justification is supposed to reveal why your belief is true.

In everyday life, people frequently worry about whether they really know something or not. Members of a jury may worry about whether they really know that the accused is guilty of the crime, or you may worry about whether you really know that your wallet is on your dresser. In such cases people are concerned about whether their beliefs (that the accused committed the crime and that your wallet is not lost) are true. What they need is evidence that establishes that what they believe is true. The beliefs can be true even without this evidence, but the believer cannot be sure of it without sufficient reasons.

SUFFICIENT REASONS

A person may make a lucky guess that happens to be true. You may believe, for no reason, that the next card in the deck is a queen, and, lo and behold, it is. In this case, there is true belief, but you do not know that the next card is a queen because you have no good reason for what you believe. A person may believe something for bad reasons and it may turn out to be true. You may believe that the next card is a queen because your horoscope predicted that today would bring you good fortune and because a queen would win the hand for you. In this case, few people would claim that you know that the next card is a queen; you again are lacking good reasons for what you believe.

Knowledge requires that you have sufficient reasons or a justification for what you believe. What exactly is a justification or sufficient reasons for what you believe? In general, a reason or a justification is something that supports or is evidence for the truth of what you believe. Good reasons are really connected with that for which they are used as reasons. Seeing that the stoplight is red is a good reason for believing that the stoplight is red, because there is a definite connection between what you see and the facts; in this case, the stoplight being red. Good reasons have some such connection that can be noticed by a reasonable person. Bad reasons are not really connected with that for which they are used as reasons. The statements in a newspaper horoscope have no apparent connection with whether the next card in the deck is a queen and so are not good reasons for believing that the next card is a queen.

Good reasons for what you believe should be recognizable as good reasons by other reasonable people. When people know something, they generally can explain to other people why what they believe is true. When you do this, you are explaining to others your reasons for accepting some fact as true. Other people may be able to point out to you why your reasons are not totally convincing, or they may be able to give you some additional reasons that you had not considered.

Sufficient reasons are enough good reasons to believe something to be true. Sufficient reasons are particularly important when there are some good reasons for each of two or more positions that are inconsistent with each other. You cannot believe both because they are inconsistent. In such a case, it is rational to accept—believe in—the position for which there is the most evidence. However, you cannot know that it is true unless you have enough evidence for its truth. How much is "enough" is a difficult question, about which philosophers disagree. Some philosophers, such as Descartes, have claimed that knowledge must be absolutely certain. For them, sufficient reasons have to prove that what is believed is true. According to Descartes, if you can in any way doubt what you believe, you do not know it. If you can think of any way in which what you believe might be false, you cannot be absolutely certain of it and so do not know it. In order to know something, you must have evidence for it that is so conclusive that you cannot even conceive that it is not true.

ABSOLUTE CERTAINTY

Those who hold that knowledge must be absolutely certain also think that deductive proof is the main way to justify knowledge. In deductive logic, a valid argument guarantees that the conclusion is true if the premises are true (see chapter 1). If you start from true premises and use only valid arguments, everything that you can deduce is guaranteed to be true. Deductive proofs, as used in geometry, provide absolute certainty for everything that you can prove. The "rationalist" philosophers (see p. 43) claimed that all knowledge is acquired by deduction from self-evident first principles.

The claim that knowledge must be absolutely certain restricts what we can know. Descartes claimed to be able to prove many things starting from the absolutely certain truth that he exists. However, there are large areas about which we cannot be absolutely certain. We cannot be absolutely certain about everyday facts, such as that this book is solid or that you have two hands. This conception of knowledge claims that we do not know such things.

Other philosophers, such as Locke, hold that knowledge does not have to be absolutely certain. We know things when we have sufficient evidence for them, but only in special types of cases, such as mathematics and analysis of definitions, does sufficient evidence approach absolute certainty. Most of what we know comes from sense perception and is justified inductively. Careful sense perception provides very strong evidence for claims about the world. If you examine something carefully from many different perspectives, you can avoid almost all mistakes. Starting from sense perception, you can build up a conception of the world whose parts can be checked against one another to see if they "fit together" (cohere). Beliefs and theories can be developed and checked for their pragmatic usefulness in our interactions with the world. This perception-based approach to knowledge, which is called "empiricism," does not produce absolute certainty, but it does produce very strong evidence.

RATIONALISM AND EMPIRICISM

Rationalism and empiricism are two contrary views about the sources of knowledge. The basic idea of rationalism is that we attain knowledge by a process of reasoning from self-evident first principles. Empiricism claims that knowledge comes from perception. Rationalism was at the height of its influence during the seventeenth century, but some elements of rationalism are still very influential. The most famous empiricist philosophers wrote during the period from the late seventeenth century to the middle of the eighteenth century, but many elements of empiricism are accepted by contemporary philosophers.

Rationalism

Rationalists, such as Descartes, Spinoza, and Gottfried Leibniz (1646–1716), think that knowledge must be absolutely certain and that it comes from reason. Deductive proof is the main way to develop absolutely certain knowledge, since a valid argument guarantees that its conclusion is true if its premises are true. Mathematical systems, such as geometry, that prove all theorems starting from basic axioms and procedures are the models for knowledge in general. All knowledge is supposed to be provable from certain original truths. The difficult part is finding absolutely certain starting points. If the first premises are false or just uncertain, even the use of valid arguments cannot give us any knowledge. Rationalists solve this problem with self-evident truths that are known by reason. They claim that there are some things, such as the fact that I exist, the nature of substance, and the basic laws of deductive logic itself, that are self-evident. We can be absolutely certain of the truth of these starting points based on our awareness or "rational intuition" of their self-evidence. From these starting points, we can then prove everything that can be known.

According to the rationalists, we know that the basic starting points are true because of their self-evidence. The rationalists consider basic principles and basic definitions to be self-evident. Basic principles are claims such as "something does not come from nothing" and "there is a sufficient reason why anything exists." Basic definitions are explications of what basic categories, such as "substance" and "identity," are. The analysis of what is already "contained in" the category of substance or identity produces self-evident judgments. Judgments about basic principles and basic definitions are "necessary truths" because it is impossible for them to be false.

INNATE IDEAS

There is a different question concerning the origin of our ideas of these principles and definitions. Rationalists hold that these ideas must be innate to the mind. They are basic features of the mind that must exist as soon as the mind exists. Without them, we could not have any of our ordinary experiences. However, the fact that these ideas are innate does not mean that we are always conscious of them. Innate ideas may not be active until something in our experience triggers them. The main point is that in opposition to the empiricists' claim that we derive all our ideas from some type of perception, rationalists hold that some ideas must already exist before perception.

Empiricism

Empiricists, such as Locke, Bishop Berkeley, and Hume, think that all knowledge comes from sense perception and "inner perception" of the operations of the mind itself. As Locke originally stated, the mind starts as a "blank tablet (*tabula rasa*) of white paper" on which ideas are written by perception. Sense perception gives us our ideas of objects in the external world, and reflection, inner perception, gives us our ideas of what exists within the mind. This is both a theory of the origin of ideas and a theory of how knowledge is attained. Knowledge, which need not be absolutely certain, can be attained by careful and systematic perception of the facts of the world. Locke argued that ideas in the mind correspond to independently real objects and that these objects cause us to have the appropriate ideas (this "causing" is perception). Berkeley denied that there were real objects over and above the ideas of them (see chapter 3), but thought that we could still have knowledge about such bundles of ideas. Hume ended up with the skeptical doubt that we may not be able to know anything about matters of fact.

Empiricists do not deny that we can reason about our ideas. We can analyze what is "contained in" some idea, such as the idea of substance or identity. We can prove something in mathematics starting from basic ideas, such as the idea of the number two or of a triangle. This reasoning gives us a type of knowledge about our ideas. It tells us how the parts of our ideas are related to one another. However, the relations among our ideas apply to the external world only to the extent that the ideas themselves apply to the external world. This is where the empiricist claim that all ideas come from perception is important. All of our ideas, even our ideas of basic mathematical things such as triangles, come from perception. While we can know with certainty that the sum of the three angles of a triangle is equal to two right angles, we can only judge from perception whether any physical thing is triangular (is an instance of a triangle).

BUILDING UP JUSTIFIED BELIEF

We ordinarily think that we can acquire knowledge about whatever interests us. In order to put aside the question whether knowledge has to be absolutely certain, we can talk about "justified belief." In everyday life, we have various ways of building up justified beliefs. The most common ways of acquiring new justified beliefs are through sense perception, forming generalizations from perceptions, forming and testing hypotheses, deducing conclusions from other justified beliefs, and learning about a subject from the reports of other people.

SENSE PERCEPTION

Learning about specific objects and facts through sense perception is an experience with which everyone is familiar. From early childhood, we learn to recognize individual objects (such as mother and the teddy bear) and facts (such as that mother is here) based on what we see, feel, hear, smell, and taste. As adults we regularly perceive new locations, people, buildings, and all sorts of other things and facts. If you want to know something about Chicago, the Pacific Ocean, or the food in a restaurant, one way to find out is simply to observe. Careful and systematic perception can avoid almost all perceptual errors. If it is especially important that we get things right, or if we have reason to suspect that we are in error, we can take extra precautions, such as using other senses—touching as well as looking—and perceiving the thing from different perspectives and under different conditions.

FORMING GENERALIZATIONS

On the basis of perceiving a number of individual instances, we regularly form (inductive) generalizations about types of things. We develop a conception of what all New York taxicabs, all Chinese restaurants, or all reactions of potassium and oxygen are like. Such generalizations are essential to developing a detailed understanding of the world. They are main sources of the types or universals (see chapter 3) that we use to classify individual things, and they tell us what to expect when we encounter something that seems to fit into some of these types. However, generalizations are also common sources of errors. One type of error occurs when we use the wrong types for classification. You may have been eating at Chinese "soup kitchens" (free food for the poor), which you mistook for restaurants. In forming generalizations about individual instances, it is important to limit the terms of the generalization as much as possible. As the terms of the generalization go further beyond what you actually observe, you are really forming hypotheses that need to be tested.

The other major source of error is generalizing from a bad sample of cases. Since the generalization covers all cases, not just the ones that you have observed, there is always the question whether the cases that you have observed are representative of all the others. Are all instances of Chinese restaurants sufficiently like the ones you have visited? You might have gone only to a particular type of Chinese restaurant, and there may be other types that are significantly different. In forming general conclusions from individual cases, it is important to work from a relatively large number of individual cases that are as varied as possible. The more cases and the more varied they are, the more likely it is that whatever they share will also be shared by other, unobserved, cases. Social scientists and mathematicians have worked out principles for scientific sampling; these try to ensure that a sample is representative of the total set of cases.

HYPOTHESES

In addition to generalizations, people form hypotheses about what is going on. In general, a hypothesis is some account of a situation that goes beyond any of the observed facts. Generalizations are a type of hypothesis, but there are other types as well. Hypothesizing that a parade must be going on because you hear the sounds of a marching band on Memorial Day is a typical example of thinking of a larger whole within which the separate parts that you experience would fit. Hypothesizing that your battery is dead because your car does not do anything when you turn the key in the morning is another example. In these cases, the information that you have makes sense if a parade is going on, or your battery is dead. The information does not require that the hypothesis be correct, but the hypothesis would explain the presence of this specific information.

Hypotheses by themselves are usually not very strongly justified by the data that first lead to their formation. The hypothesis is just one scenario that would explain why the specific data are as they are. Other scenarios that would also explain the data are possible. A hypothesis is justified by further testing. We look for other data that should occur if the hypothesis is correct but not if the hypothesis is false. To test your hypothesis about your battery, you might try to turn on the lights. If your lights do not come on, this is further evidence in support of the hypothesis that your problem is a dead battery rather than a faulty starter. Further testing might rule out all other reasonable alternatives. You then would have very strong reasons for your belief that your battery was dead.

The formation and testing of hypotheses is very widely used in developing justified beliefs about things that we cannot directly observe. Historians, natural scientists, doctors, police detectives, and everybody else form and test hypotheses in order to form justified beliefs about what must have happened, given the evidence. For example, in the case of a crime to which there were no eyewitnesses, detectives try to reconstruct what must have happened. They form a hypothesis that explains the evidence that they have. The hypothesis then tells them what other evidence to look for, that is, what other data must be there if the hypothesis is correct, and that will not be there if the hypothesis is incorrect. Complete testing of hypotheses is difficult and sometimes impossible to achieve. However, the formation and testing of hypotheses is tremendously important because it can extend justified belief beyond what people can directly observe. This is how the existence of unobservable scientific entities is established (see chapter 5).

DEDUCING CONCLUSIONS

Deducing conclusions from other justified beliefs that you already have is another way to acquire new justified beliefs. Everyone has probably had the experience of suddenly realizing something based on facts that he or she already had. In this case you derive new useful information from things which you already believed. Frequently, the trick is in putting together the right information that you already have. The power of deduction in developing new beliefs is sometimes not obvious in discussions of deductive logic (see chapter 1). The conclusions of the arguments may not seem to be large advances in our justified beliefs. This is because the conclusions can look obvious. However, in complex deductions the conclusion may not be obvious beforehand; they become obvious only after you work through each step. If you think about what is involved in solving mathematical problems, you can understand how difficult it may be to form the right conclusion.

REPORTS FROM OTHER PEOPLE

Much of what we believe about the world is not based on our own observations, but rather on what other people have told us or written in books and newspapers. Young children generally accept what their parents and other authorities tell them, and this teaching produces many of their beliefs. Writing is one of the great advances of civilization because it allows information to be stored, communicated widely, and passed on to the next generation. Those who are interested in some specialized subject, such as the plants of the American Southwest or the history of Central Africa, have sources of information on these topics available to them.

Not everything that people say or write in books and newspapers is true. We have to sort through these claims to discover which are worthy of belief. This is a complicated process that goes on continuously. It makes use of all the other ways of justifying beliefs. We check what people say against what we ourselves observe, against our generalizations, against our tested hypotheses, and against what other people say. For the purposes of justifying beliefs, our objective is to find out whose testimony can be trusted. There are many different topics about which people can tell us things and many different reasons why what they tell us may be mistaken. For example, they may have poorly tested hypotheses, or they may be lying, or they may themselves believe people who do not know what they are talking about. We try to figure out, for a large number of different circumstances and subjects, who is likely to be giving us trustworthy information. What is especially significant about having good reasons for believing what specific people say about certain subjects is that this can tremendously expand the scope of things we have good reason to believe. By being able to count on the testimony of others, we can have good reasons for things about which we ourselves have little direct evidence. By being able to find reliable authorities on some subject, we can find out about all sorts of subjects without reviewing all of the evidence ourselves. This is necessary for any modern system of education, and it allows people to specialize in one area, while relying upon specialists in other areas.

SKEPTICISM

Skepticism is the claim that we do not or cannot know. It may be absolute: We do not or cannot know anything; or relative: We do not or cannot know certain kinds of things. Absolute skepticism has been charged with self-contradiction. We can know that we cannot know anything. Skeptics have responded either by shifting to relative skepticism or by denying that skepticism itself involves a knowledge claim. Thus: This is the situation we *seem* to be in. Skepticism has traditionally accepted the view that knowledge must be absolutely certain. It is easier to raise skeptical doubts about the supposed absolute certainty of beliefs than about the sufficiency of evidence for the beliefs. However, contemporary skeptics also frequently doubt that there can be sufficient evidence, or even good evidence, for beliefs.

Denying that knowledge is possible probably seems to you to be a very strange position. Since it seems obvious that we can learn more about the world, you are probably asking yourself why anyone would want to be a skeptic. This is a reasonable question. Skeptics have usually wanted to deny the possibility of knowledge in order to direct people toward something else. Skepticism has frequently been joined with religious faith. If we cannot know anything, particularly about ultimate questions concerning God, life after death, and good and evil, we just have to have faith. Since we have to believe something, but we cannot know anything, the skeptic claims that we should believe in his favorite religious doctrine, even though there is little evidence for it. Alternatively, the skeptic may want us to turn toward some social cause without worrying about what is true, or toward practical engagement in the world that does not worry about theoretical knowledge. Finally, there are some skeptics who just consider skepticism to be an interesting and believable, though not true, theoretical position.

Arguments for Skepticism

As a philosophical position, skepticism is not just a denial of the possibility of knowledge or a tendency to doubt. Skeptics need and use arguments to support their position. One argument is based on perceptual illusions and hallucinations. Our sense perception sometimes deceives us, such as when a stick in water appears to be bent, or there appears to be water on the road ahead. The skeptic asks how we can tell at any given time that we are not being deceived. If we cannot tell at any given time whether our sense perception is accurate, we cannot be sure whether even our supposed "corrections" of illusions are accurate. For example, when we approach the part of the road on which there seemed to be water, we cannot be sure that our seeing and feeling no water on the road is correct. If we can never be sure of our sense perceptions, we can never be sure of anything concerning the external world.

A related, more forceful, argument concerns dreams. During dreams we experience all sorts of environments, people, actions, and episodes that are very different from waking life. We ordinarily consider what happens in dreams not to be real. The skeptic asks how we can tell whether we are dreaming at any given moment. Have you ever asked yourself in a dream whether you are dreaming? Have you ever answered in the dream that you are not dreaming? If we cannot be sure whether we are dreaming now, we cannot be sure about the truth of anything that we now experience and think. A version of the dream argument is the story of a Chinese philosopher who once dreamed that he was a butterfly. Thereafter, he always wondered whether he was a man who dreamed he was a butterfly, or a butterfly who was dreaming it was a man.

Descartes—who was ultimately not a skeptic—proposed perhaps the strongest argument for skepticism. It is based on a conception of how the mind thinks of things. The "picture" conception of belief claims that we are in direct contact only with ideas or representations in our minds. We are directly aware only of our own thoughts of things, not of the things themselves. Even in sense perception, we are not in direct contact with the external world, but rather with our ideas or representations of the external world. If this is the correct account of belief, then it is possible that the external world is not at all like our portrait of it. (Idealists like Berkeley even claim that there is no external world.) Whatever causes the ideas in our minds during sense perception may be completely different from our ideas. Since we have no way of telling one way or the other, skepticism is the only reasonable position.

Descartes used a striking image to present this argument. Suppose that there was an evil demon, "evil genius," who manipulated your thoughts and that the external world as you think of it did not exist. This demon might place ideas directly into your mind. You would think that these ideas came from externally real things like trees and hills, but there would be no trees and hills. The ideas would come from the demon. The more contemporary version of this is the "brain in the vat." Suppose that your brain were transplanted from your head and kept alive in a vat of fluid. A team of scientists might connect electrical wires into all of the nerve endings in your brain. Your brain would receive the same sort of electrical input that it currently receives from the nerves connected to your eyes, ears, and other sense organs. The scientists could then control all of your sense experience by controlling the electrical input. They could make you perceive all sorts of things that did not exist in the external world. The skeptic claims that in either of these cases you would have no way of telling that you were being deceived. Since you have no way to tell, you cannot be absolutely certain, or even have good reason to think, that you are not being deceived now. Hence, it is quite possible that everything you believe is false. Since you are not certain that you know anything, skepticism is the only reasonable position.

DESCARTES'S ARGUMENT AGAINST SKEPTICISM

In his *Meditations on First Philosophy*, Descartes argues that it is possible to have absolutely certain knowledge about some topics. After presenting the major skeptical arguments, Descartes presents his famous *"cogito, ergo sum"* (Latin for "I think, therefore I am") argument. He reasons that even if an evil demon were deceiving him, he, the thinker, must exist. Deception requires that there be someone who is deceived. If his mind or consciousness did not exist, there would be no thoughts that could be mistaken. In order that it be possible for him to be mistaken, he must have thoughts. Descartes uses "thought" to include all conscious experiences including perceiving and remembering. He concludes that he can know with absolute certainty that he exists and that he has thoughts, because he cannot doubt this. The alternative—that he is mistakenly thinking that he is thinking—is impossible.

Knowing Our Own Thoughts

That he exists as a "thinking thing" is the first piece of absolutely certain knowledge. The next step is to argue that he can know with absolute certainty what his own thoughts are. If he cannot be certain that there are trees and hills that he is perceiving, he can at least be certain that he is having the experience of perceiving trees and hills. Even if he has no eyes, ears, head, or torso, he nevertheless is having certain experiences that present to his consciousness his body and the external world. This also applies to the other types of "thinking." Even if he has no past, he can be sure that he is having the current experience of remembering previous episodes. Descartes uses the same argument about deception to prove that he can know what his own current conscious experiences are. Deception requires that there be experiences that are mistaken. Even if an evil demon were deceiving him, or if he were dreaming, he nevertheless must be having the experiences that portray an external world, his own body, and other things. His belief that he is having these experiences is necessarily true, because he cannot be mistaken about them.

The next step in Descartes's chain of reasoning is to consider in more detail what he knows about his own current experiences. He has just claimed that he can know whether he is having the experience of seeing, feeling, desiring, remembering, judging, and so on. However, he recognizes that he may make hasty judgments about the contents of his experiences, his ideas—what his perceiving, feeling, or judging is "of" or "about." As his wax example demonstrates, he may initially think that "the same piece of wax" is just a bunch of perceptible properties, but careful reflection shows that what he really means is somewhat different. What he really means is "a certain extended thing that is flexible and movable" and has the perceptible properties. This investigation of what he knows about the contents, the ideas, of his thoughts leads Descartes to conclude that even concerning his own thoughts he cannot know something unless he clearly and distinctly understands it. Clear and distinct understanding, "perception" emerges as the criterion or the mark of truth. When he clearly and distinctly understands what he means, the contents of his thoughts, he can tell whether his ideas are true or false.

Knowing the External World

Up to this point, Descartes has argued that he can know that he exists, that he thinks, that he is having various types of experiences, and that his experiences have specific contents or ideas. All of his knowledge concerns himself and his thoughts. He has not yet proven anything about what exists outside his thoughts. If he could go no further, Descartes would have defeated skepticism in general (he can know some things), but he would not have defeated skepticism about the external world. He would not know whether his ideas of external things corresponded to any real external things. The next step is to establish some knowledge of what exists outside the mind.

In order to know whether or not his ideas correspond to anything outside the mind, Descartes employed God. God is supposed to guarantee that clearly and distinctly understood ideas of the external world actually correspond to the external world. However, first Descartes had to prove God's existence without assuming that he knew anything other than his own thinking and ideas. He could not use most of the traditional arguments, such as the argument from design or the first-cause argument (see chapter 2), because these assume knowledge of the external world.

Descartes used three arguments for the existence of God. One of these was the ontological argument (see chapter 2), which suits Descartes's situation because it argues directly from the idea of God. Another was the causal argument, which argues that only a perfect being could be the cause of the idea of a perfect being, which each of us has. This also starts from the idea of God, but it does include claims about causation. The third argument concerns preserving the mind through time.

GOD AND THE EXTERNAL WORLD

Whether or not he succeeded in proving God's existence, Descartes used God to establish the possibility of knowledge of the external world. An all-powerful and all-good God would not deceive us, because only a limited or imperfect being has any reason to deceive anyone. God would not make us such that if we used all of our faculties properly we would still have to make mistakes. To make us such that we could not avoid mistakes would be to deceive us in a fundamental way. Hence, if we use our mental powers properly and do not judge about anything unless and until we clearly and distinctly understand it, we will not make any mistakes. We have to suspend judgment until we sufficiently understand that about which we are thinking.

We have a natural tendency to think that some of our ideas, those that we receive in perception, are caused by external, material things. We naturally think that our sensory idea of a tree on a lawn is caused by a real tree on a lawn (remember that Descartes accepted the "picture" theory, which holds that we are directly aware only of ideas in our minds.) We know that these sensory ideas are not caused by our own minds because they are not under our control and they are more vivid and forceful than ideas that we imagine. We can clearly and distinctly understand the notion of causation, so that we can know that these ideas are caused by something. We also know that God made us such that we can avoid all general mistakes if we use all of our faculties properly. Using all of our faculties, we have no way to tell that we are mistaken in thinking that external, material things cause our sensory ideas. Descartes concludes that we can know that external, material things cause our sensory ideas. Through this connection, we can then know some of the general features of the external physical world.

OTHER ARGUMENTS AGAINST SKEPTICISM

Descartes's argument against skepticism proceeded in several stages: first knowledge of ourselves and our thoughts, then knowledge of God, then knowledge of the external world. Most philosophers accept the thesis that we can know about our own thoughts (see chapter 6). However, few contemporary philosophers accept Descartes' use of God to make knowledge of the external world possible. If you accept the theory that we are directly aware only of ideas in our minds, some other connection between ideas in the mind and external reality is necessary. According to this theory of belief, knowledge of the external world would require that something guarantee that ideas in the mind correspond to the external world.

Evolution
Guarantees
Correspondence

Many contemporary philosophers think that evolution provides the necessary connection. Suppose that humans are part of the natural world and have developed over millions of years in accord with the general principles of evolution. In this case, our perceptual and cognitive abilities should aid our survival and reproduction. In order to survive and prosper in the material world, our perception would have to give us a generally accurate picture of things. Almost all of what we do is based on our perception of our surroundings. If ideas in our minds did not correspond to the external world, our behavior could not be adjusted to the circumstances of the external world. It would be completely a matter of chance whether we banged into trees and rocks, or walked around them, because what we see, hear, smell, and feel would not correspond to what was there. It would be completely a matter of chance whether we found things to eat, shelter from the elements, protection from predators, mates to reproduce, and so on. From the perspective of evolutionary biology, a species whose "picture" of the environment did not, in general, correspond to the environment could not survive. Humans, as an evolved animal species, must have a generally accurate "picture" of the relevant features of their environment.

Just as our perceptual ideas would have to correspond to the external world, so our thoughts and inferences would, in general, have to provide information that was useful for surviving and prospering. Our thoughts about the external world, our "map" of it, would have to guide our behavior in ways that were generally successful. If we had good reason to believe that fruit trees, deer, or some other source of food was in the next valley, these justified beliefs would, in general, have to correspond to reality if we were to find food. Inferences would, in general, have to produce conclusions that would guide successful actions. Otherwise, a species that made that type of inference would be less successful than one that did not, and so would tend to be replaced. Even if we are directly aware only of ideas in our minds, the survival and success of the human species show that these ideas generally correspond to reality.

Direct Awareness of External Reality

Another frequent objection to skepticism denies the basic principle that we are directly aware only of ideas in our minds. Some theories of perception consider it to be a direct awareness of external reality. We see the tree on the hill, not some idea of it in our minds. If perception is a type of direct contact with external things, many of the traditional skeptical questions do not arise. Theories of perception as direct contact still have to account for illusions and hallucinations, since these are what tempt us to think that we are directly aware only of "inner ideas" (the hallucinated things), not external objects. However, these can be explained as distorting ways of appearing of external things. We do perceive external things, but sometimes they can appear in ways that do not easily reveal what they are. For example, a flat round penny viewed at an angle will appear elliptical, and hot air rising from a warm highway will look, from a distance, like water (it appears as water on the road).

HUME'S SKEPTICISM

David Hume is most famous for his skeptical doubts about causation and induction, although he also raised questions about knowledge of the external world. Hume's empiricism was the basis for his skeptical questions. Like other empiricists, Hume thought that all knowledge about the external world must come from sense perception. Although we can know about "relations between ideas," such as mathematical truths, this knowledge is only about ideas in the mind, not about the external world. We cannot know with certainty whether there are any real instances in the external world of these ideas (see Empiricism, p. 44).

Doubts About Causation

Concerning causation, Hume asked whether there is any reasonable basis for believing that effects are necessitated, made to happen, by causes. We ordinarily think that there is some power or force in the cause that makes the effect happen (see chapter 3). Hume claimed that we never perceive this power or force. All that we perceive is that when the cause happens, the effect happens. For example, when one moving billiard ball strikes another, we do not perceive in the moving ball any power or force that makes the second ball move. Since we never actually perceive any "necessary connection" between the cause and effect, and perception is the only way to know about the external world, Hume claimed that we do not have any rational basis for believing that causation exists in the external world. Hume then offered his own theory of why we think that there are necessary connections between events in the external world. Hume's theory is that we project the notion of necessary connection onto external events. After we have observed that two events regularly occur together, we expect the second to happen whenever the first happens. The idea of the first event brings about, in our minds, the idea of the second event. That the idea of the first event makes the idea of the second event happen leads us to imagine that the first event itself makes the second event happen.

Doubts About Induction

Induction is the procedure in which we draw a general conclusion from a number of individual cases (see chapter 1). For example, from observing a number of cases in which individual pieces of balsa wood float in water, we may conclude that all balsa wood floats in water. Hume asked whether there is any rational basis for induction. Can we ever be justified in drawing general conclusions, which cover all cases that might ever occur, from a limited set of observed cases? What reason could we have for thinking that all the unobserved cases are like the observed cases? Hume suggested that if we knew that nature was uniform we might be able to justify these generalizations. However, he thought that we do not have any rational grounds for thinking that nature is uniform. In particular, we have no good reason for thinking that the future will be like the past. Hence, we have no good reason to think that relationships which we have observed in the past (such as that pieces of balsa wood float) will continue in the future.

A PRIORI KNOWLEDGE

A priori knowledge is knowledge that is not known to be true on the basis of sense perception. It is known in some other way, and it is known with certainty. Mathematical truths are the most famous example. We can be certain of mathematical truths, and this knowledge seems not to be based on sense perception. That two + three = five is known with certainty. It is not possible that two + three might sometimes be equal to six or to four. We seem to know that two + three = five in some way other than through sense perception. We might know this even if we never perceived two things, three things, or five things. The major questions about a priori knowledge are: How we can know anything a priori? How can a priori knowledge tell us anything about the world?

Rationalists claim that all knowledge is a priori. They try to develop systems of knowledge starting from self-evident basic principles, such as "everything has a cause," and basic definitions, such as the definition of what substance is. We can know these things a priori through the "light of reason" or rational intuition. A major problem for rationalists has been to explain how we can know that these basic principles and definitions apply to real, individual things. If we know, from its definition, what a substance is, how can we tell that anything is a substance? How can we know that there are instances of this universal?

Empiricists have a similar problem about "relations of ideas." Empiricists claim that mathematical truths and other a priori knowledge can be known by reasoning. However, this reasoning is not about external reality, such as numbers, the physical world, and so on. It is about ideas in our minds. Mathematical truths and basic principles concern the relations of ideas to one another. The problem is whether these relations of ideas can reveal anything about the external world. For empiricists, the connection to the world is made by sense perception. However, sense perception is always of individual instances (this tree on that hill, not trees or hills in general) and is never fully certain. Sense perception can make mistakes in classifying an individual thing under some universal (for example, that this thing is a tree) or in thinking that some relation of ideas applies to this individual (for example, thinking that this thing is a tree so that all the characteristics of trees must apply to it). Hence, empiricists are also unable to explain how we can know with certainty general truths that apply to the world.

Kant on A Priori Knowledge

Kant tried to resolve the problems of a priori knowledge. He tried to show that absolutely certain knowledge of general truths that apply to the external world is possible. He claimed that we can know, a priori, mathematical truths and the basic principles of natural science, and that these general truths apply to the physical world. Kant's explanation of a priori knowledge was that the mind structures the "external world." The mind employs the structures of space, time, number, substance, and causation in all of its perceiving and thinking. In everyday life, we consider these structures to be features of independent things that we detect. We assume that they are independent of the mind and that the mind reaches out to them. Kant claimed that they are really features of the mind, not of independent things, but that they form our conception of the physical world. They appear to be part of independent reality because we experience independent reality through them. Rather than something to which we reach out, they are part of the "reaching out" itself. They are like eyeglasses through which we can encounter independent reality. Hence, everything that we might perceive and think must conform to these structures. When we know about these structures, we know about all parts of space and time, and all individual things that we might ever encounter or imagine. Hence, we can know general truths about all spatial things, all things in time, all material objects, and all cases of causation.

Kant's most famous example of this a priori knowledge is Euclidean geometry. If you prove that the angles of a triangle add up to 180 degrees, you know something about all triangular objects in any region of the universe. Without perceiving or investigating each individual triangle, you know that the sum of its angles equals 180 degrees. Kant claimed that geometry investigates the nature of the space that we use in perception and thought. We can know with certainty about this space because it is only a structure of the mind. As a structure of the mind, it is readily available to us. However, we can also know that all physical things will conform to the truths of geometry, because all things can be perceived and thought of only through the medium of this space. They can be "seen" only through "spatial eye-glasses." Although there are things-in-themselves that are independent of the structures of our minds (see The Unknowable in chapter 3, p. 29), the world that we can investigate always conforms to the basic structures of the mind. This is how a priori knowledge that applies to the world is possible.

OBJECTIONS TO KANT

Many contemporary philosophers dispute Kant's claim that space, time, number, substance, and causation are only structures of the mind. While accepting that our conceptions of these things affect our ongoing experience, they think that these conceptions reveal something about independent reality. Independent reality (things-in-themselves) is not permanently unknowable. Our conceptions of the physical world are partially accurate depictions of independent reality. The basic structures of the world in these conceptions are not fixed and unimprovable. Our conceptions of the physical world can be improved. These improvements progressively reveal the features of independent reality. The improvements make the conceptions more accurate depictions of independent reality. Our conception of space is not just a structure of our minds; it is our best current understanding of the independently real space. On the basis of what we can perceive, detect with instruments, and determine by experiments, we can form a better understanding of the nature of the independently real space. Thus, Euclidean geometry is not unchangeable knowledge of space as a structure of the mind. It was, and for most practical purposes, still is, the best understanding of the nature of independently real space.

RELATIVISM

Kant argued that there is only one way that the mind can operate. He claimed that being conscious depends upon employing the basic structures that explain a priori knowledge. Many philosophers, anthropologists, and historians have accepted Kant's notion that the mind structures everything that it encounters. However, many of these thinkers also claim that there are a variety of structures that the mind can employ. There are different structures of space and time and different basic categories; these are like different tints and prescriptions for the "mind's eyeglasses." If different structures of space or time, or other basic categories are employed by different people, cultures, or linguistic groups, "everyday reality" will be different for them. The world that each of them can investigate will be different because of the different basic structures. Hence, the knowledge that is available to each of them will be different. This is the main argument for relativism about knowledge.

Extreme and Moderate Relativism

Relativism about knowledge claims that knowledge is not the same for all people. Knowledge is relative to something, such as a set of structures that the mind employs or the structures contained in a language or the worldview that a culture employs or the worldview of an economic class (Marxism). In its most extreme form, relativism about knowledge claims that something could be known to be true within one set of structures, or worldview, and known to be false within a different set of structures. This extreme form of relativism runs into a serious problem. How could the exact same thing be thought in two worldviews that are supposed to be so different? How could a statement that is true in one set of structures mean the same thing as a statement that is false in another? If the structures affect whatever can appear, differences in the structures should mean that the exact same thing could not appear in both sets of structures.

In response to this problem, more moderate forms of relativism claim that people with the different structures or worldviews think of somewhat different things. Something can be known to be true within one set of structures, or worldview, that cannot even be thought, or known, within another set of structures. For example, someone who understands scientific theories and modern appliances can know that electric current is a flow of negatively charged electrons, whereas someone who lived in the Middle Ages or in a primitive society has no idea what electricity is. If he saw a working electrical appliance, he would think that spiritual or magical forces were involved. The more moderate versions of relativism are sometimes joined with a metaphysical position about reality having many different types of things and properties (see Alternative Realities in chapter 3, p. 31). Some people might be more sensitive to some of these real things and properties, while other people are sensitive to different but nevertheless real things and properties.

Evidence for Relativism

The main argument for relativism about knowledge is that different structures or worldviews determine what we can perceive and encounter. What evidence is there for such different structures or worldviews? There are two major theories about what determines what we can perceive and encounter: that the structure of our language does this, and that our culture does this, or the two can be combined. That languages have somewhat different structures and that cultural conceptions of the world are somewhat different are the starting points for most defenses of relativism.

LANGUAGE

Most of our thoughts about anything employ language in one way or another. The types of things into which our perceptual fields are divided are affected by our words. We tend to pick out the things and properties for which we have words. Most of our thoughts are formulated in language. When you think about what you have to do tomorrow or the location of your home town, you formulate some linguistic question or statement to yourself, such as "What do I have to do tomorrow?" and "My home town is a suburb of Miami in Florida." Linguists and anthropologists have investigated the differences in the basic structures—grammars—of different languages. Not all languages have the same types of nouns, adjectives, verbs, and tenses of verbs as English. Relativists claim that since language is so important to our experience of the world, these differences in the grammar of a language make different worlds available to different linguistic groups. A language that is based on nouns and adjectives will consider the world to consist of enduring things (nouns) with properties (adjectives) whereas other languages may "cut up" the world differently. Verbs may not be distinguished in the same way from nouns, or the tenses of verbs may be different. In English we use the same word for falling snow, hard-packed snow, slushy snow, and blowing snow, while Eskimo languages have different words for all of these conditions. The Eskimos do not think of these as the same stuff, snow, that is in different conditions. They consider the situation as a whole, such as "slushy snow that gets your feet wet and is hard to get a sled through" and do not group the different situations under the general description "snow." The anthropologist and linguist Benjamin Whorf (1897–1941) claimed that the Hopi, an American Indian people, did not have a conception of time, because their language did not use tenses, such as the past tense "was," present tense "is," and future tense "will be." There are countless other examples of differences between languages that relativists can use to support their position.

CULTURE

People grow up and learn about the world within a culture. Different cultures may have very different views about the nature of the world. Some cultures think that everything, including plants, forests, valleys, and mountains, has a mind or spirit that controls its behavior, while others think that most things are matter without soul. Some cultures understand most events in terms of their religion, while in others God and religion are not an important part of everyday life. Given the vast differences between cultures in their practices, languages, beliefs about things, and values, relativists claim that members of different cultures live in different "worlds." Because of the differences in their general worldviews through which they experience things, members of different cultures do not encounter the exact same things.

Arguments Against Relativism

Philosophers continue to argue about the moderate forms of relativism about knowledge. Some opponents of relativism attack the idea that people's experience is really that different. They claim that there are universal features of all human perception and that there is a universal structure underlying all human languages. Some philosophers argue that we have to understand other people to perceive and to interact with the same sorts of ordinary things that we do. Otherwise, we could not recognize them as having perceptions and thoughts about the world at all. If their world were really so different from ours, we would not be able to recognize that they are conscious at all, and we would not be able to recognize that they have a language. The fact that other languages can be learned and understood by English speakers argues against the notion of different worlds.

Other opponents of relativism attack the notion that different current worldviews mean that people live in different worlds. Those philosophers who reject Kant's theory about what is available to be known reject relativism for the same reason. They think that any conception of the world can be improved. It can be changed so as to be a more accurate depiction of independent things. They argue that a current worldview does not determine what is available to be known. This is shown by the fact that there can be evidence within a worldview that indicates how it should be changed.

*P*hilosophers have summarized our common sense notion of knowledge in the formula "knowledge is justified true belief." This definition includes three features: belief, truth, and justification. There are two important features to belief: Belief portrays the world to be a certain way, and we accept this account of the facts. The strength of our acceptance of the account of the world can vary.

Beliefs are true when they depict things as they are. There are three major philosophical theories of truth. The correspondence theory claims that beliefs are true when they correspond to an independent reality. The coherence theory claims that beliefs are true when they fit together well, cohere, with one another. Idealists accept the coherence theory. The pragmatic theory claims that beliefs are true when using them allows us to accomplish our objectives in the world and to get what we want. Defenders of the correspondence theory consider coherence and practical usefulness to be major parts of the justification of beliefs.

To have knowledge, a believer needs some way to recognize that his beliefs are true. A justification is supposed to reveal why a belief is true. Sufficient good reasons for what you believe make up a justification. Good reasons are really connected with that for which they are used as reasons and can be recognized by other reasonable people. Philosophers disagree about how much evidence (good reasons) is necessary for knowledge. Some follow Descartes in thinking that absolute certainty is necessary. Others follow Locke in thinking that strong evidence without absolute certainty is sufficient.

Rationalism and empiricism are two contrary views about the sources of knowledge. Rationalists think that knowledge must be absolutely certain and comes from reason. Knowledge must be proved from self-evident truths, such as the fact that I exist, basic definitions, and basic principles. Em-

piricists think that knowledge need not be absolutely certain and comes from sense perception. The only use of reason is to make clear the relations between ideas in the mind.

The five major ways of building up new justified beliefs are: sense perception, forming generalizations from sense perception, forming and testing hypotheses, deducing conclusions from other justified beliefs, and learning about a subject from the reports of other people. Sense perception tells us about the features of individual things. On the basis of perceiving a number of individual instances, we can form an inductive generalization about types of things. Errors can occur in generalizations if we use the wrong types or have a non-representative sample.

A hypothesis is some account of a situation that goes beyond any of the observed facts. A hypothesis is justified by testing for other data that would occur if, and only if, the hypothesis is correct. The forming and testing of hypotheses is important because it can extend justified belief beyond what people can observe directly. Deducing conclusions from justified beliefs that we already have can produce information that we have not realized before. We also acquire new information from what other people tell us and write in books and newspapers. We have to sort through these claims to determine which are worthy of belief. Finding reliable authorities on some subject allows us to have good reasons for beliefs, without reviewing all of the evidence.

Skepticism claims that we do not and cannot know anything. Skeptics support their position with arguments concerning illusions and hallucinations, dreams, and the nature of belief. If we are deceived in illusions, hallucinations, and dreams, and we cannot tell at any given time whether we are having these experiences, we can never be sure that we are not being deceived. According to the "picture" conception of belief, we are directly aware only of our ideas of things, not of the things themselves. We can never tell what the independent source of our ideas is like. It could be completely different (such as an evil demon) from what the ideas picture.

Descartes's argument against skepticism starts with his claim that he must exist and have thoughts, even if he is being deceived. He then argues that if he is careful, he can know his own thoughts with absolute certainty. In order to know that the ideas in his mind correspond to anything outside of the mind, Descartes employs God. After attempting to prove that God exists, he argues that an all-perfect God would not make us so that we inevitably make mistakes, even when we are using our faculties improperly. Since we naturally think that our perceptual ideas correspond to independent things and have no way of telling that this is a mistake, they must actually correspond to independent things. Otherwise, God would be deceiving us.

Other arguments against skepticism about the external world do not use God. Some contemporary philosophers think that evolution guarantees that ideas in the mind correspond to the external world. As an evolved animal species, humans must have a generally accurate "picture" of their environment, and their thoughts must lead to successful actions. Otherwise, we could not survive, prosper, and reproduce. Another objection to skepticism denies the basic principle that we are only directly aware of ideas in our minds. If perception is directly aware of external things, not of ideas, many skeptical questions do not arise.

Hume raised skeptical doubts about causation and induction on empiricist grounds. Hume claimed that we never perceive a power or force in a cause that makes an effect happen. For this reason, we have no rational basis for thinking that one event necessitates another event. Hume also claimed that we have no rational basis for developing generalizations. We have no good reason for thinking that all unobserved cases are like the observed cases.

A priori knowledge is known with certainty in some way other than by sense perception. Mathematical truths are the most famous examples. Both rationalists and empiricists had trouble explaining how we can know, a priori, general truths that apply to the world. Kant argued that a priori knowledge of geometry, arithmetic, and the basic principles of natural science is possible because the mind structures what we take to be the external world. Space, time, number, substance, and causation are structures of the mind through which we experience things. In knowing about these structures of the mind, we know certain features of anything that we might ever encounter. Many contemporary philosophers dispute Kant's claim that space, time, number, substance, and causation are only structures of the mind.

Relativism claims that knowledge is not the same for all people. Knowledge is relative to worldviews or structures of the mind and language. The most extreme form of relativism about knowledge runs into a serious problem. More moderate forms of relativism claim that something can be known to be true within one worldview that cannot be thought or known in a different worldview. Relativists argue that since language is so important to our experience of the world and languages have different words and grammars, different linguistic groups live in different worlds. They also argue that the worldviews of different cultures affect everything that can be experienced, so that members of different cultures live in different worlds. Opponents of relativism about knowledge claim that there are universal features of human perception and language. They also argue that people's current worldviews do not determine what is available to be known, because worldviews can change.

Selected Readings

Carr, B., and D. J. O'Connor. *Introduction to the Theory of Knowledge.* Minneapolis: University of Minnesota, 1982.

Dancy, J. *An Introduction to Contemporary Epistemology.* Oxford: B. Blackwell, 1985.

Descartes, R. *Meditations on First Philosophy.* (Several good translations).

Gifford, N.L. *When in Rome: An Introduction to Relativism and Knowledge.* Albany: SUNY, 1983.

Hume, D. *An Inquiry Concerning Human Understanding.* (Several editions are available).

Kant, I. *Prolegomena to Any Future Metaphysics.* (Several good translations.)

5

Science

*S*tarting in the early 1600s, science replaced religion and classical texts as the authority on most issues of fact. If we want to know something about the facts of the world, we do not consult the Bible or our church. We consult what science says about the matter. We usually assume that whatever natural science claims about some issue is true. However, there are a number of issues in which the complete authority of science is questioned. In order to understand the disputes between natural science and other claims to knowledge, it is helpful to know how scientific claims are developed and justified. This chapter examines the nature of scientific knowledge, the differences between scientific entities and our common-sense conceptions of real entities, the dispute between evolution and creationism, and the question of relativism about scientific knowledge.

SCIENTIFIC KNOWLEDGE

Contemporary scientific theories can be very complicated and difficult for a lay person to understand. When we learn about scientific developments in the news, most of us do not fully understand how the claims about the world are justified. Generally, the truth of scientific claims is accepted by people on the authority of the group of scientists. Most people do not have a very good idea how scientists justify their general laws and theories, which are sometimes about strange entities, such as quarks and quasars.

Scientific knowledge is built up in the same way that any kind of knowledge is developed (see chapter 4). Scientists justify their claims in the same general ways that people justify their non-scientific claims about the world. Scientists observe individual things, form generalizations about types of things, form and test hypotheses, deduce conclusions from what they already know, and rely upon the results of other scientific investigations. That scientific ways of knowing are not, in general, different from our everyday ways of knowing is frequently not realized. There are three main reasons for this. One reason is that in some areas of science, particularly physics, hypotheses are formulated using a lot of mathematics. The mathematical expression of a hypothesis makes it somewhat foreign to a lay person. A second reason is that many of the things that science investigates are different from the things we deal with in everyday life. Some scientific theories concern strange and unobservable entities. People frequently do not have any idea how someone would determine whether these non-ordinary things exist, or how they work. The third reason is that scientific hypotheses are usually tested by experiments that are themselves complicated and require an understanding of other scientific theories. While we are all familiar with forming hypotheses and testing them, we are not all familiar with the specific experimental ways in which scientists test their hypotheses.

Sensory Observation

The basis of scientific knowledge is sense perception. Scientific knowledge always starts from and returns to observable facts of the world. Biologists investigating the variety of plants and insects in a specific environment have to observe individual specimens to learn about their features. The Italian physicist and mathematician Galileo Galilei (1564–1642) made many observations of how cannonballs and other objects move through the air as a first step toward formulating general laws about moving objects (you may have heard the famous story about Galileo dropping two iron balls of different size from the top of the Leaning Tower of Pisa to see whether they fell at the same speed.) Scientists observe individual things in order to develop knowledge about types of things. The observations of individual things are a means of developing generalizations about all similar things and forming hypotheses that explain why the individual things behave as they do. These generalizations and hypotheses have to apply to other individual things, so sensory observation is also employed in the testing of generalizations and hypotheses.

On the basis of many observations, an empirical law about the behavior of some type of thing can be formed. Empirical laws are well-confirmed generalizations that employ only observational terms—terms for what can be observed. Empirical laws do not use any terms defined only in a theory. Consider the law about gases:

$$P \text{ (pressure)} \times V \text{ (volume)} = T \text{ (temperature)} \times K \text{ (a constant)}$$

If a gas is in a sealed container and you compress it with a piston so that its volume is reduced, either the pressure the gas exerts on the piston and the container will become greater, or the temperature of the gas must be reduced. Alternatively, if you heat the gas, either the gas must expand, increase its volume, or its pressure will become greater. This law concerns the relationship between three features of gases that can be directly observed. We can feel pressure and temperature, and we can see, and feel, volume. To determine the exact value of the constant, we have to use measuring instruments that are more exact than our unaided senses, but these instruments measure features that we can perceive.

Scientific Theories

Hypotheses and the testing of hypotheses are particularly important for scientific knowledge. Science seeks laws and theories that go beyond what is actually observed. Empirical laws go beyond what is ever observed, because they are generalizations that concern all cases, not just the ones that have been or will be observed. For this reason, the justification of empirical laws is subject to the problems of justifying inductive generalizations (see Hume's Skepticism in chapter 4). Scientific theories go even further beyond what is observed, because they involve things and properties that cannot be directly observed with our senses. The terms that refer to things and properties that are defined within a theory are called "theoretical terms."

Scientific theories frequently introduce entities that are different from ordinary things and properties. Scientific theories hypothesize that there are realms of non-ordinary entities that interact with one another in specific ways, and that these interactions produce the effects in ordinary things that we can observe. We can observe when a cut on our skin becomes red, swollen, and tender to the touch. We consider the cut to be "infected." Well-justified medical theories hypothesize that there are microscopic substances, bacteria, that get into such a cut and multiply there to produce the infected state. The bacteria cannot be observed with our unaided senses. We cannot learn about bacteria just by careful sensory observation. We need to think in terms of a theory or hypothesis about what is there (bacteria) and what happens (that these multiply in a cut to produce infection).

Theories contain laws about how the entities of the theory behave. Laws that concern the interactions of theoretical entities with one another are theoretical laws. A law that concerns what makes bacteria multiply, die, or change form is a theoretical law. Theories also contain correspondence rules, or "bridge laws," that connect the theoretical entities to what can be observed. A simple correspondence rule would be, "enough bacteria in a cut produce: redness, swelling, and tenderness." The theoretical laws and the correspondence rules together make up the theory. The correspondence rules, by connecting the condition of theoretical entities to observable conditions, allow the theory to be applied to individual cases.

Testing Theories

Scientific theories are hypotheses that are designed to explain and predict certain things. Scientific and other hypotheses have to be tested to determine whether they are true. The most important part of testing a scientific theory is determining whether it accounts for all of the available data. The theory should explain what we have actually observed to happen and predict the occurrence of things on which we can check. If what the theory predicts does in fact happen, this is evidence for the theory. The more unlikely are the theoretical predictions that actually occur, the stronger is the confirmation of the theory. If a theory predicts that the sun will rise tomorrow, that the sun rises is not particularly strong evidence for the theory because we already expected the sun to rise. However, if the theory predicts that the sun will not rise tomorrow, and the sun does not rise, that would be strong evidence for the theory.

The most common way of understanding explanation and prediction is the covering law model, also called the "deductive-nomological" model. According to this model, results are deduced from the laws of the theory and a statement of the initial, usually observable, conditions. The theoretical laws—about the interactions of theoretical entities and correspondence rules of the theory, together with a statement of the relevant particular conditions, imply a statement about a specific result. This result is what is explained by being deduced from the theory plus the conditions. In the case of a prediction, a result is deduced from the theory plus the relevant initial conditions. We then observe whether the actual occurrence fits the predicted result.

Many factors can affect what happens. Experiments are attempts to test a theory by controlling the factors that might affect the result of the experiment. The point of an experiment is to be able to rule out factors other than those that will bear on the truth or falsity of the theory. If the influence of extraneous factors can be ruled out, then whether the result predicted by the theory occurs or not will be evidence for or against the theory.

Scientific knowledge has been built up over several centuries. Most of what individual scientists claim to know about the world has been learned from other scientists, and most of this knowledge is theoretical. In engaging in scientific research, scientists assume the truth of many scientific theories about the world. The testing of almost all current scientific theories presupposes other scientific theories. Any experiment involves more than the theory that is being tested. It also involves other theories about how the instruments work, what the initial conditions for the experiment are, and how to prevent extraneous factors from influencing the result. In terms of the covering law model, the result of an experiment is deduced not only from the theory being tested, but also from all the other accepted theories that go into setting up the experiment, called "auxiliary hypotheses." Sometimes, one of these auxiliary hypotheses later turns out to be mistaken. In this case, the result of an experiment may turn out not to be the evidence that it was initially thought to be, for or against the theory being tested.

The testing of scientific theories is an ongoing process. A theory can never be proven, once and for all, to be totally true. The more varied the things that the theory explains and predicts, the better confirmed the theory is. Many theories become so well confirmed, and are presupposed so much in the testing of other theories, that they are taken to be just facts about the world. However, it is always possible for new evidence to require that a theory be revised or even abandoned. Sir Isaac Newton's (1642–1727) theory of gravitation and motion was accepted and used for over two hundred years, before Albert Einstein's (1879–1955) theory of relativity showed that it had to be revised (Newton's laws apply only approximately under certain conditions).

At any given time, more than one theory may explain all the currently available data, or one theory may do a good job in explaining some of the data, but a competing theory may better explain some of the other data. In addition to explaining the data, there are other factors that determine which of several competing theories is a better theory. Precision makes a theory better. A theory that can make more precise predictions is better than one that can make less precise predictions. The preciseness of the predictions makes testing more accurate. Opening up new types of evidence—this is sometimes called "serendipity," which means "happy chance"—makes a theory better. A theory that predicts the existence of previously unknown phenomena is better than one that predicts only known types of phenomena. Theoretical support "from above" makes a theory better. A theory that can be deduced from more comprehensive theories that have an independent evidential basis is better than one that cannot. (If it disagreed with more comprehensive theories, something would have to be revised.) Finally, simplicity makes a theory better. Complexity that is not necessary to explain the data should be avoided. The simpler theory that accounts for all the available data is the better.

Instrumentalism

Instrumentalism is the claim that scientific theories do not portray reality. Scientific theories are only useful instruments for predicting what will happen if specific conditions are satisfied. According to instrumentalism, there is no reason to think that the non-ordinary entities of a theory, such as bacteria or genes or quarks, exist. These entities and the theory about how they interact are just a useful way of thinking in order to predict observable happenings. Instrumentalists think that the observable evidence for a theory is all that is real. Since it is always possible that even a well-justified scientific theory may have to be revised or even abandoned, there is no reason to believe in the independent existence of the entities the theory postulates. It is better to consider these to be mere devices for predicting observable states of affairs.

One major objection to instrumentalism is that it is hard to draw a sharp line between what can be observed and what is only a theoretical entity. Some things we can see with our unaided senses; other things can be seen only with a low-power telescope or a microscope; other things can be seen only with a high-power telescope or microscope. Many things that are initially unobservable can later be observed, as our instruments are improved. Things which initially are understood only through a theory, such as bacteria, may later become observable with more powerful instruments. For this reason it seems unwise to consider observable things to be real, but unobservable things to be just useful ideas.

SCIENTIFIC REALITY VERSUS EVERYDAY REALITY

If scientific theories portray reality, and current scientific knowledge—the set of well-justified theories—is at least approximately true about some things, then many non-ordinary entities exist. Questions then arise about the relationship between these scientific entities, the entities hypothesized by scientific theory, and the enduring things with properties that we deal with in everyday life. Do both scientific entities and ordinary entities exist in reality? Are scientific entities what are ultimately real, while ordinary things and properties are only our mistaken conceptions of what is real?

Properties of Physical Things

Material things can be divided into spatial parts. The smaller parts of a physical thing may not be able to do what the whole thing can do; for example, a twig separated from a tree cannot continue to grow leaves. Nevertheless, we commonsensibly think that the smaller parts of material things continue to have the basic properties of material things. Smaller parts have size, shape, weight, color, temperature, and so on.

In the early 1600s, Galileo and other scientists developed the scientific theory that material things are made up of tiny parts, atoms, that do not have many of the properties that we perceive ordinary physical things to have. Atoms have size, shape, location, weight, and motion, but they do not have many other sensible properties, such as color, taste, smell, sound, or being hot or cold. The arrangements and movements of atoms cause us to have all of our sensory ideas. However, the sensory ideas of size, shape, location, weight, and motion correspond to what atoms really are, while the sensory ideas of color, taste, smell, sound, and being hot or cold do not. These latter sensory ideas are produced in our minds by the motions of atoms affecting our sense organs. If there were no sense organs, there would be no color, taste, smell, sound, or being hot or cold.

Scientific theory about what makes up normal-sized physical objects has changed, in some ways, since the early atomists, but the basic dispute about the properties of material things has continued. Those properties that atoms—or matter, according to Descartes—really have come to be called "primary qualities." Those properties that atoms cause us to perceive, because of our sense organs and minds, but that are not in the atoms themselves came to be called "secondary qualities." The debate about whether normal-sized physical objects really have some secondary qualities, such as color, still goes on.

The scientific investigation, not only of physical things, but also of how our sensory apparatus works, has supported the view that some sensory properties are not really in things. It has become widely accepted that the sensory properties of taste and smell are not really in physical objects. The taste of an apple is not really in the apple. What is in the physical object are different atoms arranged into complex molecules. These complex molecules act upon the tissues inside our mouths and noses to cause us to perceive the distinctive taste and smell of an apple. That taste and smell are secondary properties dependent upon our sense organs and minds does not bother most people. However, that color is a secondary property is still a matter of debate. Bishop Berkeley claimed that we cannot think of an extended surface without its having some color, including gray. We cannot think of something having primary qualities without its also having color. Although Berkeley's argument seems to be false for blind people, whose idea of extended surfaces is based mainly on touch, the idea that colors are real properties of surfaces has some supporters.

Scientific Reductionism and Emergent Properties

Chapter 3 raised the question of whether scientific entities were an ultimate reality that "lies behind" our ordinary world. Some philosophers and scientists think that scientific entities, such as atoms, neutrons, protons, electrons, and quarks, are what basically exist. Everything else is made up of these basic scientific entities. This position is called "scientific reductionism" because everything real is "reduced" to scientific entities. According to scientific reductionism, solid objects and fluids and gases, are nothing more than complex arrangements of atoms, or other scientific entities. Normal-sized objects, such as apples, are made up of atoms bonded together into molecules. The properties of real things—normal-sized solid objects, gases, fluids, and so on—are only the properties of their parts and of the arrangements of their parts. Thus, the size, shape, and weight (mass) of an apple depend upon the number of atoms that compose it and how they are formed (bonded together). An apple can be solid, even though individual atoms are not solid. This is because atoms can be bonded together so as to produce solid structures, or fluid structures. However, neither the individual atoms nor the arrangements of atoms has color, smell, or taste. Color is like smell and taste. Atoms bonded into molecules are not a smell or a taste, but can cause an experience of smell or taste through our sense organs. Surfaces made of bonded atoms do not have color, but they do reflect different frequencies of electromagnetic radiation ("colored light" is not really color either). These frequencies can cause the experience of color through our sense organs, eyes in this case. Color is only a secondary quality, which we perceive, but which is not really in things. Scientific reductionism eliminates color from the reality that is independent of our minds.

Defenders of the view that colors are real properties of surfaces generally think that colors are emergent properties. Emergent properties are properties that a complex system has, but which its component parts, taken individually, do not have. Individual atoms do not have color. However, a large number of atoms bonded together to form a surface may have color as an emergent property. The bonding of the atoms into a surface is not itself color, but this complex organization allows a new type of property, color, to exist. Emergent properties are dependent upon the complex organization of their parts. They could not exist without the organized parts, but they are not identical with the organized parts. They are something more, just as color, as we ordinarily understand it, is something more than the light-reflecting characteristics of a surface.

Many philosophers accept the reality of both scientific entities and emergent properties. Whether or not color is a real case of an emergent property, many philosophers think that there are real cases. They think that there are some emergent properties that are not reducible to basic scientific entities. Some philosophers and scientists think that biological life includes emergent properties. According to this view, all of the properties and behaviors of living things cannot be fully explained only in terms of physics and chemistry. The most widely accepted emergent properties are those that make up conscious life.

The Brain and Consciousness

Scientific knowledge about how our brains work has increased dramatically in the last fifty years. We know that the brain is made up of nerve cells, neurons, that pass on electric charges to one another through a complex network of connections. We know that specific regions of the brain process information from particular sense organs, that other regions are the centers of emotions, and that other regions control the muscles throughout the body that produce all of our physical movement. The progress in understanding the biology and chemistry of the brain has led some philosophers and scientists to claim that eventually all features of human life will be explainable by laws about how the brain works. Human perception, emotion, memory, thought, language use, and everything else will be explained by physical and chemical laws about brain structures and events. Since these laws will be physical and chemical laws, they will not include anything about consciousness or experience "from the inside." They will deal only with physical and chemical properties, such as how electrical charges move through the complex connections of neurons, and how chemical transmitters and hormones affect things. This is frequently compared to how the inner workings of a computer involve only physical properties.

The possibility that the brain is only an incredibly complex physical-chemical system can be illustrated by a "perception machine." In order to check its new wines, a company might use a human wine-taster or a "tasting machine." The tasting machine would take a sample of wine and determine the amounts of the various components, such as acid, tannin, sugar, and so on. It would then make a decision according to an internal program about whether these were properly balanced, and make suggestions for improving the balance. The machine would do all this by electrical and chemical means. It would do everything that the human wine-taster does, without having the experiences we normally associate with tasting.

Scientific reductionists claim that humans are really just like the tasting machine, only much more complex. Humans are wholly natural entities that possess only the properties that physics and chemistry describe. Since biology should ultimately be reducible to physics and chemistry, according to the reductionists, biological properties will be nothing more than complex arrangements of physical-chemical entities. Scientific reductionists claim that the same is true for all human properties. The complex behavior of humans in their environment is the result of an incredibly complex internal control system (chapter 6 discusses the computer account of the mind). This control system, like everything else in the physical world, has only the physical-chemical properties of its parts and the arrangements of its parts. We may think that we have all sorts of other special properties, such as having experiences and consciously perceiving the world (or wine), but this is a mistake.

The scientific reductionist account of human beings clearly conflicts with what most people understand themselves to be. People consider themselves and others to be consciousnesses in a body. Conscious experiences are thought to be central to what people are. Most people care more about their conscious experiences than about anything else. They care about whether they will feel pain or be uncomfortable, and whether changes in their careers will make them feel more happy or more depressed. Given the importance of the properties of consciousness to probably all people, most philosophers oppose scientific reductionism. This can be done in several ways: by attacking the notion that scientific theories portray reality at all (instrumentalism does this); by attacking the notion that physics and chemistry provide an accurate account of reality, by denying that biology and psychology are reducible to physics and chemistry (emergent properties would be one form of this); or by supporting some form of duality of the physical and the mental (see chapter 6).

EVOLUTION VERSUS CREATIONISM

Many religions have some account of the creation of the world, of plants and animals, and of humans. Judaism and Christianity share the accounts in the Bible (there are two accounts that differ somewhat). Many religious people consider these accounts from the Bible to be metaphorical. On such a metaphorical reading, the Bible accounts need not conflict with the scientific view that the Earth formed over four billion years ago, and that the first forms of life arose over three billion years ago. However, some religious people consider the Bible accounts to be literally true. According to this reading, the entire universe, the sun and the stars, the Earth and all life forms, was created by God within seven days and is only approximately six thousand years old. Defenders of the literal truth of this claim are called "creationists." Creationists have argued that evolutionary theory should not be taught in public high schools because it conflicts with their religious views. They think that if evolution is taught, the creationist theory should also be taught as an alternative. They claim that their creationist theory is just as scientific as evolutionary theory. This claim raises issues about what it is to be a scientific theory and what the evidence is for evolutionary theory.

Evolution

Charles Darwin's (1809–1882) original theory of evolution has been altered and supplemented in many ways. Contemporary, Neo-Darwinian, evolutionary theory is a basic unifying feature of modern biology. It is part of the general explanatory structure that biologists use to explain a large number of very different things. There is not a small set of precise "laws of evolution" that make up the theory. Evolution is, rather, a general principle that is applied in understanding and explaining practically everything about living things.

The general principle of evolution is that types of organisms change because of the operation of natural selection on a population of organisms that have somewhat different genes. Genetic changes may be produced by many different factors. Whatever produces the genetic changes, some of these produce changes in the body or the behavior of the offspring that make them more able to survive, reproduce, and pass on these genes to their offspring. Other changes may make other offspring less able to survive and reproduce. Over long periods of time, the organisms that are more able to survive and reproduce, with their changed bodies, behavior, and genes, become more and more numerous, while the others become less numerous and perhaps entirely extinct. This is "natural selection." Certain body or behavior characteristics, with the genes that produce these, are "naturally selected" in that they become the predominant characteristics of that type of organism. The type of organism changes, at least in that vicinity. An overly simplified example would be to explain how giraffes came to have such long necks. There were mutations in the genes of some members of the short-necked giraffe population. These produced long-necked giraffes, which were in general better equipped to eat the leaves of trees. With more food, they lived longer, produced more offspring, who had the genes for long necks, and had healthier offspring. Given the pressures of survival, eventually only the long-necked giraffes remained.

From the preceding sketch you can understand why the application of evolution to specific cases becomes so complicated. The exact way that natural selection works for any given population of organisms depends upon all of the factors that can affect survival and reproduction. These have to be investigated for each particular population of organisms. For example, if long necks made giraffes easy targets for predators, or if the original giraffes had genes that made them mate only with short-necked giraffes, long necks might not have made their owners more able to survive and reproduce.

A major application of evolution is to the origin of the diverse life forms on Earth. According to evolutionary theory, all the different species of living things—including humans, animals, fish, insects, plants, and microorganisms—evolved from the original single-celled self-replicating entities that can be considered to be the first forms of life. This process took over three billion years. Many of the stages in the development of living things can be traced in the fossils laid down in rock strata of different ages.

Is Evolution Scientific?

Creationists have claimed that evolutionary theory is not scientific because the process of evolution cannot be observed by anyone and cannot be tested by experiment, and because evolutionary theory makes no definite predictions that can be tested. Major changes in the types of organisms are supposed to take very long periods of time. Everyone agrees that no individual biologist lives long enough to observe such changes. However, biologists, paleontologists, and geologists claim that the changes in the types of organisms can be seen in the progressively older layers of rock that make up the Earth's surface. Fossils—preserved skeletons, imprints of body parts, such as footprints, and other remains—of ancient living things are found throughout the world in these strata. The record of fossils shows a transition from only simpler organisms to progressively more complex types of organisms, along with continuing simpler organisms. The wealth of detail in the fossil record does not show what mechanism produced the changes, but it does show the changes. In addition to the fossil evidence, biologists have been able to observe the effects over many generations of new characteristics, presumably caused by genetic changes, in populations of organisms that reproduce very quickly (such as bacteria).

The general principle of evolution by itself does not make specific predictions. It makes predictions only in combination with a large amount of specific information about the population of organisms in question and their environment. All the factors that might affect the survival and reproduction of the organisms have to be taken into account. If a prediction does not agree with an observed result, it may be because some of this other information (auxiliary hypotheses) used in making the prediction was mistaken. For this reason, no single failure of a prediction would show that evolutionary theory was false. However, consistent failure to make correct predictions using the best specific information would show that evolutionary theory was wrong. Failures in certain types of cases have in fact required that Darwin's original theory be modified. Darwin's original theory of evolution has been replaced by a somewhat different theory, because it did not explain and predict all of the observed phenomena.

SCIENTIFIC OBJECTIVITY

Without thinking much about it, some people consider scientific knowledge to be a fully accurate depiction of real entities. As you have seen in earlier sections, this is a mistaken view. Scientific knowledge is not fully accurate, and it may not include all the properties of real entities. Well-established empirical laws—observed relationships between observable properties—are rarely changed, but new instances can reveal flaws in these generalizations. Scientific theories are more changeable. At best, accepted scientific theories are only hypotheses about certain features of reality, which have the most evidence for them. In principle, any scientific theory could be overturned if further evidence provided more support for an alternative theory. Instrumentalists even deny that scientific theories portray reality at all.

In the last thirty years, there has been more consideration of whether scientific knowledge is relative to historical periods (see chapter 4 concerning relativism about knowledge in general). Some philosophers and historians of science claim that scientific knowledge always operates through a framework that structures whatever can appear. This framework, which is called a "paradigm," changes throughout history. A paradigm is the accepted set of theories, theoretical entities, empirical laws, instruments and their use, agenda of problems to be solved, and ideas of what a successful solution is to a scientific problem. These are accepted by a group of working scientists and taught to those who learn the science. The question of historical relativism is raised by major changes of paradigm, which are also called "scientific revolutions." In a scientific revolution certain fundamental theories, with their claims about theoretical entities, are replaced by other theories. Examples are the shift from Ptolemaic astronomy to modern astronomy, in which the earth and the other planets move around the sun; the change from Newtonian physics, in which mass is constant, to special relativity theory, in which mass is convertible to energy; and, in chemistry, the replacement of phlogiston theory with John Dalton's atomic theory. These changes of theory are, according to the relativists, accompanied by changes in all the other factors. Relativists claim that because the paradigms before and after the revolution are so different, the scientific views before and after the revolution are really not comparable. The later view is not a more accurate account of the world than the earlier view; they do not deal with the same world. Those operating in the later paradigm do not ask the same questions as those operating in the earlier paradigm, and they have different criteria for when a scientific question has been answered.

Scientists and many philosophers consider changes of paradigm to be progress. They think that later theories explain and predict the observable data better than earlier theories. Relativists deny this. They claim that the same data cannot occur in different paradigms. This is because the paradigm structures what can appear. Data are always determined by the theories, and the rest of the paradigm. What is observed within an earlier paradigm is always different from what is observed in a later paradigm; for example, mass in Newtonian physics is not the same as mass in relativistic physics. The later theories do not explain and predict all of the data of the earlier theories and more. Rather, they deal with different observable data. For this reason, scientific revolutions are not really progress. During a revolution, the decision to abandon the earlier paradigm for the later one is made on non-scientific grounds. A later paradigm is accepted for all sorts of social reasons other than the "official" criteria: whether it accounts for all the data, is precise, opens up new types of data, has theoretical support from more comprehensive theories, and is simple.

Critics of scientific relativism claim that scientists with different theories, or even paradigms, accept much of the same observable data and do disagree with one another about what they take to be one shared world.

Scientific knowledge is built up in the same way that any kind of knowledge is developed. Scientists observe individual things, form generalizations about types of things, form and test hypotheses, deduce conclusions from what they already know, and rely upon the results of other scientific investigations.

Sensory observation is the basis of scientific knowledge. The observation of individual things is a means to develop generalizations about all similar things and to form hypotheses that explain why the individual things behave as they do. Empirical laws are well-confirmed generalizations that employ only observational terms. They do not use any terms defined only in a theory.

Hypotheses and the testing of hypotheses are particularly important for scientific knowledge. Science seeks laws and theories that go beyond what is actually observed. Scientific theories frequently introduce things and properties that cannot be directly observed with our senses. Scientific theories hypothesize that there are realms of non-ordinary entities that interact with one another in specific ways, and that these interactions produce the effects in ordinary things that we can observe. Theories contain both theoretical laws that concern the interactions with one another of these non-observable entities and bridge laws that connect these entities to what can be observed.

Scientific hypotheses have to be tested to determine whether they are true. The most important part of testing a scientific theory is determining whether it accounts for all of the available data. The theory should explain what we have actually observed and predict the occurrence of things on which we can check. The more unlikely are the theoretical predictions that actually occur, the stronger is the confirmation of the theory. According to the covering law model, results are deduced from the laws of the theory and a statement of the initial, usually observable, conditions. Experiments are attempts to test a theory by controlling the factors that might affect the result of the experiment. The testing of almost all current scientific theories presupposes other scientific theories. Hence, the result of an experiment is deduced not only from the theory being tested, but also from all the other accepted theories (auxiliary hypotheses) that are presupposed in setting up the experiment.

The testing of scientific theories is an ongoing process. A theory can never be proven, once and for all, to be totally true. In addition to explaining the data, the other factors that determine which of several competing theories is better are: precision, the opening up of new types of evidence, theoretical support from "above," and simplicity.

Instrumentalism is the claim that scientific theories do not portray reality. Scientific theories are only useful instruments for predicting what will happen if specific conditions are satisfied. One major objection to instrumentalism is that it is hard to draw a sharp line between what can be observed and what is only a theoretical entity.

Questions arise about the relationship between the entities hypothesized by scientific theory and the enduring things with properties, with which we deal in everyday life. Are scientific entities what is ultimately real, while ordinary things and properties are only our mistaken conceptions of what is real? Some philosophers and scientists claim that the parts of normal-sized physical objects do not have many of the properties that we perceive the objects to have. Atoms have primary qualities, such as size, shape, location, weight, and motion, but they do not have many other sensible properties, such as color, taste, smell, sound, or being hot or cold (secondary qualities). The scientific investigation of how our sensory apparatus works has supported this view.

Scientific reductionism is the position that scientific entities, such as atoms, are what basically exists. Everything else is made up of these basic scientific entities. The properties of real, normal-sized physical objects are only the properties of their parts and of the arrangements of their parts. Color is neither of these, so it is not a real property of things. Emergent properties are new properties of complex systems. They are properties that the parts of the system, taken individually, do not have and that are more than arrangements of the parts. Reductionists deny that there are any emergent properties. Other philosophers and scientists think that biological life and consciousness involve emergent properties.

Scientific reductionists claim that the brain is only an incredibly complex physical-chemical system. Human perception, emotion, memory, thought, language, and everything else will eventually be explained by physical and chemical laws about brain structures and events. Since these laws will be physical and chemical laws, they will not include anything about consciousness or experience "from the inside." The complex behavior of humans will eventually be shown to be the result of a very complex physical-chemical control system that is like a computer. This scientific reductionist account of human beings clearly conflicts with what most people understand themselves to be. To provide a place for consciousness, the truth of scientific theories can be attacked, or emergent properties or dualism of the mental and the physical can be defended.

Creationists take the Bible accounts of the creation of the universe, the Earth, and all life forms in seven days to be literally true. God created everything within seven days about six thousand years ago. Creationists oppose evolutionary theory, because evolutionary theory claims that all the different species of living things evolved from non-living chemicals over a period of more than three billion years.

Contemporary, neo-Darwinian, evolutionary theory is a basic unifying feature of modern biology. The general principle of evolution is that types of organisms change because of the operation of natural selection on a population of organisms that have somewhat different genes. Those that are more able to survive, reproduce, and pass on their genes become the predominant type.

Creationists claim that evolutionary theory is not scientific because the process of evolution cannot be observed by anyone and cannot be tested by experiment, and because evolutionary theory makes no definite predictions that can be tested. Biologists respond that evolution can be seen in the record of fossils and in certain fast-breeding organisms. Biologists also claim that evolutionary theory, in conjunction with specific information, does make testable predictions.

Some philosophers and historians of science have claimed that scientific knowledge is relative to historical periods. They claim that scientific knowledge always operates through a framework (paradigm) that structures whatever can appear. When paradigms change in scientific revolutions, the scientists before and after the revolution have different worlds of observable data. Since they are dealing with different worlds, a later theory is just different from an earlier theory. It is not a more accurate account of reality. Defenders of scientific objectivity deny this. They claim that scientific knowledge is an account of reality that can be improved and that there is progress in science.

Selected Readings

Giere, Ronald. *Understanding Scientific Reasoning*. New York: Holt, Rinehart & Winston, 1979.

Hempel, Carl. *Philosophy of Natural Science*. Englewood Cliffs, NJ: Prentice-Hall, 1966.

Kitcher, Philip. *Abusing Science*. Cambridge, Mass.: MIT, 1982.

Kuhn, Thomas. *The Structure of Scientific Revolutions*, 2nd edition. Chicago: University of Chicago, 1970.

O'Hear, Anthony. *Introduction to the Philosophy of Science*. New York: Oxford, 1989.

6

Mind

Both your mind and your body are important to you. You are probably concerned about your physical health as much as your mental health. Although you regularly distinguish mind and body, you may have a difficult time stating exactly how they are different from each other. Many philosophers have attempted to specify the nature of mind and body. Are they really that different from each other, and if they are different, how can our minds affect our bodies and vice versa?

CONSCIOUS EXPERIENCE

In everyday life, we consider ourselves to be conscious. We think that humans and some other animals have an ongoing experience of the external world and of their own inner life of feelings, thoughts, and emotions. We think that there is a difference between the conscious experience of seeing a tree on a hillside and the detecting of a tree on a hillside by a television camera hooked up to a computer. The difference is not in the information that is detected, but rather in the "how" of the detecting. Conscious perceiving is a particular way of detecting, so that there is an experience of detecting. We can imagine ourselves perceiving in different ways. We can even imagine ourselves to be a conscious computer that perceives through a television camera. However, we cannot imagine being a non-conscious computer, because there is no experience of being a non-conscious computer.

Feelings are another central example of consciousness. Conscious animals have feelings of different sorts, but non-conscious computers do not. We prohibit cruelty to animals, but not cruelty to computers, because animals can feel pain and computers cannot. This is not just a matter of their internal "detecting systems." A computer may have an excellent system for detecting internal malfunctions but still not feel pain. The same holds for humans. A sharp, stabbing pain in your elbow depends upon nerves and tissues. If a doctor is checking out the injury of an athlete, she may ask him whether something hurts and what sort of pain it is. The doctor may be interested in the damage to tissue, bone, or nerve. She may be interested in the particular type of pain only because it is indicative of a particular type of injury. A complicated non-conscious monitoring system could report on the athlete's physical injury perhaps better than the athlete's feeling of pain. However, the feeling of pain is something more than just a report on the state of the body's tissue and nerve systems. It is hard to give a full description of what that "something more" is, but we all know it in our own cases. We know how pain hurts, whether or not it also reports on some physiological event in the body.

Features of Conscious Experience

Philosophers try to describe what makes up our first-person conscious experience. They try to specify the major features of any "stream of consciousness." If we consider our consciousness at any given time, there is always at least one "mental act" with its coordinate "object of consciousness." Any conscious experience includes both what the experience is "of" or "about"—the object of consciousness—and the way in which we are conscious of the object—the mental act.

OBJECTS OF CONSCIOUSNESS

When we see or imagine something, the something-as-seen or the something-as-imagined is the object of consciousness. If you see a bluish-green tree on a wooded hillside, the "bluish-green tree on a wooded hillside" is the object of your experience. The object of consciousness is what your experience portrays as it is portrayed; the object of consciousness is also called the "intentional object." If your experience distorts the real world in some way—for example, the tree is really yellowish-green, or there are two trees close to each other—it is the distorted appearance that is the object of consciousness. Theories of knowledge consider how the object of believing consciousness is related to the world (see chapter 4).

MENTAL ACTS

There are different ways in which you can be conscious of a bluish-green tree on a wooded hillside. You might see it, remember it, imagine it, or think of it without imagining it. These are different mental acts. Experience always involves at least one mental act that is directed at some object of consciousness. Seeing, hearing, smelling, imagining, remembering, desiring, being anxious, being happy, being angry, and fearing are some of the types of mental act. Frequently, more than one mental act is going on at the same time. You may be seeing the tree on the wooded hillside, hearing what your friend is saying to you, and worrying about the paper due tomorrow, all at the same time.

PROCESSES

Processes are another feature of consciousness. We may experience ourselves to be thinking about a movie, following through the steps of a rational argument, or letting our imaginations run free. In all these cases, there is not one single mental act with its object, but rather a particular type of sequence, or process, of mental acts. In different types of process, the later conscious experiences follow the earlier conscious experiences in different ways. We experience these "different ways of following." There is an experiential difference between how new experiences arise when we are engaged in free association of ideas (whatever "pops into your mind") and when we think about a problem to find a solution.

SENSE OF ABILITIES

Another feature of conscious experience is our sense of our abilities and capacities. We all seem to have some sense of what we are able to think but are not now thinking. We have a sense of various courses that our experience could follow if we wanted to think that way. For example, upon seeing a page of a book in English, you have the sense that you could read it, whereas if the book is in some foreign language that you do not know, you have the sense that you could not read it. Similarly, while watching a city landscape, you may have the sense that you could imagine an entirely different scene, even though you do not go on to imagine the different scene. These senses of our abilities and capacities make the changes in our experience understandable to us. It is not a shock or a complete surprise to us when our experience goes in some direction because we were aware beforehand that it was possible. For example, if while watching a city landscape you do start to imagine an entirely different scene, you understand the switch and are prepared for it. It would be quite different if the city landscape suddenly disappeared and was replaced by an entirely different scene. That would startle us.

These are some (maybe not all) of the main experienced features of conscious experience. There are other features of mental life that may be noticed from an external point of view, but which are not themselves experienced by the consciousness that has them. Tendencies and habits are frequently not experienced by the consciousness that has them. A person who has a tendency to get angry at anyone who mentions his family life may not have any experience of this tendency, although he does experience the anger. The same can hold for habits and causal relations. Too much coffee or too much pressure may make a person irritated or angry, without the person himself having any experience of the source.

Knowledge of Our Own Conscious Experience

Just having conscious experiences is not the same thing as knowing about them. Many people think that having conscious experiences is necessary for knowing about them, but that knowing requires something more. Descartes claimed that we could know with absolute certainty about our own current conscious experiences (see chapter 4). However, he recognized that just having conscious experiences does not provide certain knowledge of them. According to Descartes, we know our conscious experiences only when we clearly and distinctly understand them. This includes both understanding the mental act and understanding what our thoughts are about. (According to Descartes, the objects of consciousness are ideas in the mind that represent things.)

Conscious experiences are experienced by someone. They are "present to his or her mind," although they may be very much in the background of consciousness rather than something on which we are focused. That they are experienced is what makes them available in a special way to us—this availability is frequently called "privileged access." We usually can focus on them if we want. Through reflection on our own experiences, we can mentally observe the various features of our experience. When we are clear about some feature of our own experience, we know about it.

Knowledge of Other Minds

The connection between having conscious experiences and knowing about them raises questions about knowing anyone else's conscious experiences. Any individual conscious experience occurs only in one consciousness. Only one person has it. Several people may think the exact same thing or feel an exactly similar pain, but each of them has his or her own instance of the thought or the pain. For this reason, one person's conscious experiences are not available for another person to observe, at least not in the way that they are available for the person who has them (privileged access). This raises the question of whether we can ever know about the conscious experiences of other people. Can we even know that they have conscious experiences at all? Could it be that others are just non-conscious computers or zombies?

Most people respond to the problem of knowledge of other minds by saying that we can tell that other people are like us, and that we have conscious experiences. Therefore, others must have conscious experiences, too—this is sometimes called "the argument from analogy." Knowledge that other people have experiences, and knowledge of what those experiences are, can be considered to be well-justified hypotheses. Even though Jennifer cannot directly observe Jason's experiences, she can hypothesize that he has them. On the basis of the circumstances, his bodily similarity to her, and his behavior, she can hypothesize that he is now having experiences that are like those she would have under the given conditions. If Jason has been running around in the hot sun, is dripping with perspiration, and pours himself a glass of cool water, she can hypothesize that he feels thirsty. She thinks that he has an experience of being thirsty that is like her experience of being thirsty when she has been in similar conditions. She can test her hypothesis by seeing whether he goes on to act as she acts when she feels thirsty. For example, does he slowly savor the water, like a fine wine, or drink it down quickly and pour some more? She can ask him to describe his experiences to see whether his description is similar to her descriptions. As in the testing of most complex hypotheses, auxiliary hypotheses are necessary for these tests (see chapter 5). She has to assume that he is not faking his behavior or lying when he describes his experiences.

The more, and the more varied, the testing of hypotheses about someone else's experiences, the more justified are her claims about what his experiences are. If Jennifer thinks that Jason is having the experience of remembering their trip to Venice last year because he is looking at posters that they bought in Venice, she can test this by asking him. The more that he is able to tell her about their trip, the more it is likely that he remembers these episodes just as she remembers them. Similarly, if Jason shows creativity in solving problems and is able to explain to her how he solved them, if Jason shows real sensitivity in describing his experiences, and if Jason shows sensitivity to what Jennifer must be feeling, Jennifer has further evidence that Jason has a conscious life like hers. This testing can also reveal ways in which someone's experiences are different from one's own.

Criticisms of This Solution to the Problem

Some philosophers have attacked this account of knowledge of other people's experiences. They have argued that we can know about the inner causes of other people's behavior, but we cannot know whether these inner causes are conscious or how they are experienced. We cannot distinguish between inner non-conscious causes, such as those a sophisticated robot might have, and inner conscious causes. We cannot tell whether the perceptual process that guides Jason in pouring the water into the glass is a non-conscious process or a conscious one. We can tell that this perceptual process can cause further behavior, such as talking about what he saw, but we have no way to find out "what it is like" for Jason or whether it is conscious at all.

Critics of this sort can be divided into two groups. Some accept the existence of conscious experiences, but think that we cannot really know about other people's experiences. Others deny that there are conscious experiences at all (see Materialism, p. 93). They claim that all that we are and should be concerned about are the inner causes of humans' incredibly complex behavior. These causes are the physical-chemical characteristics of the human brain and nervous system, not some private experience to which only one person has direct access.

A different sort of criticism is that our belief that other people have experiences is not a hypothesis at all. Some philosophers and social theorists claim that the consciousness of other people is as evident as our own consciousness. George Mead (1863–1931), Martin Heidegger (1889–1976), Sartre, and others have pointed out that the acceptance of other consciousnesses is central to most of our interactions with other people and to our whole understanding of ourselves. We feel proud or ashamed of ourselves in the presence of other consciousnesses, but not before non-conscious things. We evaluate ourselves partly in terms of how we think that others feel about us. The importance of our belief in other minds to our sense of self has led these philosophers to deny that our belief in others' experiences is only a hypothesis for which there is a lot of evidence. This belief is too definitive of us to be a hypothesis. However, their alternative accounts of how we know about other minds differ from one another and are too complex to be discussed here.

MIND VERSUS MATTER

Conscious experience is the main reason for distinguishing mind from matter. In earlier times, people knew little about how complex material things work. Material things seemed to be inert and inactive, so that matter was conceived to be a "stuff" that did not do much on its own. Complex movement and structure were considered to belong only to living things and conscious things. Life and consciousness were thought to involve something more than matter, a non-material soul or life force.

With the growth of natural science in the seventeenth century, most of the natural world came to be regarded as a complex material system. Many scientists and philosophers, such as Descartes and Thomas Hobbes (1588–1679), claimed that living things are only "complex machines," that is, that they are only complex arrangements of matter that operate according to the laws of matter. According to this view, living things do not have any emergent properties and are not animated by any life force or soul. Descartes denied that any animals are conscious. Animals might look as if they are thirsty or feel pain, but all their behavior can be explained by internal mechanisms. Only humans actually have conscious experiences. Conscious experiences occur in a distinct non-material type of thing, a mind or soul.

Whether or not other animals have minds, mind has been thought to be something different from matter. Mind has been thought to have many characteristics that matter does not have.

Not Located and Non-Divisible

Descartes and many other philosophers have thought that material things have to be extended in space, while the mind is not spatial. Since we cannot touch, handle, or see the mind, there is an initial plausibility to the idea that, in this way, the mind is different from physical things. There are actually two claims included in the claim that mind is not spatial: that the mind does not have a location in space, and that the mind cannot be divided in the way spatial things can be divided.

All physical things have some type of location in space. If the mind and mental things did not have some type of location in space, this would be a strong reason for considering them to be very different from physical things. However, our minds are strongly connected with our bodies and nervous systems. We see, hear, and smell things from the perspective determined by where our bodies are. We act on the world through our bodies and their powers and limitations. We feel pains, itches, exhilaration, and other things throughout our bodies. Damage to the brain can result in decreased mental abilities. For all these reasons, and others, our mind does seem to be located in space. It is where our body is.

However, there is a second claim: that the mind and mental things are not divisible in the way spatial things are divisible. Any region of space can be divided into as many small parts as one wants. An extended physical thing can, in principle, be divided along with the space that it occupies. This is not true of thoughts and other mental things. The thought that the room is hot cannot be divided into eight equal parts in the way that a room might be divided into eight equal parts. Although some thoughts may be divisible into smaller parts, such as words or simple ideas, they cannot be divided into smaller and smaller parts. This character of being a non-divisible whole, the "wholistic" character, seems to distinguish thoughts from ordinary physical things.

Not Explainable by the Laws of Physics and Chemistry

The laws of physics and chemistry deal only with physical and chemical properties. Mental properties, such as being in pain or being angry at Jason, are not included in any physical or chemical laws. Since minds seem to have different properties from physical things, minds cannot be fully explained only by the laws of the basic physical sciences. For this reason, minds seem to be different from ordinary physical things. However, scientific reductionists (see chapter 5) claim that physical and chemical laws will eventually be able to explain everything about the mind. Their claim that the mind is nothing more than a complex physical-chemical control system for the body is explored in Materialism, p. 93.

Location of Secondary Properties

We perceive many properties that physical things may not really have. These are called "secondary properties" (see chapter 5). Secondary properties, such as color, smell, and taste, are supposed to exist just in our minds, not in independent physical things. According to this view, redness does not really exist in the apple, but only in our minds. The perception of secondary properties seems to require that the mind be different from matter. Secondary properties have to exist in some way. If secondary properties do not exist in physical things, but they do exist in the mind, it follows that the mind is not just a physical thing. If the mind were just a physical thing, secondary properties could not exist in it either.

One response to this argument is to appeal to the mind's "aboutness," or intentionality. According to this response, a secondary property such as being red exists neither in an apple nor in the mind. What exists in the mind is only the "idea of red," not a red property. Since we can have ideas of many things that do not exist at all, we can have an idea of redness, even though red properties do not exist in the mind. Critics of this response claim that the mind contains "qualia," such as redness (and tastes and smells), which are more than just ideas of something. We can think of red without having the sensory qualia of redness. (For example, someone gives you the direction "turn right at the red sign.") However, when qualia occur (when you imagine or see a red sign), the red qualia must exist in the mind.

Being About— Intentionality

Minds and many mental states and events are intrinsically about something. Conscious experiences contain a mental act that is "of" or "about" the object of consciousness, also called "the intentional object." This feature of being about, or "intentionality," is necessary for most, and maybe all, mental things. Mental acts cannot exist without their intentional objects.

The relationship of a mental act to its intentional object is not a physical relationship. A physical relationship, such as one thing causing another or being three feet from another, requires that both things actually exist. For a match to cause a fire, both the match and the fire must exist in reality. However, an object of consciousness need not exist in reality, although frequently it does. We can think of many things that do not exist in reality. In understanding fiction, we think of casts of characters and even whole worlds that do not exist in reality. In being afraid of a nuclear holocaust, we are afraid of something that does not now exist and with luck never will exist.

A second way in which intentionality differs from physical relationships is that objects of consciousness are dependent upon certain "descriptions." An intentional object only has the characteristics that the mind ascribes to it. An intentional object is only what the mind portrays or describes.

Although the real object that we perceive probably has many other properties, over and above those that we now attribute to it, our intentional object
is only the real object as portrayed, or described, in our perception. Thus,
when you see a bluish-green tree on a wooded hillside, your intentional
object is only what you see (and think) to be there. The real tree may be
hollow, but unless you actually see or think of its hollowness, your intentional object does not include its hollowness. You are not seeing the tree as
hollow. This feature of intentional objects also distinguishes the intentional
relationship from physical relationships. The two things that are related in
physical relationships are not dependent upon certain descriptions. If a
match causes the tree to burn, and the tree is hollow, the match causes the
hollow tree to burn.

Intentionality seems not to be a physical relationship. However, some
material things seem to be about something. Clouds on the horizon may be
a natural sign of an approaching storm. A book, which is a material thing
made of paper and ink, seems to be about something. A book of fiction seems
to be about the same fictional world as that which our thoughts are about
while reading it. How then can intentionality distinguish mind from matter?
The usual response to this question is that only minds are intrinsically, or by
themselves, about something. Books, natural signs, and other material things
can be about something only because minds use them in special ways.
Without writers and readers, the book is not about anything. It is about
something only because a writer produces it and readers can use it to direct
their thoughts to something.

Privacy

Privacy refers to how available conscious experiences are for observation. Some people think that we have no access to other people's thoughts
and experiences. These are available to be observed only by the person who
has them. They are thus completely private. This contrasts with the non-
privacy, or publicness, of physical facts and events. In principle, anyone can
observe a physical fact or event as well as anyone else.

Most philosophers think that we have some access to other people's
thoughts and experiences. This access is our basis for knowing about others'
thoughts. However, we do not have the same access to another person's
thoughts and experiences that the person herself has. According to this view,
conscious experiences are not completely private, but they are partly private,
because a person has privileged access to them. This privileged access to
one's own thoughts and experiences distinguishes them from physical
things, to which everyone, in principle, has equal access.

Rationality

From the beginning of philosophy, rationality has been thought to be a
distinctive feature of human minds. Humans have been thought to be the
only animals that can reason. Humans have the ability to solve complex

problems, to think about the evidence for a conclusion, and to speak and understand language. Humans' flexible intelligence, which can adjust to new situations, has been contrasted with the inflexible "instincts" of animals and the mechanical behavior of material things. This broad range of abilities that are grouped under the term "rationality" has seemed to be a characteristic that only minds can have. Descartes even thought that rationality was necessary for having a mind at all. Animals must be only complex machines, he thought, because they are incapable of rational thought.

In recent years, the development of sophisticated computers has challenged the claim that material things without minds cannot be rational. Computers can prove theorems in mathematics, beat almost all humans at chess, diagnose illnesses from symptoms, translate sentences (roughly) from one language to another, and many other things. A computer can be designed to perform any task that can be precisely defined. These developments show that the ability to do tasks that require "rationality" is not a characteristic only of minds. Computers may not understand what they are doing, but they can do most of the things that rational humans can do.

Desire and Value

Conscious beings feel pains and pleasures, have desires, aversions, and other wants, and have emotional highs and lows. Some of what they do is motivated by these factors. Conscious beings do many things for a purpose. They not only have an objective in mind, but they also want to do what they do. They are frustrated or pained if they are prevented from doing these things. Material things, even complex computers, seem not to have any pleasures or pains, or desires or aversions. Although computers can do very complex tasks, they seem to do them automatically, not because they want to do them. Computers also seem not to have pains or pleasures and not to be frustrated if they are prevented from doing something.

Normal adult humans have standards by which they judge situations and actions. These are their values. A person may judge his own action or someone else's action to be wimpy, courageous, immoral, unjust, artistically beautiful, or many other things. Values guide what a person does and how he evaluates other people. Material things, even complex computers, seem not to have values. Just as they do not desire to do things, they do not do things in order to fit their values. They do not act so as to be moral or courageous or to fit any other value.

DUALISM

Dualism claims that mind and matter are two distinct types of existing things. Mind must be something different from matter because it has all these characteristics that matter does not have. The traditional forms of dualism include the claim that mind and matter are two distinct substances. Substances are things that can exist on their own and support properties. Matter is a spatially extended "stuff" that has physical properties. Mind is a non-spatial, conscious thing that has the distinctive mental properties. Each individual mind is a substance and is distinct from other minds.

Mind and Body

According to the traditional forms of dualism, the human body is only a complex material thing. Humans have both a mind and a body. Throughout a person's lifetime, her mind and her body are connected. However, the mind, or soul, is a substance that is entirely distinct from the body. The mind, with its mental properties, is not dependent upon the material body. For this reason, continued mental life is possible after death. The mind can continue to exist without being connected with the body. When the material body no longer functions, the mind may continue to operate independently of the body.

Interaction

If mind is a substance that is distinct from the material body, the nature of their connection is an issue. A living person's mind and body are very closely connected. We perceive the world through our bodily sense organs. We feel pains, pleasures, tensions, exhilarations, and other things in our bodies. We act on the world through our bodies and their powers. What is the exact connection of mind and body that explains these things?

Descartes provided the traditional answer to this question. Mind and brain causally interact. Each causally affects the other. Information from the sense organs travels through nerves to the brain. All of this occurs within the body. Brain events cause events in the mind. Brain events cause us to have the experiences of perceiving things. Brain events also cause us to have all of the feelings that seem to be in the body. The experience of a pain in the foot or of a general feeling of bodily energy occurs in the mind but is caused by appropriate events in the brain. Mental events also cause brain events. Decisions to do something cause events in the brain that are transmitted by the nerves to the appropriate muscles. The mind can control some of the behavior of the body through these pathways.

Questions About Interaction

Some philosophers have thought that causal interaction between the mind and the brain is not possible. They think that there is no way for entirely distinct substances to affect each other. They cannot "get a grip" on each other because one is wholly material and the other is wholly mental. One material thing, such as a rock, can affect another, such as a glass window, because they are both material and have similar properties. We can understand this causal relation in terms of the mass, momentum, and force of the rock and the makeup of the glass window. However, we cannot develop a deeper explanation of mind-matter causal relations. Hence, proponents of this view think that something is wrong with the whole notion of mind-matter causal interaction. Some seventeenth century philosophers, such as Leibniz and Nicolas Malebranche (1638–1715), proposed alternative accounts of what seem to be causal interactions. Leibniz claimed that mind and matter run in parallel order, as two clocks that seem to work in connection with each other but really operate independently. Malebranche claimed that God causes the appropriate events in mind or matter that seem to be caused by events in the other substance.

Problem of Dependence

The most serious challenge to dualism is the mounting evidence that everything mental depends on a properly working brain and nervous system. All experiences and mental capacities seem to be dependent upon the material brain. This is shown by what happens to people's minds when they suffer brain damage or disruption, or are born with brain defects. A dualist might expect that perceptual experiences would be seriously affected by disruptions of normal brain functioning. This is because perceptual experiences are, according to interactionism, caused by events in the brain. However, every type of mental event and capacity is affected by some type of deficiency in or damage to the brain, or disruption of normal brain functioning. The ability to remember things, the ability to recognize specific types of things, the ability to do mathematics, the ability to understand language, the capacity to have certain types of desires and emotions, the ability to restrain oneself from acting on some desires, even the unification of experiences into one stream of consciousness are all dependent upon the proper functioning of the brain. All of these, and many other things, disappear if the brain is damaged or disrupted in specific ways. In light of these facts, it appears that mind is not a separate substance that could exist on its own. If mind were a distinct substance, all of its important properties should not be so dependent upon events and states of matter.

Dualism of Properties

Many philosophers think that mind is not a substance distinct from matter, but that mental properties are distinct from physical properties. They think that mental characteristics occur in the brain rather than in a nonmaterial substance. A properly functioning brain has both material properties and mental properties. Mental properties are emergent properties of brains (see chapter 5). As emergent properties, they are dependent upon the complex organization of the parts of the brain, but they are also something more than this organization. The "something more" is all of the distinctive characteristics of being conscious.

Mental Causes

If mental properties are dependent upon the brain and its material properties, do mental properties cause any part of our behavior? Is our intentional action partially caused by our conscious experiences, or is it entirely caused by brain events and structures? There are two distinct views about this. Some philosophers think that the brain events and structures that control the movements of our bodies are a closed system. These brain events and structures are not affected by conscious experience. Specific brain events and states are caused by earlier brain events and states, but not by conscious events and states. Conscious experience accompanies many brain events, states, and structures, but it has no causal input. Conscious experience just occurs alongside the real causes of bodily behavior. Conscious events and states do not even cause other conscious events and states. All of these are just byproducts of brain events, states, and structures. In the past, positions like this have been called "epiphenomenalism."

Some philosophers think that conscious events and states must have some causal affect both on bodily behavior and on later conscious events and states. They think this because, in everyday life, conscious experiences seem to affect behavior and later conscious experiences. However, no one has a very good idea precisely how this influence works.

MATERIALISM

Materialism claims that only matter and the physical properties of matter exist. There is no non-material substance (mind), and there are no non-material properties. Materialists emphasize an external, and usually scientific, approach to people. They do not emphasize how each person's mind appears to the person himself. They think that what have appeared to be minds and mental properties will be ultimately shown to be only complex physical systems.

Behaviorism

Behaviorism claims because introspection involves first-person "privileged access" (p. 84), it is not a suitable basis for developing a science of psychology. What is publicly accessible and observable is human behavior. Methodological Behaviorists have concluded that scientific psychology must rely on observationally established linkages ("dispositions") of environmental stimuli and behavioral responses. Metaphysical Behaviorists have gone further, and maintained that "that is all there is," and that there are no non-material minds or mental properties. Hence, they consider all of our talk about minds and mental characteristics to be really about people's behavior and dispositions to behave. To say that someone is intelligent, generous, or angry is just to say that the person is likely to behave in intelligent, generous, or angry ways. A person's belief that there is a greenish tree on a wooded hillside is nothing more than a disposition or tendency to act in specific ways, such as saying "there is a greenish tree on the wooded hillside over there" or walking toward the tree when asked to stand under a greenish tree. A person's being in pain is nothing more than a disposition to behave in specific ways, such as holding the injured part of the body, crying or wincing, and saying "it hurts." There is nothing more to pain than these behaviors and dispositions. There is no experience of pain over and above them.

Behaviorism was an influential movement in psychology. Its objective was to be scientific in investigating behavior. Behaviorists thought that being scientific required that nothing be included in scientific laws that was not accessible to public observation. All scientific laws had to be empirical laws. Since the thoughts and experiences of other people and animals are not publicly observable, behaviorists formulated laws that included only what could be publicly observed, behavior in specific circumstances.

Inner Causes of Behavior

The contribution of behaviorism is its focus on the connection of mental characteristics with publicly observable behavior. Behaviorism's one-sided emphasis on behavior counteracts the one-sided emphasis of some dualists on private conscious experience. Part of what we mean in thinking or talking about people's mental characteristics are internal features that produce behavior. We do not mean just their private conscious experiences. Rather, we think that there are internal entities that interact with one another to produce their behavior. Their wants, beliefs, emotions, and other mental characteristics are expressed in bodily changes, such as blushing, shaking, or sweating, and in intentional action, such as doing what you believe will satisfy your desire. On the basis of these expressions, which are publicly observable, people can know about the inner causes.

Other forms of materialism emphasize the connection between inner causes and publicly observable expressions. All non-behaviorist forms of materialism claim that what have been called "mind" and "mental charac-teristics" are really the complex system of inner causes of human behavior. These inner causes are entirely material. In normal life, we cannot observe the system of inner causes. We can observe only the effects. According to materialists, people have speculated for thousands of years about what these inner causes must be like. They have hypothesized that the inner causes must be something non-material and spirit-like. This is because they did not understand complex material systems. Materialists think that our common-sense understanding of mind and mental characteristics is only a mistaken hypothesis about the characteristics of the inner causes of the outer expressions.

Brain as a Computer

Sophisticated electronic computers provide materialism with a model of the system of inner causes of human behavior. The human brain is considered to be a computer that controls everything about the body. What have been called "mind" and "mental characteristics" are really the operations, stored data, and programs of this computer. Perception is the process of putting data into the system. This data can be used right away or stored. Memory is the retrieval of stored information for use in the system. Thinking is the running of programs whose results can be used in directing behavior or stored for later use. Desires and wants are the objectives of the programs. They specify what the programs are to bring about or accomplish. Intentional action is the movement of the body as directed by the system using its information to accomplish its objectives. All "mental things" are really some part of this information-processing system that controls the human body.

Two Levels of Description

Electronic computers can be described in two ways. They can be described purely in terms of their physical characteristics, such as how their material parts are arranged, what parts have what electric charges, and how new electric charges will affect things. Such a physical description would be incredibly complex, but in principle it could be given. Computers can also be described in terms of running programs and processing information. Instead of describing all of the physical states and events that are involved, we can describe the computer as "adding two plus two and arriving at the sum four." There is some physical condition of the computer that is its instance of "two" and some physical condition that is its instance of the process of adding two and two. These conditions and processes produce its output, either on a screen or through a printer. Adding two plus two is actually nothing more than these complex physical conditions and processes.

Materialists think that biologists' descriptions of the brain are like the physical description of the computer. In charting the incredibly complex arrangement of neurons (nerve cells) in the brain, neuroscientists are investigating the physical structure of the human computer. Psychological descriptions are like the description of the computer in terms of information and running programs. Psychology investigates how we process information, such as adding two plus two, perceiving the structure of our environment, or deciding whether to go to medical school. All of these psychological things are actually nothing more than the incredibly complex physical conditions and processes that produce the "outputs" in the human body, everything that the body does. However, for practical purposes, we have to use the psychological level of description because the biological and physical levels are just too complex.

Functionalism

Functionalism is an account of the nature of psychological things, what we ordinarily consider to be mental characteristics. Functionalism claims that psychological things are defined in terms of performing a function. Perceptions, memories, beliefs, thinking in all its forms, desires, wants, feelings, and emotions are parts of a system of inner causes of bodily responses and behavior. Each of these is defined in terms of the role it plays, its function, in the system of inner causes. Since psychological things interact with one another as part of this system of inner causes, each is partially defined in terms of its relations and interactions with the others. Thus, functionalism considers a belief to be, roughly, an inner state that is caused by perceptions of the right kind, that can cause other beliefs, through "thinking," and that interacts with wants and desires to cause intentional action. Desires are similarly defined as interacting with one another, beliefs and perceptions to cause intentional action. Functionalism tries to provide such "system accounts" of all psychological states, events, and processes.

Functionalism defines psychological things in terms of a system of causes. It does not say in what "stuff" this system of causes occurs. Thus, functionalism is not itself a form of materialism. However, it is consistent with materialism. The things that realize these functional relationships can be material things. The things that form the system of inner causes can be the carbon-based nerve cells that make up our brains. They can also be silicon-based structures of computers or Martians. However, they can also be non-material features of a spirit or soul. Almost all functionalists think that in the case of humans it is a material brain that realizes these relationships.

In everyday life, we consider ourselves to be conscious. Consciousness is something that is experienced. We can imagine our perception to be very different from how it is, but we cannot imagine being a non-conscious detecting mechanism. Feelings, such as the feeling of pain, are another central example of being conscious.

Important experienced features of conscious experience are mental acts, objects of consciousness (intentional objects), processes, and our sense of our abilities and capacities. Mental acts are different ways of being conscious, such as perceiving, imagining, remembering, desiring, fearing, or being happy. Objects of consciousness (intentional objects) are what consciousness is "about," as portrayed by the mental act. Processes are types of sequences of mental acts, such as free association or rational thinking. Our sense of our abilities is our sense of what we are able to think but are not now thinking. This sense makes the changes in our experience understandable to us.

Many people think that having conscious experiences is necessary for knowing about them. Our own conscious experiences are available to us to be known. Knowing about them requires that a person mentally observe them and clearly understand what is observed.

The conscious experience of one person is not available for other people to observe. To know that other people have experiences and to know what these experiences are requires the use of hypotheses. On the basis of the circumstances, bodily similarity, and a person's behavior, we can hypothesize that he is now having experiences that are like what we would experience under the given conditions. We can test this hypothesis by observing whether he goes on to act as we would act and by asking him to describe what his experiences are like. The more varied the testing of these hypotheses, the more justified are our claims about what his experiences are.

Some critics of this account of our knowledge of other minds claim that we can know only about the inner causes of someone's behavior. We cannot know whether these inner causes are conscious, or how they are experienced. Other critics claim that the consciousness of other people is as evident as our own consciousness.

Conscious experience is the main reason for distinguishing mind from matter. Minds have been thought to have the following characteristics that matter does not have. Minds are non-spatial. They are not located at any specific place in space, and thoughts are not divisible into as many small parts as one wants. Mental properties, such as being in pain or being angry at someone, are not explainable by the laws of physics and chemistry. Minds are where secondary properties exist. Since secondary properties, such as redness, do not exist in physical objects, the "qualia" of redness, and of tastes, smells, and other properties, must occur in the mind. Minds are intrinsically about something. Mental acts are about intentional objects, which are special in that they need not exist in reality and that they are dependent upon certain descriptions. Some material things, such as books, seem to be about something, but this is only because minds use the material things in special ways. Mental things are private in that a person has an access to her own conscious experiences that outsiders do not have. Minds are able to reason, solve complex problems, think about the evidence for conclusions, and understand language. However, the development of sophisticated computers has shown that material systems can also do rational tasks. Finally, minds feel pains and pleasures, have desires, aversions, and other wants, and have emotions. These features and humans' values motivate what people do. Computers seem to do things automatically.

Dualism claims that mind and matter are two distinct types of existing things. The traditional forms of dualism include the claim that mind and matter are distinct substances that support different properties. These dualisms also claim that the human body is only a complex material thing. The mind with its mental properties could exist without the material body.

A living person's mind and body are very closely connected. Many people think that mind and body causally interact. Events in one substance cause changes in the other substance. Some philosophers reject this causal interaction because the two substances and their properties are so different.

The most serious challenge to dualism is the mounting evidence that everything mental depends on a properly working brain and nervous system. All experiences and mental capacities are disrupted by damage or disruption of the material brain. In light of these facts, it appears that mind is not a separate substance that could exist independently of the body. Many philosophers think that mental properties are distinct from physical properties but are supported by the brain. If the brain has both physical and mental properties, there is the question of whether mental properties cause any brain events and bodily behavior, or whether they just accompany brain events and states.

Materialism claims that only matter and physical properties exist. There are no non-material minds and no non-material mental properties. Behaviorism is a form of materialism. Behaviorism claims that all our talk about minds and mental characteristics is really about people's behavior and dispositions to behave. There is no conscious experience, just behavior and dispositions to behave in specific ways under certain circumstances.

Other forms of materialism claim that what have been called "mind" and "mental characteristics" are really the complex system of inner causes of human behavior. These inner causes are entirely material. Since we cannot observe the system of inner causes, people have speculated about their nature. People have hypothesized that they must be something non-material and spirit-like. Materialists think that our commonsense understanding of mind and mental characteristics is only a mistaken hypothesis about the characteristics of the inner causes of the outer expressions.

Materialism considers the human brain to be a computer that controls everything about the body. Computers can be described either at a physical level or in terms of information and programs. These two levels apply to descriptions of the brain, as well. Neuroscience investigates the arrangements and interactions of the neurons that make up the brain. Psychology investigates how we receive information, process it, and use it to direct our bodily behavior. The entities and processes of psychology, such as perceptions, memories, beliefs, thinking, desires, wants, feelings, and emotions are just part of a system of inner causes of bodily responses and behavior. Each of these is defined in terms of the role it plays, its function, in the system of inner causes. Such functionally defined things could, in principle, occur in different types of "stuff," including human brains, the "brains" of extrater-

restrials, silicon computer chips, or a non-material mind. Almost all functionalists think that in the case of humans it is a material brain that realizes these relationships.

Selected Readings

Campbell, Keith. *Body and Mind*. Garden City, NY: Anchor Books, 1970.

Churchland, Paul. *Matter and Consciousness*. Cambridge, MA: MIT, 1984.

Dennett, Daniel. *The Intentional Stance*. Cambridge, MA: MIT, 1987.

Flanagan, Owen. *The Science of Mind*. Cambridge, MA: MIT, 1991.

Haugeland, John. *Mind Design*. Cambridge, MA: MIT, 1981.

Margolis, Joseph. *Philosophy of Psychology*. Englewood Cliffs, NJ: Prentice-Hall, 1984.

Shaffer, Jerome. *Philosophy of Mind*. Englewood Cliffs, NJ: Prentice-Hall, 1968.

7

Persons

People are aware of themselves, as well as of other things. How people conceive of themselves makes a major difference in how they feel and act. We consider ourselves and other people to be persons. Philosophers have tried to figure out what the basic features of a person are, and what the basic features of a person's sense of self are. They have devoted the most attention to what makes someone the same person over a long period of time.

WHAT ARE WE?

The most basic issue is what type of entity we are. Few people ask themselves this question, probably because they think that the answer is obvious. We are persons. Persons have both a mind and a body. Human persons have psychological, biological, and physical characteristics. However, not all beings with psychological or mental characteristics are persons. Most animals are not persons, although many are conscious, feel pain, and have some emotions. Persons must have specific mental capacities and abilities, such as the ability to solve complex problems, to control the expression of their desires, and to speak and understand language. Such rational characteristics distinguish human persons from most, maybe all, other animals.

That each of us is a person means that each of us is one thing. You are not a conglomerate of different features that just happen to exist together, like all the items in a storeroom. A person is a type of unified thing. Characteristics have to fit together and operate together in specific ways to make up a person. That each of us is a person also means that you are not only, or primarily, an insignificant part of some larger whole. Although you may also be part of an organization, a state, or a culture, you have an existence as an individual person. As an individual thing, rather than just a performer of functions in a larger whole, you cannot be totally replaced by some other performer of the same functions.

Characteristics of a Person

We encounter many persons in everyday life. They all have both mental and bodily properties. Both mental and bodily characteristics seem to be essential to what we are. However, some philosophers and religious thinkers claim that we are only our minds or souls. They think that our bodies are not essential to us. We could continue living without our bodies or any bodies at all. Two responses can be made to this claim that we are only our minds. First, it is very unlikely that we could continue to live without any body or brain because mental life is so dependent on a properly functioning brain (see chapter 6 on the problem of dependence). Second, if it occurred, such disembodied life would be very different from our current life. In everyday life, our bodies are involved in practically everything that we do. For these reasons, having a body should be included in what we are.

Materialists claim that matter is all that exists. They think that there are no mental properties over and above physical properties. Speaking precisely, materialists would claim that persons do not have mental properties. However, they recognize that there are features of persons that we common- sensibly call "mental" features. Materialists do not deny that it is essential to persons that they have features that we commonsensibly consider to be mental. However, they consider these features really to be functionally defined, causal properties of complex physical systems (see chapter 6).

Many animals have psychological characteristics, but few, if any, non-human animals are persons. Specific mental capacities and abilities are necessary to be a person. There is not general agreement on the exact set of mental capacities and abilities that make someone a person. The following are the features that are most frequently considered to distinguish persons from merely conscious animals.

PLANNING AHEAD AND ACTING ON THEIR PLANS

Normal humans think about their futures and act now so that things will turn out better later. They control present desires and emotions for the sake of obtaining larger rewards later. They do things that they do not presently feel like doing because they realize that the actions will benefit them later. Dogs and other animals seem not to think about what will happen next week.

IDEALS

Normal humans have ideals for their behavior, such as requiring that their actions conform to morality or to other standards, such as being noble, "cool," or "liberated." On the basis of ideals, they control the expression of their desires and emotions. Other animals seem not to have ideals such as being moral.

A SENSE OF THE PAST

Normal humans have a sense of their own past and of history. This understanding of the past affects many things that we feel and do, such as feeling proud of past accomplishments or "paying someone back" for something. Other animals seem not to have this understanding of the past.

ABILITY TO REASON

Normal humans can modify their conceptions on the basis of new information, solve complex problems, and think about the evidence for a conclusion. Other animals do not have the same abilities to reason.

ABILITY TO COMMUNICATE THROUGH LANGUAGE

Normal humans speak and understand at least one language. Speaking a natural language enables someone to express an infinite number of things. Other animals can communicate, but they do not join symbols together, according to a grammar, or syntax, to express complex meanings.

COMPLEX SELF-CONCEPTION

Normal humans have complex conceptions of who they are, what their characteristics are, and what they want to become. Many animals seem to have some sense of themselves, because they realize where they stand in a social hierarchy—which are, for example, who is dominant among a group of dogs. However, these animals seem not to have the complex conceptions of themselves that persons have.

COMPLEX EMOTIONS

Normal humans have many complex emotions that build upon some of the preceding features. Persons can be nostalgic for the past or have a sense of adventure concerning the future. Persons can be indignant about some slight to their self-esteem or resent another's success. Other animals seem to have simpler emotions, such as fear, devotion, or anger, but not to have these more complex emotions.

Mentally Defective Humans

Normal humans have all of the preceding mental characteristics. However, there are many humans who will never have some of these characteristics. Children who are born with brain deficiencies or are severely retarded may never plan for their futures, develop a sense of morality, show much ability to reason, learn a language, and so on. The most mentally defective humans may have none of the distinctive features of persons. Others may have some degree of some of the distinctive features. Are such mentally defective humans persons?

There are rights and privileges that come with being a person. We generally think that persons have a right to life and liberty, a right to develop their capacities, and a right to choose their own way of life. The classification of some being as a person or not has practical importance because it affects the application of these, and other, rights and privileges. Chickens can be slaughtered for food and have their lives controlled by others because they are not persons, with rights to life and liberty. Whether we consider mentally defective humans to be persons affects how we think they should be treated. Should they be considered to have the rights and privileges of persons?

Some philosophers think that being a person is a quality of a species of animals. The characteristics that make something a person apply at the level of species, such as humans, dogs, chickens, and lizards, rather than at the level of individual animals. Since normal humans are persons, mentally defective humans are persons, even though as individuals they lack the mental characteristics of persons. To hold that all members of the human species are persons is one way to preserve rights for mentally defective humans. Many people consider mentally defective humans to have rights and privileges that other animals, with similar or greater mental abilities, do not have. Pigs are relatively intelligent animals. A pig may come closer to fulfilling the mental qualifications for being a person than a severely retarded human does. Nevertheless, pigs are frequently eaten, whereas everyone would consider it monstrous to treat severely retarded humans in the same way. This difference in treatment can be justified if personhood is a quality of a species. However, critics of this position consider it to be just a prejudice in favor of members of our own species. They think that we just have to accept the hard fact that some humans are not persons.

Becoming a Person

There are other controversial issues about who is a person. Normal newborn infants will develop all of the mental characteristics of a person, but they do not yet have all of them. Should newborn infants be considered to be persons? Should they be considered to have all the rights and privileges of persons? Some philosophers think that, as developing toward being a person, infants should have some, but not all, of the rights of persons.

The status of unborn fetuses is a more controversial issue because of abortion. A fertilized egg develops over a period of nine months into a fully functioning human baby. The brain and nervous system, which seem to be necessary for mental characteristics, develop during this period. At the earliest stages of development, there is no brain and nervous system, and there seems to be no mental life. Just before birth, however, the fetus seems not to be significantly different from a newborn infant. If a newborn infant is a person, the fetus just before birth may be a person as well. If the fetus just before birth is a person, when in the developmental process does the fetus become a person?

Philosophers who consider the newborn infant to be only developing toward being a person consider the fetus in a similar way. The fetus is not a person. It is only developing toward being a newborn infant. Throughout the period of biological development, it gradually acquires more of the features of a newborn infant. Rights and privileges are also gradually acquired.

Some religious thinkers consider being a person to be a matter of having an immaterial soul or mind (see chapter 6). The soul is something distinct from the brain and its functioning. The soul is created by God and is implanted in the developing body. In principle, the fetus could receive a soul at any time during the developmental process or even after birth. Many religious thinkers claim that the soul is implanted at the moment an egg is fertilized. For this reason, they think that a person with a right to life begins to exist at this time.

Ceasing to Be a Person

Another controversial issue is whether a human may cease to be a person without being entirely dead. Brain injury and deterioration, such as Alzheimer's disease, may remove the distinctive features of persons. A conscious human, who was once a person, may no longer have or be capable of the complex mental life of normal persons. Does the person continue to exist in such cases? Has the person disappeared, leaving only a non-personal but conscious being?

Physical and brain injury may remove all features of conscious life, including the distinctive features of persons. Modern medical techniques make it possible to keep a body alive in which there is no consciousness at all and none of the features of persons. Does this body continue to be a person? Is the person still alive? These are serious practical issues that affect the type of medical treatment that is given.

SENSE OF SELF

Part of being a person is having a complex self-conception. All normal people are concerned about who they are. Some people are relatively secure in their sense of self, while others are uncertain and feel somewhat "lost." What is the "self" of which we can have or lack a secure sense? Philosophers, sociologists, and psychologists have tried to figure out what a self is and what a sense of self is. However, there seem to be several different, but overlapping, meanings of "self." At different times, people may be concerned about different aspects of themselves when they wonder who they are.

Identifying Characteristics

On job and school applications there is always a section that asks for basic information to allow others to identify you. This information includes your name, where you live, your age, gender, height and weight, race, religion, color of your eyes and hair, other family members, educational background, work experience, and other things. These facts about you help other people to pick you out from a crowd. They also tell other people some things that they can expect from you. If you are older than five, people expect that you can tie your own shoes and go to the bathroom on your own. If you have graduated from high school, they expect that you know the basic things that people normally learn there.

You may feel that these "external facts" are not who you really are. Nevertheless, they are part of your identity. These are things that people conceal when they "hide their identities"—for example, when a fugitive or someone in a witness protection program hides his or her identity. That they are part of a person's sense of self is shown dramatically in cases of amnesia. People who lose all memory of their previous life, and do not even know their own names or family, feel that they do not know who they are.

Social Roles

When asked to say who they are, people frequently provide a list of their social roles. They think of themselves as a worker in a particular business, a college student with a particular major, an athlete, a rock or classical musician, a member of a political group, a member of a church or religion, the husband or wife or lover of someone, and so on. Social roles include socially defined ways of behaving and interacting with people. For example, there are normal—standardized—ways of behaving that go with being a college student, which are different from the normal ways of behaving of someone in the army. People act as someone in these roles is supposed to act (hence, the analogy with characters and roles in a play).

A self, according to this conception, is the organization of all of someone's social roles. Some of them define you more than others. A person's roles tend to affect one another, and the self is this unity of the roles. Your sense of self is your sense of the importance of various roles to who you are and of how they modify one another. When someone suffers an "identity crisis," they have, at least partially, lost this sense of the organization of roles that should guide their behavior.

Core Self

Many people think that the organization of their social roles is not their real self. They think that their "core self" is something distinct from their roles. They can take on new roles and abandon old ones because of this core self. They remain the same person throughout these changes, because it is the core self that they really are.

Different philosophies and religions have proposed different theories of the core self. One theory is that your core self is your mind or soul, which is the subject of all your experiences. Your mind or soul can think different thoughts and play different roles, but it is the continuing basis of your self. Existentialists, such as Heidegger and Sartre, have a somewhat different theory. They consider the core self to be the decision-making feature of a person. The decision-making feature is an activity of choosing all of your objectives and of choosing to accept or reject social roles. Psychoanalysts, such as Sigmund Freud (1856–1939), consider the core self to be the organization of unconscious instincts, internalized prohibitions that are acquired from your parents in early childhood, and ego structures. This organization makes up a person's basic psyche and affects everything a person feels and does. A fourth theory is that your core self is your body. Whatever changes you may go through, you remain the same self so long as you have the same physical body.

Buddhism denies that there is any continuing core self. Selfish desire—desiring something for yourself—is the source of unhappiness, and selfish desire is based on the idea of a continuing self. To overcome unhappiness, a person must give up selfish desire. This is accomplished by realizing that there is no continuing self to which things happen or for which things might be gotten. To be "enlightened" is no longer to believe the illusion of a enduring self or soul. Living with this "selfless" attitude is living in accord with what you really are.

PERSONAL IDENTITY THROUGH TIME

We consider ourselves, and everyone else, to be one person who exists throughout a long period of time. Many characteristics of the person may change, but he or she continues to be the same person. Money deposited in a bank account for a baby may rightfully be collected seventy years later by an old woman who is the same person as the baby. Philosophers have offered different theories of what makes someone the same person over a long period of time.

Same Body   The simplest way to identify other people is by their bodily charac- teristics. One living human body exists over a long period of time. It exists from infancy until death, when the body normally starts to degenerate. One theory of personal identity is that having, or being, the same body is what makes someone the same person. Even though a person's personality may change completely throughout her lifetime, she remains the same person because she is, or has, the same body.

The human body changes in dramatic ways from early infancy, through adolescence and adulthood, to old age. If there are such dramatic changes, what makes the body of a baby the same body as that of an eighteen-year-old man? What makes the body of the eighteen-year-old man the same body as that of an eighty-year-old man? One important factor is that one living body passes through a continuous spatial-temporal path. A human body inside a room at ten o'clock and a human body that is outdoors ten minutes later are the same body if at every moment in between there is a similar human body that occupies a spot in space that is the same spot or is right next to the spot occupied a moment earlier. If we were observing the body all during this period, we would not see any gaps. We would see one body that moves from inside the room to the outdoors. The same applies to long periods of time. A continuous path through space over time connects a baby's body with that of the eighty-year-old man. A second important factor is causal continuity. What happens to the earlier body has effects on the later body.

Problems for the Same-Body Theory

Locke proposed the classic objection to the same body theory of personal identity. The objection is that it is, in principle, possible for one person to switch bodies while remaining the same person. Switching bodies may never happen, but we understand what it would be. We understand science fiction and fantasy stories, in which someone gets a body different from the one that she had. Furthermore, neuroscience may someday make it possible to transplant someone's brain into another, healthier and younger, body. In the case of a brain transplant, or, perhaps better, a body transplant, we think that the same person would get a different body. Hence, being the same person cannot be just a matter of having the same body.

A second type of objection is that the same body might, in principle, be home to two or more persons during the same period. In unusual but real cases of multiple personalities or division of the two hemispheres of the brain, it makes sense to ask whether two or more persons exist in the one human body. In such cases, the psychological entities that exist in the body seem to belong to two, or more, different systems. Psychological entities—desires, wants, beliefs, thoughts, memories, and so on—in one system work together with one another, but they do not work together with those in the other system. For example, one personality does not experience the desires of the other, does not perceive what the other perceives, and does not remember the actions of the other personality. This type of mental separation is more like the mental life of two people than the mental life of one person. Whether these real cases involve two persons or not, the fact that there is just one body is not sufficient to prove that there must be just one person.

Same Brain

In light of the evidence that mental properties depend upon a properly working brain (see chapter 6), some philosophers have proposed that being the same person over time is a matter of having the same brain. In all real (rather than imagined) cases, having the same body includes having the same brain. The advantage of the same-brain theory over the same body theory is that it also covers the future possibility of brain transplants. If it ever becomes possible to remove a living brain from its body and keep it alive outside of any body (a "brain in a vat"), or implant it in a new body, the person would continue to exist with the brain. If the brain in one body were switched with the brain in another body (a double transplant), the person would follow the brain. Each person would acquire a new body, rather than a new brain.

Problems for the Same-Brain Theory

The same-brain theory has some of the same problems as the same body theory. It seems to be in principle possible for one person to switch brains while remaining the same person. There may be no proven cases in which someone has moved from one brain, and body, to another brain, but it seems to be possible. Even some materialists (see chapter 6) think that it is possible. If what we ordinarily consider to be a mind is really the "computer program" of the brain, this "program" in principle could be transferred from one brain to another. The person would follow the "program," rather than remaining with the brain.

The same-brain theory also has the problem that one brain might be home to two or more persons during the same period. If two separate systems of mental or psychological entities exist in one brain, there may be two persons rather than one.

Same-Mind Substance

Most people think that personal identity over time is a matter of having the same mind. All previous experiences that were experienced by the same continuing, mind are part of the same person. Even though you are very different now from what you were at the age of fourteen months, the experiences of the fourteen-month-old baby are your past experiences, because the same mind experienced them. Characteristics of your body belong to the person that you are because of the connections between mind and body.

The mind or soul is frequently thought to be a non-spatial, conscious substance that has mental properties (see chapter 6). A mind substance is supposed to be distinct from any material thing, such as a brain or body. If a person is a mind substance, it would be in principle possible for a person to switch bodies and to switch brains. The mind substance which causally interacted with one body and brain might, for some unknown reason, start to interact causally with a different body and brain. Whether or not this ever actually happens, as in reincarnation after death, a person *could* acquire a new body and brain, because the mind could become connected to the new body and brain.

The mind-substance theory of personal identity makes life after death very understandable. Since a person is a non-material mind or soul, the person can continue to exist without any connection with a material body. There is no reason that the death of the body should harm the person—the mind—in any way.

Problems for the Same-Mind Theory

The major problem for the same-mind theory is that recent evidence indicates that mind is not a separate substance. All experiences and mental capacities seem to be dependent upon a properly working brain (see chapter 6). Brain damage can remove a person's ability to remember, to speak and understand language, to have emotions, and other things. If there is no distinct mental substance, it cannot be the basis of personal identity.

Locke argued that even if there were a distinct mental substance or soul, it could not be the basis of personal identity. He claimed that what makes you you is your personality and consciousness of yourself, and not the substance in which these occur. If your personality and consciousness of yourself were somehow to switch from one mind substance to another, you would follow your personality and consciousness of yourself. You would not continue to be your former mind substance that now had an entirely different personality, memories, desires, beliefs, goals for itself, and so on. If God were to substitute a new mind substance for your former mind substance, but leave everything else the same, you would not notice any difference.

Mental Connections

The mental-connections theory tries to retain the basic idea that personal identity is a matter of having the same mind, while rejecting the idea of a mind substance. The mental-connections theory claims that a person is basically the unity of his mental or psychological characteristics. This unity is not provided by something, such as a mental or physical substance, that has all of the characteristics. The characteristics are not unified just by being in the same mind substance or in the same body. Rather, the psychological characteristics are united directly with one another. They connect with one another, somewhat like the threads woven into a fabric or the links of a chain. The unity is a matter of the psychological characteristics working together in a system and being aware of one another. Hence, personal identity over time is a matter of these connections between the psychological characteristics of different stages of a person.

MEMORY

Locke claimed that memory was the only psychological connection between person-stages; a person-stage is that portion of a person that occurs at a particular time. A person now is the same person as an earlier person-stage (person at an earlier date) if she can remember, "from the inside," the experiences and actions of the earlier person-stage. A person can remember in this first-person way only her own experiences. If you can remember, "from the inside," filling out applications for college, you are the person who filled out those forms for college. It is not necessary that you actually recall to mind the previous experiences. At any given moment, we actually recall to mind very little of our past lives. All that is necessary is that you are able to remember them.

CONTINUITY OF CHARACTER

Contemporary defenders of the mental-connections theory appeal to other mental connections in addition to memory. Continuity of character and personality is an important mental connection between the stages of a person. When the character and personality of a later stage are similar to that of an earlier stage and have been produced in an appropriate way from the earlier stage, there is continuity of personality and character. Even though there may be some changes over time, there is one person throughout because the later moments of the personality and character develop out of the earlier ones.

OTHER MENTAL CONNECTIONS

Other mental connections are those between earlier intentions and later actions, and between stages in the normal development patterns of mental characteristics. People make plans for the future and decide now to do something later. There is a psychological connection between person-stages when a later action is produced by this earlier planning and deciding. There is another type of psychological connection between person-stages when a later mental condition is a normal outgrowth from earlier ones. For example, in memorizing a poem, or facts for a test, you probably repeat them to yourself. The normal result of this memorizing is that later you are able to recite the poem, or the facts. Many emotions that extend over time similarly involve normal patterns of development. For example, the sense of shock at the death of a friend usually develops over time into grief and then into acceptance. The person-stage that accepts the friend's death has a mental connection with the earlier person-stage that was shocked by the death.

Most mental-connections theories use both direct and indirect mental connections. Being able to remember the experiences of an earlier person-stage is a direct connection between the later person-stage and the earlier one. An indirect connection is an overlapping chain of direct connections.

If you are now able to remember what you experienced five years ago, and five years ago you were able to remember what you experienced five years before then, there is an overlapping chain of memories connecting you now with what you experienced ten years ago. There are overlapping chains (indirect connections) of the other specific mental connections, such as earlier intentions to later actions, as well as of memory.

Problems for the Mental-Connections Theory

One problem is that it is difficult to state mental connections exactly without presupposing personal identity. This is frequently called the "problem of circularity," because in trying to define personal identity in terms of mental connections, specific mental connections may be defined in terms of personal identity. For example, it is not easy to define "being able to remember" without presupposing personal identity. "Being able to remember" does not mean "actually recalling to mind." What we "are able to remember" has sometimes been thought to mean "what it is logically possible for us to remember." However, "what it is logically possible for us to remember" may presuppose the concept of personal identity, because it may be logically possible for us to remember only our own experiences, the experiences that are part of our personal past.

Another problem is that the body may be more important to personal identity than this theory recognizes. If your entire system of unified mental characteristics were somehow moved into an entirely different sort of body, such as into a brain in a vat or into the body of a tortoise, your personal identity might be affected. If this relocation does change what the person is, personal identity cannot be just a matter of mental connections.

We consider ourselves and other people to be persons. A person is a unified thing that has both mental and physical characteristics. As an individual thing, a person is more than just a performer of functions in a larger whole, such as a state. As having physical properties, a person needs some type of body. A person also needs to have specific mental capacities and abilities.

Many animals have mental characteristics, but few, if any, non-human animals are persons. Although there is not complete agreement, the features that are most frequently considered to distinguish persons from merely conscious animals are: the ability to plan ahead and act on their plans, ideals for their behavior, a sense of the past, the ability to reason, the ability to communicate through language, a complex self-conception, and complex emotions.

Normal humans have all of the preceding mental characteristics. Mentally defective humans may never have some or all of these characteristics. Are such mentally defective humans persons? Should they have the rights and privileges of persons? Some philosophers think that being a person is a quality of a species of animals. Since normal humans are persons, mentally defective humans are persons, even though as individuals they lack the mental characteristics of persons. Other philosophers think that mentally defective humans are not persons or are only partially persons.

There are other controversial issues about whether normal newborn infants and unborn fetuses are persons. Some philosophers think that, as developing toward being a person, infants should have some, but not all, of the rights of persons. These philosophers also think that as fetuses develop, they gradually acquire the rights and privileges of newborn infants. Other philosophers think that a person exists from the moment an egg is fertilized, because God creates a soul at that time.

Another controversial issue is whether a human may cease to be a person without being entirely dead. If brain injury and deterioration remove the mental features distinctive of persons, has the person disappeared, leaving only a living body?

Part of being a person is having a complex self-conception. Philosophers, sociologists, and psychologists have tried to figure out what a self is and what a sense of self is. However, there seem to be several different, but overlapping, meanings of "self." One meaning of "self" is the set of basic facts about a person that help other people identify him. Another meaning of "self" is the organization of all of a person's social roles. People frequently think of themselves in terms of their social roles, such as being a college student or a member of a particular church. A third meaning is that of a core self that can take on new roles and abandon old ones. Some philosophers think that your core self is your mind as a substance. Others think that the decision-making feature of a person is the core self. Some psychoanalysts consider the core self to be the organization of unconscious instincts, internalized prohibitions, and ego structures. Buddhism denies that there is any continuing core self.

We consider each normal human to be one person who exists throughout a long period of time. Philosophers have offered different theories of what makes someone the same person despite time and change. One theory of personal identity is that having, or being, the same body is what makes someone the same person. This raises a question about what makes the body of a baby (at an earlier time) the same body as the body of an eighty-year-old man (seventy-nine years later). The two most important factors are passing through a continuous spatial-temporal path and having causal continuity.

One objection to the same-body theory of personal identity is that it is in principle possible for one person to switch bodies while remaining the same person. A second type of objection is that the same body might in principle be home to two or more persons during the same period.

Another theory of personal identity is that it is a matter of having the same brain. If a living brain could be removed from its original body, the person would follow the brain rather than the body. The same-brain theory of personal identity has many of the same problems as the same-body theory.

Many people think that personal identity is a matter of having the same mind substance. The mind, or soul, is frequently thought to be a non-spatial, conscious substance that has mental properties. If a person is a mind substance, it would be in principle possible for a person to switch bodies and to switch brains. Life after the death of the body would also be very understandable.

The major objection to the same-mind theory of personal identity is that recent evidence indicates that the mind is not a substance separate from the brain. Another objection is that it is personality and consciousness of self that define a person, not the substance in which these occur.

The mental-connections theory claims that a person is basically the unity of his mental or psychological characteristics. These psychological characteristics are united directly with each other, somewhat like the threads woven into a fabric. Personal identity over time is a matter of psychological connections between different stages of a person. The most important psychological connections between stages of a person are memory, continuity of character and personality, movement from earlier intention to later action, and normal development patterns. Most mental-connections theories use both direct and indirect mental connections. An indirect connection is an overlapping chain of direct connections.

One problem with the mental-connections theory is that it is difficult to state mental connections, such as memory, exactly without presupposing personal identity. Another problem is that our bodies may be more important to our personal identities than this theory recognizes.

Selected Readings

Mischel, Theodore (ed.). *The Self*. Oxford: Basil Blackwell, 1977.

Noonan, Harold. *Personal Identity*. London: Routledge, 1989.

Parfit, Derek. *Reasons and Persons*. Oxford: Oxford, 1984.

Perry, John. *A Dialogue on Personal Identity and Immortality*. Indianapolis: Hackett, 1978.

_____. (ed.). *Personal Identity*. Berkeley: University of California, 1975.

Shoemaker, S., and R. Swinburne. *Personal Identity*. Oxford: Basil Blackwell, 1984.

8

Freedom and Responsibility

People are thought to be responsible for many of the things that they do. A person is normally responsible for the action of stealing a watch from a department store, but someone else is not responsible for breaking a display case if the thief pushes him against it. Despite these clearcut cases, there are more difficult cases in which people disagree about whether someone should be held fully responsible for something that he does. Philosophers have attempted to specify what sort of factors make someone responsible for what he does. Freedom has frequently been thought to be necessary for responsibility. There is continuing debate about what type of freedom persons may have and how this affects responsibility.

COMMON SENSE AND LEGAL CONCEPTIONS

In everyday life and in our legal system, many distinctions are made about types of human behavior that affect responsibility. A person is normally considered to be morally and legally responsible only for voluntary actions.

Voluntary Action

Voluntary action is behavior that is in your control. Voluntary actions are the things that you do willingly—voluntary action is sometimes called "free action." For the action to be a voluntary action, it is not necessary that you explicitly consider and decide to act. Actions that you perform out of habit, such as plugging in the coffeepot as soon as you get up in the morning, are normally voluntary actions. What makes something a voluntary action is that you have some sense of what you are doing and consent to do it.

Human bodies do many things that are not voluntary actions because the person does not control what is done. The beating of your heart and the digestion of your food are not voluntary actions. Reflex movements, such as your hand jerking away from a very hot object, are normally not voluntary actions. In general, anything your body does that you do not realize it is doing or that you do not consent to do is not a voluntary action.

Aristotle noted that an action may be involuntary for either of two reasons: The person is ignorant of what he is doing, or he acts under compulsion.

IGNORANCE

If you do not understand the circumstances in which you are acting or the likely causal results of your immediate movements, you probably do not know what you are doing. If you do not know that scratching your nose is an obscene gesture in a particular society, you do not realize that in scratching your nose you are insulting your hosts. If you do not know that gasoline vapor explodes, you do not realize what you are doing in using a lighted match to help you see down into the gas tank of a car. As these examples indicate, ignorance of what you are doing normally involves a distinction between your immediate movements and a "larger" action. The person normally realizes that he is moving his body in some way (scratching his nose or lighting a match), but he does not know what, from a larger point of view, he is doing. He may be unaware of the larger situation and causal laws, or he may have false beliefs about them. For example, he might think that scratching his nose is a sign of gratitude in this society. In this case, there is a difference between what he thinks he is doing and what he is actually doing.

COMPULSION

Compulsion exists when a person is forced to do something; she does not do it "of her own free will." Aristotle considered an action to be compulsory when it originates in an external cause to which the doer contributes nothing. For example, a sea captain does not follow his course because a storm blows his ship off course. According to Aristotle's account, threats and unusual circumstances that "force" you to do something that you would not otherwise do are not clear cases of compulsion. This is because you do have it in your power to resist the threat or to ignore the circumstances. However, other accounts of compulsion consider external factors, such as threats or unusual circumstances, to reduce the degree of voluntariness of an action. The more important the external factors are, the more "force" or coercion they exert on a person. If a criminal threatens to shoot you, or your mother or someone else, unless you give him a quarter, the threatened action is so serious in contrast with giving him a quarter that you have little choice. In this case, your action of giving him a quarter is largely involuntary. However, if the criminal threatens to take your quarter unless you shoot your mother, the threatened action is very minor in contrast with what you are to do. In this case, your action, either of shooting or refusing, is voluntary.

Responsibility

Being responsible for something is being rightfully subject to reward or punishment, or praise or blame for that something. You are liable to responsive actions by other people based on the something for which you are responsible. They hold you responsible for it. Most issues of responsibility concern responsibility for acting, or for failing to act. We want to know when it is proper for someone to be rewarded or punished, or praised or blamed (held responsible) for an action that she did.

In our system of criminal law and morality, people are responsible only for voluntary actions and their results (what a normal person would understand to be the results of the voluntary action). Other people and legal authorities can rightfully hold you responsible only if your behavior was in your control. If you can show that your action was not voluntary, you have a defense against being punished or blamed for it. If you were forced to commit a criminal act, for example, someone forces your hand to hit someone, or if, through no fault of your own, you did not realize that what you were actually doing was against the law, you are not responsible for the violation of the law. Similarly, you are not responsible for violations of moral law if you acted under compulsion or in ignorance.

Compulsion and ignorance remove moral and criminal responsibility for an action if these conditions are not your own fault. Moral and criminal responsibility are not removed if a person is responsible for being in the condition of compulsion or ignorance that makes his action involuntary. A person may be at fault for not realizing that he is violating a moral or criminal law. When someone is drunk, or is on other drugs, he may not realize what he is doing, but he is responsible for putting himself in that condition. Similarly, someone may be at fault for being subject to compulsion. A person may fail to take the normal degree of care so that he "invites an accident" (failing to take a proper degree of care is called "negligence"). For example, if someone carries a powerful acid or poison in a coffee cup onto a crowded bus, he is not excused from all responsibility if someone hits his arm and forces him to spill the acid on an innocent person.

In some religious, moral, and legal systems, people have been held responsible for what they did, regardless of whether it was voluntary. This is called "strict liability." Within a system of strict liability the person is responsible for her behavior whether or not it was in her control. A person might be held responsible by gods, priests, or believers for violating a command not to visit a sacred island, even if her boat were blown there by a storm or if she did not know about the command. In our legal system, there are a few areas in which civil laws and regulations hold people, or companies, strictly liable for their behavior. The person or company is rightfully subject to punishment or blame for a violation, regardless of whether or not the action of violating was voluntary.

Ability to Choose

We normally think that people are able to choose what to do. People may do many things out of habit, but they always have the ability to decide to do something different. They have the power to consider what they are about to do and choose either to do it or something else. Furthermore, a person does not automatically act because she desires something. That she has a specific desire does not dictate that she act to satisfy it. Rather, she is able to choose whether to act from her desire or not. People are free in that they are able to choose what they do.

The ability to choose what to do is complicated, but it includes at least three features: being able to think about acting before acting; being able to think about the results of an action; and being able to think about the motives for acting. That you are able to think about what to do before doing it allows you to consider different possible courses of action. You can consider alternatives and then decide to do one of them. That you are able to think about the results of an action allows you to take into account more than just the immediate bodily behavior. You can consider what your bodily behavior will be in the specific circumstances (for example, that it might be an obscene gesture), and what it will cause (for example, that lighting the match will cause an explosion that injures people). That you can think about motives for acting allows you to detach yourself from any current desire or emotion. You can weigh different desires and wants against one another and consider the priority of different types of motives. Thinking about motives allows you to consider what morality or duty might require of you, and whether you will act to satisfy your desires if these conflict with morality, or the law.

Most people think that being able to choose either to do or not to do an action is necessary for being responsible for it. They think that responsibility requires more than understanding what you are doing and consenting to do it. You have to consent to act while being able not to consent. Responsibility for a voluntary action requires that you could choose not to do it. If someone acts voluntarily but is not able to choose not to do the action, he is not responsible for it. He should not be rewarded or punished, or praised or blamed for it. However, if the person is at fault for being unable to choose (the person has put himself in this condition), responsibility is not removed.

Inner Compulsion

External compulsion forces a person to act. External compulsion makes a person's action involuntary because she does not consent to it. Inner compulsion occurs when some inner psychological factor forces a person to act. A craving for water may force someone dying of thirst to drink all of the water, rather than share it. A craving for heroin may force an addict to take the drug. An extraordinary fear of heights may force someone to cancel her flight. Mental "illness" of various sorts may make a person subject to inner forces over which she has no control. Most people think that there are cases in which psychological factors force someone to act, although there is dispute about which are real cases of inner compulsion.

Inner compulsion removes a person's ability to choose. If someone is dying of thirst and is overcome by a craving for water, he does not have the ability to choose not to drink the water. Although he consents to drink the water, he is not able not to consent. He does not have freedom of will, because his desire for water controls him. Therefore, he is not responsible for drinking the water, according to one conception of responsibility. If responsibility for an action requires that the person could choose not to do it, and inner compulsion means that one could not choose not to do it, inner compulsion removes responsibility. If an inner force can really overwhelm a person and force him to act, the person should not be held responsible, unless he is at fault for making himself subject to the inner force. Some type of treatment to remove the inner compulsion may be a better idea.

Mental Deficiencies

Some humans, and probably all animals, do not have the ability to choose that normal persons have. They may be under the control of some inner compulsion, or they may lack some of the mental abilities necessary for the ability to choose. Young children, mentally retarded people, and various types of insane people are usually considered not to be responsible for some of their actions. They are not responsible because they are not able to choose these actions. They lack freedom of will. A very young child is not able to consider alternative courses of action before acting. He does not choose between possibilities that he considers beforehand. Rather, he acts according to whatever "comes into his mind."

Young children, and others with more permanent mental deficiencies, are not able to think much about the results of their behavior. They may realize how they are moving their bodies and what the immediate effects of this movement are, but they do not realize what their "larger" action is. For example, a young child may realize that she is painting a picture on a surface, but not realize that she is ruining an expensive tablecloth. The insane frequently have beliefs about the results of their action, but these are wildly false beliefs. They frequently act in response to an "imagined world"—for example, they think their action is necessary to prevent space aliens from taking over the government. Hence, they do not fully realize what they are doing in the real world.

DETERMINISM

Determinism is the theory that all events are caused or determined, by antecedent conditions. Whatever happens is caused to happen by previous facts. Nothing happens "by mere chance." There are laws of nature according to which whatever happens, happens because of what happened before. If we know these laws of nature and the antecedent conditions, we can know what will happen. In principle, we could know beforehand about any event.

Determinism is widely accepted in most areas of natural science. However, many philosophers and religious thinkers claim that not all human actions and decisions are causally determined. They oppose determinism because it seems to conflict with our ordinary understanding of people as able to choose. Determinism means that people do not have free will in the traditional sense.

Physical Determinism

Some philosophers think that determinism must apply to human action and decision-making because our brains control our bodies. Our brains direct our bodies to do certain things and not to do others. Brain processes are physical events that are caused by antecedent physical factors. Any later condition of the brain could, in principle, be explained by the immediately preceding condition of the brain plus any physical input. If all brain events occur according to natural laws, then human action must also occur according to natural laws. There is no room for anything non-deterministic because all brain events are caused by antecedent physical factors.

A related argument for physical determinism is that making a decision must be causally determined because the mental states involved are totally dependent upon brain states. The earlier mental state (of considering various alternatives) is dependent upon a specific state of the brain, and the later mental state (of intending to do one of the alternatives) is dependent upon a specific state of the brain. This later state of the brain is causally determined by antecedent physical factors. Hence, the later mental state that is dependent upon this brain state is also causally determined by these antecedent physical factors.

Objections

Scientists who study the brain hope to discover all the scientific laws that concern brain events. There is still much to be understood about how the brain works. Physical determinism of brain events has not been proven. No one knows for sure whether all brain events are causally determined by antecedent physical factors. One area of natural science in which determinism is controversial, and indeterminism has been asserted, is quantum physics. Thus, it is claimed that the behavior of very small particles involves an element of chance. Whether one quantum event or another will occur is not strictly determined by antecedent physical factors. It is possible that some brain events are results of quantum effects. If so, these brain events would not be causally determined by antecedent physical factors. There would be an element of chance involved. But it is not obvious that this would support or sustain the claim of free will.

Free will requires more than indeterminism of brain events by physical factors. Defenders of free will claim that mental decisions affect brain states. The mental decision must cause the right brain states in order to control the behavior of the body. How a mental decision can cause changes in the brain is an unresolved problem for free will (see chapter 6 on Interactionist Dualism and Mental Causes).

Psychological Determinism

Psychological determinism is the theory that all psychological (mental) states and events are caused by antecedent psychological states and events. All decisions are caused by previously existing psychological factors. There are causal psychological laws that govern everything that a person thinks, decides, and does. The human mind is very complicated, so the psychological laws can be very complicated. However, the general relationships are already known. We already have a good idea how desires, wants, emotions, morals, and a sense of duty interact to produce a person's decision. In everyday life, we regularly predict how people will feel and decide about things. Based on our knowledge of a person's personality and character, we regularly predict that she will do certain sorts of things and not others. If you know that someone loves opera and hates football, you can be fairly certain that she will watch the opera, on television, rather than the football game. We even try to influence people's decisions by manipulating the causal factors. Advertising, for example, relies on this idea.

Psychologists try to improve on our commonsense understanding of the factors that cause decisions. They investigate in more detail how emotions, moods, desires, wants, values, a sense of morality, and other factors influence people's decisions and actions. They also look for causal factors that are not usually recognized, such as unconscious desires and prohibitions. If psychology ever discovers the complete set of causal factors that determine decisions, psychological determinism will be shown to be true.

Psychological determinists frequently argue that a person's current psychological makeup is a causal result of his heredity and environment. They claim that a person's mind, character, and personality are produced by the causal interactions of the inherited features determined by his genes—heredity—with all the external forces to which he is exposed, including his upbringing—environment. A person's character is as causally determined by antecedent factors as specific decisions are.

Objections

The main objection to psychological determinism is that in many cases we seem to be able to choose any of several alternatives. We all have this sense of being free to decide between several possibilities. If you are deciding whether to read assigned course work or go to a movie tonight, you have the sense of being able to choose either one. Both before you make the decision and afterward, your choice seems to you not to be forced by antecedent factors. However, if this decision is causally determined, there are antecedent factors that cause you to choose one specific alternative (to do your course work, of course). Because of these causal factors, you could not choose any of the other alternatives.

A related objection to psychological determinism is that it makes people not responsible for their actions. Most people think that being able to choose either to do or not to do an action is necessary for being responsible for it (see Ability to Choose, p. 117). A person must be able to choose either to go to a movie or not to go to a movie in order to be responsible for going to a movie. Many philosophers think that if you are causally determined to do an action, such as going to a movie, you are not able to choose not to do it. Hence, according to the above notion of responsibility, you are not responsible for your action because you were not able to choose either to do or not to do it.

A different objection is that human behavior is too unpredictable. Although some of a person's actions and decisions follow a pattern, some do not. It is not currently possible to know what a person will decide to do in every case. Psychological determinists think that this is only because individual people are so complex that we cannot know all the relevant facts about them. However, opponents claim that this is because people's decisions are not strictly determined by antecedent factors.

DETERMINISM AND RESPONSIBILITY

Philosophers have disagreed about the exact conditions that are necessary for responsibility. According to different conceptions of what is necessary for responsibility, a person may be responsible or not responsible for a decision that is caused by antecedent factors.

Hard Determinism

Hard determinism is the position that people are not responsible for their actions and decisions because these are causally determined. Hard determinists think that responsibility requires the power to choose either to do or not to do an action. They think that free will is necessary for being responsible; they share this conception with defenders of free will. Hard determinists also claim that this power to choose does not exist because all decisions are causally determined by antecedent factors. Only the causally determined alternative is available to the person. Hence, no one is responsible for any decision or action. No one is responsible because everyone lacks the free will that is necessary for responsibility. Everyone is in a position similar to that of the person who is forced by inner compulsion.

Hard determinists think that people should not be blamed or punished for bad actions. This is because no one is responsible for her actions. Many hard determinists think that the proper response to bad actions is some type of treatment. Society should try to change the factors that cause the person to act. The person's psychology should be changed in some way so that her decisions and actions will not be unacceptable to society. This will not make the person any more responsible, because no one can be responsible. However, it will eliminate the burden on other people of the person's bad actions.

Soft Determinism

Soft determinism is the position that people are responsible for their actions and decisions even though these are causally determined by antecedent factors. Soft determinists think that to be responsible for an action a person need only do what he decides to do. If a person decides, in the normal way, to go to a movie rather than read the text for his class tomorrow, he is responsible for what he does. So long as his action follows from his character, his current desires, and his fairly accurate understanding of his circumstances, he is responsible for it. It makes no difference that his decision was caused by antecedent factors. He did decide to go to a movie, and so his action is a free action.

Soft determinism is also called "compatibilism," because it claims that freedom is compatible with determinism. Freedom of action is being able to do what you want and decide to do. Your action is free if you could have done some other action had you chosen to do it. Freedom of choice is deciding in the normal way, without either external or inner compulsion. A person who considers the alternatives and decides, without anything seeming to force his decision, makes a free choice. However, this free choice is not a case of free will in the traditional sense. There are antecedent factors that cause him to choose the alternative that he chooses. These causal factors, such as his character, wants, and beliefs, are part of the chooser. Hence, his choosing is free in that nothing outside of him forces him to choose one alternative rather than another. His decision is an expression of (is caused by) the person that he is.

Soft determinists claim that psychological determinism of decisions and actions is compatible with being responsible for the actions. They disagree with hard determinists and free will defenders on this point. In defense of their position that free will is not necessary for responsibility, many soft determinists argue that psychological determinism (of a particular type) is necessary for responsibility. They argue that an action must derive from a person's character and personality for the person to be responsible for it. It is only when an action is an expression of someone's character and personality that it makes sense to hold her responsible for it. She should be subject to reward or punishment, or praise or blame for an action if the action is caused by her character and personality. If an action or a decision to act did not have any connection to the person's character and personality, there would be no good reason to hold her responsible for it. Soft determinists argue that free will, in which there is no causation by antecedent factors, such as character and personality, provides no basis for responsibility.

FREE WILL

Free will is the power to detach yourself from any inner motivation and to choose any of several alternatives. The theory of free will is that some decisions are both controlled by a person herself and not totally caused by antecedent factors. The person is not caused by antecedent psychological factors to decide for one possibility over another. She has the power to "step back from" any psychological factor, such as a desire or an emotion, that pushes her toward one possibility. She can then decide to follow that motivation or to pursue any of the other alternatives. Even with her desires and emotions, she is free to choose to go to a movie tonight, to read the material for tomorrow's class, or to do anything else she may consider. A person uses free will when she exercises this power to make a decision.

Free will is supposed to be the basis for responsibility. Although antecedent factors do not totally cause a decision to act, neither is the decision to act completely arbitrary. A totally arbitrary and spontaneous action is not a case of free will. If a person suddenly jumped on the table and started dancing, and this was totally unconnected with his character and previous thoughts, this action would not be done out of free will. From the person's point of view, the arbitrary action would be a surprise and would not be under his control. According to the theory of free will, a decision to act has to be an expression of the person who makes it. The person must take motivational factors into account in deciding but not be causally determined by them. The person must control the decision in order to be responsible for it.

Many defenders of free will admit that they do not have a fully detailed account of what "goes on" in free will. They claim that we all experience our own power to control our inner motivations and to freely decide, but that it is very difficult to describe this power in great detail. The reason that free will is so difficult to describe is that it is so different from ordinary events. We cannot say exactly what is happening when we exercise our free will, but we can recognize when we are using free will and when we are not.

Considering Yourself to Be Free

Defenders of free will want people to consider themselves to be free in deciding how to act. People normally do consider themselves to be able to resist acting on some desires, to be able to control the expressions of their emotions, and to be able to choose any of several different possibilities. Defenders of free will—they are sometimes called "libertarians"—think that considering yourself to be free is essential to having a sense of active control over what you do. Our sense of ourselves as acting, rather than merely passively observing, requires that we consider ourselves to be free. Considering ourselves to be free to control our desires, emotions, and any other inner motivational factors is the main feature of being an active agent.

Defenders of free will claim that we cannot consider our own decisions and actions to be causally determined by antecedent factors without changing ourselves. We would have to give up the standpoint of active agency in order to accept determinism completely. We can consider other people's decisions to be causally determined. However, we can never really consider our own decisions to be causally determined. We cannot apply determinism to our own cases without changing our own cases.

One argument to support the claim that we cannot apply determinism to our own decision-making is the following. To apply a causal law to some situation, you have to know what the law is and how the law fits the situation. To apply causal psychological laws to your own current decision-making, you would have to know the psychological laws and your own antecedent psychological factors that are supposed to cause your decision. However, once you know what the laws predict, you may—out of defiance, spite, or a love of free will—want to do something else. Whatever psychological factors, according to the psychological laws, are supposed to cause the specific choice, once you know about the laws and about how they apply, some new psychological factors (your knowing) have been added. These new psychological factors, particularly if you are a defiant person or a lover of free will, may make the original laws no longer applicable to the new situation (the old situation plus the new psychological factors).

LEGAL PUNISHMENT

Punishment is the infliction of penalties on offenders by authorities, those authorized by the system to impose penalties. Punishment occurs within a system. The system includes rules for behaving and ways to enforce the rules by imposing burdens on those who break the rules. For example, a parent, the authority, may prevent a child from watching television as a punishment for breaking a household rule. Legal punishment is the infliction of penalties by legal authorities on people who break the laws.

Penalties are unpleasant, and people would prefer not to have penalties placed on them. This is why the system of legal punishment needs to be justified. We want to know why a part of our government should impose penalties on some people. Why should criminals be punished for breaking laws? There are five major theories of why legal punishment is justified, although many thinkers use more than one of them.

Vengeance

The simplest theory is that legal punishment is a form of revenge. When someone harms you, you may want to harm them in return. Throughout human history, people, along with their families and friends, have sought revenge against others who have harmed them. According to the theory of vengeance, legal punishment is a good thing because it is a controlled form of revenge. Legal authorities, rather than the people who were harmed, impose the punishment. This satisfies people's desire for revenge but prevents continuing feuds and excessive punishment.

Retribution

Retribution is giving someone what he deserves. Most people think that legal punishment is a good thing because the law-breaker is given what he deserves. A person who voluntarily breaks the law deserves to be punished. The punishment is deserved because of the offense against society. Hence, the law-breaker deserves punishment whether or not anyone wants revenge on him. Although some people who want revenge may be pleased by the punishment, the punishment is given because the person voluntarily broke the law.

Society has set up legal authorities, such as courts, to impose penalties on law-breakers for their offenses. The offense is against society, not primarily against the people who are directly harmed by a criminal's action. For example, a person whose car is stolen is not allowed to hunt the criminal down and inflict harm on him. Our system of government includes laws against stealing someone's car and authorizes courts and judges, with the assistance of the police and others, to enforce the laws.

Deterrence

To deter someone is to discourage or prevent her from doing something by threatening her with harm. Many people think that legal punishment is a good thing because it deters law-breaking. The threat of punishment by legal authorities discourages people from committing crimes. If you know that you will suffer if you break the law, you will probably not do so. When a person does commit a crime, she must be punished in order that other potential law-breakers take the threat of punishment seriously. If individual criminals were not punished, the threat of punishment would not deter other people from committing crimes.

Deterrence alone might allow excessive punishments (people would be strongly deterred from committing minor crimes by knowing of the imposition of brutal punishments) or the punishment of innocent people (people would be more deterred from committing crimes if they knew that they would be punished if there was the slightest evidence connecting them with the crime). Hence, deterrence is usually combined with retribution and with some theory of the proper amount of punishment for various crimes. The contribution of retribution to deterrence is that only law-breakers (not possibly innocent people) deserve punishment. Hence, the legal system should be concerned not just with deterring crimes but also with finding out who is guilty, in order to punish only the law-breakers. Punishment should also correspond to the severity of the crime, so that brutal punishments should not be given just in order to deter law-breaking.

Reform

Some people think that the point of legal punishment is to reform law-breakers. Legal punishment should be a type of treatment that changes the offender's character so that he will not break the law again. Legal punishment is a good thing if the penalties do tend to reform the offenders. This reform both improves the offenders and makes the society safer. Penalties that do not tend to reform the offenders (for example, living in current prisons makes some offenders worse) should be replaced by more effective techniques of reform.

Most theories of reform already contain an element of retribution, namely, that it is only law-breakers who deserve to be forced to reform. Other people who are likely to break laws but have not done so are not to be forced to reform. However, some philosophers think that treatment that changes a person's character is an invasion of the person's rights, unless the person voluntarily undergoes the treatment. They claim that the legal system should not force a person to reform against her will.

Protection

The protection theory is that legal punishment should protect society and its members from further crimes by offenders. Legal punishment is a good thing if penalties do protect society from further crimes. Reform of offenders will protect the society from further crimes when the offenders are released. However, there are many other ways to protect society, besides reform. Simply locking offenders up protects society. The offenders cannot commit further crimes while they are confined. Executing offenders or making them incapable of committing crimes after they are released also protects society.

Protection theories normally contain an element of retribution. Legal punishment to protect society should be imposed only on law-breakers, because they deserve punishment. Protection theories are frequently combined with deterrence theories, so that the threat of punishment, as well as the actual punishment, also protects society by deterring crimes in general.

A person is normally considered to be morally and legally responsible only for voluntary actions. Voluntary action is behavior that is in your control. What makes something a voluntary action is that you have some sense of what you are doing and consent to do it. In general, anything your body does that you do not realize it is doing or that you do not consent to do is not a voluntary action. If you act in ignorance of what you are doing, or if you are forced by external causes to do something (compulsion), your action is involuntary.

Being responsible for something is being rightfully subject to reward or punishment, or praise or blame for that something. In a system of strict liability, a person is responsible for his behavior whether or not it was in his control. In our system of criminal law and morality, people are responsible only for voluntary actions and the results of these actions. If you can show that your action was involuntary because of ignorance or compulsion, you have a defense against being punished or blamed for it. However, moral and criminal responsibility is not removed if a person is responsible for being in the condition of compulsion or ignorance that makes his action involuntary. Being in these conditions may be your own fault.

We normally think that people are able to choose what to do. The ability to choose what to do includes at least three features: being able to think about acting, before acting; being able to think about the results of an action; and being able to think about the motives for acting. That you can think about motives for acting allows you to detach yourself from any current desire or emotion. Most people think that being able to choose either to do or not to do an action is necessary for being responsible for it. Responsibility for an action requires that you consent to do it while being able not to consent.

Inner compulsion and mental deficiencies may make someone not responsible for his actions. Inner compulsion occurs when some inner psychological factor forces a person to act. Inner compulsion removes a person's ability to choose. If an inner force can really overwhelm a person and force him to act, the person should not be held responsible, unless he is at fault for making himself subject to the inner force. Young children, mentally retarded people, and various types of insane people are usually considered not to be responsible for some of their actions. They are not responsible because they lack some mental abilities that are necessary for being able to choose their actions.

Determinism is the theory that all events are caused (determined) by antecedent conditions. Whatever happens is caused to happen, according to natural laws, by previous facts. If we know these laws of nature and the antecedent conditions, we can know what will happen. Physical determinists claim that human action and decision-making are causally determined because the states of our brains are causally determined. Brain processes are physical events that are caused by antecedent physical factors. Our brains control the behavior of our bodies and our thoughts are totally dependent upon the states of our brain. Hence, what our bodies do and what happens in our thoughts are also causally determined by antecedent physical factors. The main objections to physical determinism of our actions and thoughts are that brain events may include quantum effects, and that thoughts may not be completely dependent on brain states.

Psychological determinism is the theory that all psychological (mental) states and events are caused by antecedent psychological states and events. There are causal psychological laws that govern everything that a person thinks, decides, and does. In everyday life, we already have a fairly accurate conception of how people will feel and decide about things. Psychologists try to improve on our commonsense understanding of the factors that cause decisions. They develop more detailed theories and look for causal factors that are not usually recognized, such as unconscious desires and prohibitions. A person's character is as causally determined by antecedent factors (heredity and environment) as specific decisions are. The main objections to psychological determinism are our sense of our freedom to decide, the current unpredictability of many decisions, and the danger that it makes people not responsible for their actions.

Philosophers have disagreed about the exact conditions that are necessary for responsibility. Hard determinism is the position that people are not responsible for their actions and decisions because these are causally determined. Hard determinists think that free will is necessary for being responsible, but that this power to choose does not exist because the person is able to choose only one alternative. Many hard determinists think that the proper societal response to bad actions is some type of treatment to change the person's character.

Soft determinism is the position that people are responsible for their actions and decisions even though these are causally determined by antecedent factors. Soft determinists think that responsibility for an action requires only that a person does what she decides to do. Soft determinism is also called "compatibilism," because it claims that freedom, but not the traditional "free will," is compatible with determinism. Freedom of action is being able to do what you want and decide to do. Freedom of choice is deciding in the normal way, without either external or inner compulsion. Many soft determinists argue that psychological determinism (of a particular type) is not only compatible with but also necessary for responsibility. They argue that an action must derive causally from a person's character and personality for the person to be responsible for it.

Free will is the power to detach yourself from any inner motivation and to choose any of several alternatives. The theory of free will is that some decisions are both controlled by a person herself and not totally caused by antecedent factors. Free will is supposed to be the basis for responsibility. A decision made from free will cannot be totally arbitrary. It has to be an expression of the person, who takes motivational factors into account in deciding but is not causally determined by them. Many defenders of free will claim that we all experience our own power to control our inner motivations and to freely decide, but that it is very difficult to describe this power in great detail.

Defenders of free will think that considering yourself to be free is essential to having a sense of active control over what you do. They claim that you cannot consider your own decisions and actions to be causally determined by antecedent factors without changing yourself. Assuming that you want to be free, it is not possible to figure out what your own decisions will be by using psychological laws.

Legal punishment is the infliction of penalties by legal authorities on people who break the laws. There are five major theories of why legal punishment is justified. According to the theory of vengeance, legal punishment is a good thing because it is a controlled form of revenge. According to the theory of retribution, legal punishment is a good thing because the law-breaker is given what he deserves. According to the theory of deterrence, the threat of punishment by legal authorities discourages people from breaking the law, which is a good thing. According to the theory of reform, legal punishment is a good thing if the penalties tend to change the offender's character so that he will not break the law again. According to the theory of protection, legal punishment is a good thing because penalties protect society from further crimes by offenders. Many philosophers use or combine several of these theories.

Selected Readings

Dennett, Daniel. *Elbow Room: The Varieties of Free Will Worth Wanting.* Cambridge, MA: MIT, 1984.

Hook, Sidney (Ed.). *Determinism and Freedom in the Age of Modern Science.* New York: Macmillan, 1961.

Kenny, Anthony. *Free Will and Responsibility.* London: Routledge, 1978.

Morris, Herbert (ed.). *Freedom and Responsibility.* Stanford: Stanford, 1961.

Sartre, Jean-Paul. *Existentialism.* B. Frechtman (tr.). New York: Philosophical Library, 1947.

Williams, Clifford. *Free Will and Determinism.* Indianapolis: Hackett, 1980.

9

The Good Life

*H*ow do you live a good life? What things are worth doing and what things are not worth the trouble? Are some things required of you? Everyone at some time thinks about the best way to live. How a person should live is probably the most frequently considered issue of philosophy. Throughout history, philosophers and other thinkers have defended very different conceptions of the good life.

SELFISHNESS

A frequent approach to the good life is "to look out for yourself." Selfishness is concern only for yourself. A thoroughly selfish person does not care much about anyone else, about the good of society, about the progress of knowledge, or about following God's plan. There are different forms of selfishness that correspond to different ideas about what people's selfish interests are.

Hedonism

Hedonism is the view that the only good in life is pleasure. A person should try to get as much pleasure out of life as possible. Different things may bring pleasure. Eating, drinking, having sex, and sleeping are pleasurable, and some hedonists focus their energies on these things. More sophisticated hedonists obtain pleasure from other things as well, and recognize that we may have to suffer some pain in order to get a greater amount of pleasure. Sophisticated hedonists enjoy the company of other people, enjoy humor, music, movies, and other arts, enjoy perceiving and knowing about the world, so long as it is interesting, and may enjoy practically anything, so long as it brings them pleasure. Sophisticated hedonists also realize that it is usually not possible, in real life, to experience pleasure continuously. It is usually necessary to put up with some unpleasant things that are an unavoidable means to pleasurable things. The point is to get the greatest overall amount of pleasure. This may involve cultivating a wider knowledge of what sorts of things are pleasurable, but also especially an appreciation for the need to balance the attractions of short-term pleasure with those of long-term pleasure.

Hedonism advises people to pursue pleasurable experiences and anything else that contributes to pleasurable experiences. Egoistic hedonists are selfish in that only their own pleasurable experiences count. A person pursues her own pleasure, not the pleasure of anyone else. Sometimes the pleasure or welfare of someone else may contribute to her own pleasure. In such cases a hedonist will care about another's well-being, but this is only because another's welfare contributes to her own pleasure. What a consistent egoistic hedonist will not have is commitment to something, other than her own pleasure, for its own sake. An egoistic hedonist will not care about the good of others or about art, science, the environment, or God except insofar as these bring her pleasure. She will never sacrifice any portion of her own pleasure for these "causes." Other versions of hedonism may be altruistic or even universalistic in character. It depends on whose pleasure is ultimately valued.

The theory of psychological hedonism is one way in which hedonists have defended the claim that a person should try only to get the most pleasure out of life. This theory claims that it is a fact about people that they pursue only what they think will bring them pleasure. Pleasure is the only "positive reinforcement," so that the things that become associated with pleasure are the things that a person automatically pursues. However, this pursuit of pleasure is largely unconscious, because people do not realize that this is what they are doing. Hedonists claim that if people, without realizing it, are going to pursue pleasure anyway, it is better to embrace hedonism and to pay more attention to what actually brings you pleasure.

The two main objections to hedonism are that it is immoral and that it is self-defeating. Hedonism is immoral in that it is totally selfish. The interests of other people are never more than means to one's own pleasure. A hedonist will treat other people in the most terrible ways if doing so contributes to his pleasure. The claim that hedonism is self-defeating is based on the idea that constantly pursuing pleasure is not a good way to obtain it. Most of a person's pleasures occur in taking pleasure in some activity, or in taking pleasure in the well-being of other people and the success of various "causes." To take pleasure in these things requires that one care about them, not simply about the pleasure they may bring. For example, to take pleasure in a game or a sport requires that you care about playing it well and about the goal of the game or the sport.

Self-Development

Self-development is "becoming all you can be." The good life for a person is to develop his abilities and talents to their fullest extent. A person should achieve as much as possible in whatever fields he can. You should strive for accomplishment in athletics, music, science, politics, business, or any other field. People who are very talented and who successfully develop their talents may produce great results. However, recognition from other people or great accomplishments are not the goal. The goal is to do the best with what you have—that is, to develop yourself.

Self-development is an attractive idea. Self-development, like the pursuit of pleasure, need not be selfish if it is restricted by other "goods." Most philosophers who advocate self-development do not endorse the purely selfish form of it. The purely selfish notion of self-development is that developing your abilities is the only thing that counts for you. Developing other people's abilities or making their lives better is not the selfish person's concern. He will not let anything get in the way of his self-development. He develops his talents and strives to accomplish without any concern for other people. Some "creative geniuses" have this single-minded devotion to developing themselves at any cost, including any cost to other people.

SELF-INTEREST

Self-interest is the view that the good life consists of fulfilling your interests. A person should act so as promote her own interests. According to one frequent interpretation of self-interest, a person's self-interest consists of satisfying her desires or getting what she wants. This will make her happy. According to a second interpretation, a person's self-interest includes both the maximum satisfaction of informed wants and self-development.

Satisfying Wants

One interpretation is that self-interest consists of the maximum satisfaction of your desires and wants. Satisfying desires and wants makes you happy, and your self-interest is to be happy. A person should act so as to bring about the greatest amount of satisfaction of his desires and wants. Any person wants or desires many different things. Some of these wants and desires are stronger or more intense than others. It is good to satisfy any desires and wants, but it is best to satisfy some combination of the most numerous and strongest desires and wants. This will produce the greatest happiness for you. To have the greatest amount of satisfaction of desires and wants is to live the best life possible.

This theory of self-interest says that you should act so as to maximize the satisfaction of your desires and wants, but it does not tell you what to desire and want. What you want can be something for yourself, something for other people, something for the world or environment, or something for God. A self-interested person may have many different concrete attitudes depending upon what sort of wants she has. One self-interested person may mostly have wants for things, such as pleasure or self-development, for herself, so that her self-interest is to be selfish. Another self-interested person may mostly have wants for the welfare of other people, so that her self-interest is to be altruistic or "self-sacrificing" (sacrificing some selfish interests for the welfare of others).

Self-interest is sometimes equated with selfishness. This is because it is assumed that the person's wants and desires are for things only for himself. Innate or "natural" desires are always selfish, according to this theory, so that pursuing your "natural" desires is to be selfish. It is this selfish version of self-interest that Gautama Buddha (563–483 B.C.) attacked. He claimed that selfish desire was the source of all our dissatisfaction with life and that the good life required abandoning all selfish desire.

Self-interest need not be selfishness, because a person need not want only things for herself. Perhaps all people do have some selfish desires, but practically all people want or desire things for other people as well, at least for their mother, friends, or family. A self-interested person may want a natural park to be preserved or the environment to be cleaned up, even though this will bring no direct advantage to her. These are not selfish desires, but the satisfaction of these desires will please her. Acting to satisfy such non-selfish desires can contribute to the maximum amount of satisfaction of her desires.

The "maximum satisfaction of wants" theory of the good life is frequently defended by appealing to facts of human psychology. The argument is similar to the psychological argument for hedonism. It is a psychological fact about humans, the argument claims, that their actions are produced by their strongest current desires or wants. Whatever a person does must be motivated by her wants in order to be a voluntary action (see chapter 8), and her strongest current wants, or some combination of these, motivate her actions. Since a person's actions are always attempts to satisfy her desires anyway, it is better to realize this fact. It is better to embrace acting from self-interest as the right or good way to live. This allows you to do a better job of figuring out which combinations of desires and wants will bring the most satisfaction.

Objections

The main objections to the "maximum satisfaction of wants" theory of the good life are: that it does not tell you what to want; it does not distinguish between good wants and bad wants; and it does not promote self-development. To satisfy wants and desires, you must already have wants and desires. People always do have wants and desires, but they are also able to develop new wants and to strengthen or weaken old ones. Parents, educators, and friends try to cultivate the right desires and wants in children and other people, and people try to develop the right desires and wants in themselves. This theory of the good life, however, does not tell you much about which wants to encourage in other people and in yourself. Should you try to develop an appreciation of art or an appreciation of torture? This theory would tell you only to develop wants that contribute to the maximum satisfaction of wants. It would tell you to cultivate those wants that can reasonably be satisfied and to weaken those wants that cannot be satisfied without sacrificing too many other satisfactions. For example, if your desire to torture is likely to result in your suffering legal punishment, the desire to torture should be weakened or eliminated. Critics of the theory think that it should provide more specific guidance than this.

The "maximum satisfaction of wants" theory considers wants primarily in terms of how much satisfaction they might bring. Wants differ in their strength, in their prospects or chances of being satisfied, and in their compatibility with other wants of the person. However, this theory does not distinguish wants or desires for good things from wants for bad things. Many people consider this to be a serious flaw. Some wants may be for things that would be harmful or painful to a person if the wants were satisfied. You may desire some food that in fact will make you ill. Satisfying such wants cannot be in the person's self-interest. A person may also not have wants for some things that he really needs or that would benefit him if he had them. In this case also, self-interest seems to be more than the maximum satisfaction of a person's actual wants. Finally, this theory gives no priority to moral wants over selfish wants. It does not require that a person want to be moral at all, and if he does want to be moral, it does not require that moral wants have priority over other wants when there is a conflict. According to this theory, a person can be totally selfish and treat other people horribly, and yet live a good life.

Maximum Satisfaction of Informed Wants and Self-Development

This interpretation of self-interest tries to remove the features that produced the objections to the "maximum satisfaction of wants" theory. Wants for things that would be harmful or painful to a person are to be excluded from his self-interest. If a person realizes that the outcome of satisfying a particular want would be harmful or painful to him, he would not try to satisfy that want. His self-interest will include the satisfaction of informed wants only. Informed wants are those that are informed about what a person needs and what the result would be of satisfying a want. Wants that are informed by this knowledge will not be for things that are harmful or painful. Informed wants will include wants for things that the person needs and for things that would benefit him.

This interpretation also includes self-development as part of a person's self-interest. It is in a person's interest to develop his abilities and talents, whether he particularly wants to do so or not. His life will be better if he develops himself. Since developing his abilities and talents would benefit him, his informed wants should include wanting to develop his abilities and talents.

Morality and Self-Interest

Many philosophers have claimed that it is in a person's self-interest to be moral. They claim that informed self-interest does not conflict with leading a moral life, but rather supports it. There are different accounts of how treating other people morally is in a person's self-interest. The most famous account was given by Plato in *The Republic*. Plato claimed that the happiest life belonged to the person whose soul had a good inner harmony—justice in the soul. Just actions toward other people contribute to and follow from justice in the soul. They build up a good inner harmony in the person. Unjust actions toward other people destroy the soul's inner harmony and ultimately make a person unhappy. Therefore, in order to be happy, a person must cultivate a just and harmonious soul and so must treat others justly.

There have been many other accounts of how being moral is in someone's self-interest. If someone has been raised to live a moral life, she may have very strong wants to act morally. To act immorally might produce a "bad conscience," which would make her unhappy. For such a person to satisfy her informed wants to the greatest degree, she will have to act morally. Other accounts emphasize the necessity of order in a society for any person to be able to satisfy her wants. Few people would be able to live a happy and successful life if no one in society accepted moral restrictions on their actions. A "war of all against all" would exist if there were no moral, and legal, restrictions. You could not satisfy many of your wants if everyone was trying to rob, cheat, kill, or take advantage of you for their selfish gain. According to "social contract" theories, it is in everyone's self-interest to have moral social rules that restrict selfish behavior. It is in your self-interest to have and to support such moral rules, and laws. It is only through supporting morality that you can have any good chance of satisfying your wants. Therefore, it is in your self-interest to live a moral life.

MORALITY

Many philosophers have claimed that the good life is to be moral. The best way to live is to treat other people and oneself according to morality. Since there are different theories of exactly what it is to be moral (see chapter 10), there are corresponding differences concerning the best way to live. However, all theories of morality share some basic features. They all claim that your actions must take the interests of other people into account, not simply your own selfish interests. Morality always includes requirements on how people are to be treated by other people. It always imposes some restrictions on acting from selfish interests. For example, morality prohibits harming other people just because you enjoy doing so. Morality also includes requirements on how a person is to treat himself. It sets some goals for what you should and should not do with your life.

Why is living morally the best way to live? There are two main types of answers to this question. Some philosophers claim that living morally is in a person's self-interest. Living morally brings the person the most satisfaction of her informed wants and provides for the proper treatment of other people, as well. There is no conflict between morality and enlightened self-interest, according to this first position. The second answer is that living morally is the intrinsically right or good way to live, whether or not it allows you to satisfy your wants. You ought to be moral even if it makes you unhappy or imposes severe burdens on you. Being moral is always more important than selfish interests or concern for anything else, such as art, science, or the environment. Being moral always has priority over any other interest when there is a conflict. The second position is frequently expressed in terms of morality commanding you without conditions (without the condition that your wants be satisfied). You should do your moral duty, and this "should" is an unconditional requirement (a "categorical imperative" in Kant's terms; see chapter 10).

Justifications of Morality

If being moral sometimes conflicts with your self-interest, why should you be moral? Why should you follow morality and not simply do what you want or what will make you happy? Four major types of justification of morality have been proposed. (A fifth type of justification is that morality does not conflict with self-interest.)

DIVINE COMMAND

Many people think that God is the source of morality. God requires you to be moral whether or not being moral makes you happy in this life. You ought to be moral regardless of the costs, because being moral is following God's commands or acting in accord with God's wishes. Some divine-command theories stop at this point: You ought to obey God's commands because God is all-powerful, all-knowing, and all-good (see chapter 2). However, some divine command theories claim that you ought to obey God's commands because God will, in an afterlife, reward those who obey and punish those who disobey. The notion of reward or punishment in an afterlife makes obeying God's commands a matter of enlightened self-interest. When you include the afterlife, not just your worldly life, it is in your long-term self-interest to be moral. Other divine command theories claim that you ought to obey God's commands because this is the only way that humans can fulfill their natures. Finite beings yearn for a relationship with God and can be deeply satisfied in this world only through following God's wishes.

INTUITION OF OBJECTIVE GOODNESS

Some philosophers have claimed that moral goodness is an objectively existing characteristic that somehow "attaches" to actions and states of affairs in this world. People can detect which actions and results of actions are objectively good or objectively evil with a special mental sense, which is called "moral intuition." Moral intuition tells you which actions are morally good, and their moral goodness requires that they be done. Moral intuition also tells you which actions are morally bad, and their moral badness requires that they not be done. Doing morally good actions and avoiding morally evil actions is required of a person by objective moral goodness and badness. Some people may be better at determining whether an action is morally good, morally neutral, or morally bad, but everyone is obligated in the same way by objective moral characteristics. Objective moral characteristics require that you live a moral life.

NATURAL LAW

This is another theory of objective moral characteristics and of how people know about them. According to natural law theory, there are laws that govern the behavior of all things. Some have combined this with the notion that God is the source of natural law (Thomas Aquinas). These "natural laws" concern the proper functioning of all things, including people. An animal body may function as it should or have diseases or deficiencies. Your heart may be doing its job well or may have defects. Similarly, there is a naturally good way, or ways, for a human life to go on, and there are deficient and deviant ways for a human life to go on. Using their reason and powers of observation, people can discover what the naturally good ways of living are. Being moral is living in agreement with the natural laws for human behavior, the naturally good ways of living. A person should live according to the morality of natural laws, even when he might receive some benefit from disobeying the laws. For example, a person should not keep other people in slavery—slavery violates their "natural rights"—even if he can make a large profit from it. Moral natural laws require a person to live a moral life.

TRUE SELF OR DEEP SELF

A true self is an inner nature that is different from your everyday understanding of yourself. A true self is what you most truly are. Many moral and religious theories are based on the idea that people have a fundamental nature, such as to be rational, to be loving, or to be free, which needs to be developed. To develop your inner nature, or true self, is your ultimate self-interest. Your ultimate self-interest is to live in agreement with your "deep self." According to different versions of the true-self theory, your ultimate self-interest may be to be fully rational, to love others fully, or to choose freely your values and perspectives. However, your ultimate self-interest is not the same as the maximum satisfaction of your normal informed wants. This is why being moral can sometimes conflict with what you normally consider to be your self-interest. Being moral is part of living in agreement with your true self. In different theories, being moral follows from being rational or being loving or being free. You should be moral even when it harms your everyday interests, because being moral is necessary for becoming your true self.

RELIGION

Many people think that being religious is the best way to live. The good life is a life in relation with God or gods. People need God in order to have an ultimate meaning for their lives (see chapter 2). Without a relationship with God, even the most happy and successful life lacks something. God completes human life by providing the ultimate meaning that people by themselves lack. A relationship with God shows people their place in the universe and tells them how to act in this world. God provides the direction for human development and is the source of morality.

That people need a relationship with God is sometimes described in terms of people's "true selves" (see above). Human nature is such that people can be fulfilled only through a relationship with God. This religious relationship is in their ultimate self-interest, although it may not always promote the satisfaction of their "worldly" wants. Different religions, and different approaches within religions, have very different views about the satisfaction of "worldly" wants and the attainment of happiness in "this life." Some claim that people have to follow God's, or the gods', commands, even if this makes them unhappy. Others claim that the relationship with God, or gods, will make a person more happy in this life. Others claim that this life is not particularly important in comparison with a life after death, so that unhappiness in this life can be endured as a pathway to a better afterlife.

CLOSE PERSONAL RELATIONS

Most people think that close personal relations with other people are an essential part of the good life. Having friends, loving and being loved, and identifying with family and community are not all that there is to living well, but they are an important part of it. These close and emotionally charged relations partly form and remake a person's psychological makeup. They strongly influence what a person wants, what interests him, what his emotional reactions are, and what specific things will make him happy. Because they change a person, including what a person wants, positive personal relationships are not the same as the satisfaction of wants. The lives of people who do not particularly want positive personal relationships would still be improved by these relationships. Many people do want to have positive personal relationships, but when they do have them, they do not simply have their wants satisfied; they are altered by the relationships.

Love

Love is the strongest positive attachment between two people. The term "love" can be applied both to a mutual relationship—the love between two people—and to the feelings of one person for another—Jason loves Jennifer, whether she loves him or not. There are different types of love relationships. There is the love between parent and child, in which the parent may love the child differently from how the child loves the parent. There is the love between members of a family, in which it is usually assumed that a sister loves a brother in the same way that a brother loves a sister. There is the love between friends, and there is romantic love, which is traditionally between a man and a woman.

Romantic love is a major concern of most people. This is shown by popular culture, in which there is an extraordinary number of songs, stories, movies, and television programs about people's attempts to find a romantic love relationship. Romantic love normally includes a desire for sexual union, but there is much more to it than sex. Some philosophers have tried to state what our society's conception of an ideal romantic love relationship is and why love is so valuable. Some of the main features of an ideal love relationship are equality, intimacy, mutuality, and admiration. The equality of romantic love is that each lover considers the other to be his or her equal, regardless of differences in wealth, power, attractiveness, social standing, or education. The intimacy of romantic love is the detailed understanding the lovers have of each other's conceptions and evaluations of the world. Lovers strive to develop and to help the other lover to develop this intimate understanding of all their most personal features. The mutuality of romantic love is the partial merging of two minds by each lover partially adopting the outlook and evaluations of the other lover. The two "I's" try to become a "we." The admiration of romantic love is the high regard and respect that, ideally, each lover has for the other. By being loved by such an admirable person, each lover gains a type of confirmation of his or her own worth. In loving and being loved, a person feels that there is a meaning to his or her life.

Friendship

Friendship can be considered to be love between friends. Friendship differs from romantic love in that there is not usually any urge toward sexual union. Perhaps for this reason friendship is much more common between members of the same sex, although it is possible between members of different sexes. Friendship also differs from romantic love in the degrees of equality, intimacy, mutuality, and admiration that are involved. Friendship allows more inequality. Friendship is less wholistic (the friend is loved for specific features rather than as a whole), and it can tolerate more separation and distance than romantic love. Friends do partially adopt each other's views, which is one reason why they care so much about what their friends think about things. In this way, friends partly transform each other, but to a lesser degree than lovers. There is more independence from your friend than from your lover.

Selfishness is concern only for yourself. A thoroughly selfish person does not care much about anyone else or about the good of anything else. Two selfish conceptions of the good life are hedonism and self-development at any cost. Hedonism is the view that the only good in life is pleasure. A person should pursue pleasurable experiences and anything else that contributes to pleasurable experiences. Hedonists are selfish in that only their own pleasurable experiences count. A hedonist will never sacrifice any portion of his own pleasure for the good of others or for art, science, the environment, or God. Hedonists frequently use the theory of psychological hedonism to defend their view of the good life. The two main objections to hedonism are that it is immoral and that it is self-defeating.

The good life of self-development is the development of your abilities and talents to their fullest extent. A person should achieve as much as possible in whatever fields she can. Self-development need not be selfish if it is restricted by other "goods." The purely selfish notion of self-development is that developing your own abilities is the only thing that counts for you.

Self-interest is the view that the good life consists of fulfilling your interests. One interpretation is that self-interest consists of the maximum satisfaction of your desires and wants. Satisfying desires and wants makes you happy, and your self-interest is to be happy. You should satisfy some combination of the most numerous and strongest wants. Self-interest need not be selfishness, because a person need not want only things for himself. The "maximum satisfaction of wants" theory is frequently defended by appealing to the supposed fact that humans always act according to their strongest current wants. The main objections to the "maximum satisfaction of wants" theory are that it does not tell you what to want; it does not distinguish between good wants and bad wants; and it does not promote self-development.

Another interpretation of self-interest is that it is the maximum satisfaction of informed wants plus the development of a person's abilities and talents. Informed wants are those that are informed about what a person needs and what the result would be of satisfying a want. Many philosophers have claimed that in this expanded sense of self-interest a person's self-interest includes being moral. Plato claimed that the happiest life belonged to the person whose soul has a good inner harmony, which requires treating others justly. Social contract theories claim that it is in everyone's self-interest to have moral social rules that restrict selfish behavior. It is only through supporting morality that you can have any good chance of satisfying your wants.

Many philosophers have claimed that the good life is to be moral. Morality always includes requirements on how people are to be treated by other people. It always imposes some restrictions on acting from selfish interests. Why should you follow morality rather than just do what you want or what will make you happy? Four major types of justification of morality have been proposed. The divine command position claims that God is the source of morality and that God requires you to be moral, regardless of the costs. The intuition of objective goodness position claims that moral goodness is an objectively existing characteristic that people can detect with a special mental sense. Objective moral characteristics require that you live a moral life. The natural law position claims that there are naturally good ways for a human life to go on and that moral natural laws require a person to live a moral life. The true self position claims that your ultimate self-interest is to live in agreement with your true self and that being moral is necessary for becoming your true self.

Many people think that being religious is the best way to live. People need God, or gods, in order to have an ultimate meaning for their lives. They think that human nature is such that people can be fulfilled only through a relationship with God.

Most people think that close personal relations, such as having friends, loving, and being loved, are an essential part of the good life. These close and emotionally charged relations partly form and remake a person's psychological makeup. There are different types of love relationships. Romantic love is a major concern of most people. Romantic love normally includes a desire for sexual union, but an ideal love relationship also has the features of equality, intimacy, mutuality, and admiration. Friendship differs from romantic love in the degrees of these four features and in the absence of an urge toward sexual union.

Selected Readings

Butler, Joseph. *Five Sermons*. Indianapolis: Hackett, 1983.

MacIntyre, Alasdair. *A Short History of Ethics*. New York: Macmillan, 1966.

Plato, *The Republic* (Several good translations.)

Rand, Ayn. *The Virtue of Selfishness*. New York: New American Library, 1964.

Solomon, Robert. *Love: Emotion, Myth, and Metaphor*. New York: Doubleday, 1981.

10

Moral Theories

The behavior of organizations and individuals is frequently criticized for being immoral. Charging a high price for a life-saving drug or selling a used car without revealing all its defects is sometimes said to be immoral. People are told that they should treat other people in a moral way. Being moral is thought by many to be an essential part of a good life. All of this praise of being moral and criticism of being immoral presupposes that we know what it is to be moral. In everyday life, people normally do have a "rough and ready" sense of which actions would be moral and immoral, but there are also many areas of dispute. Philosophers have tried to state more precisely what it is for an action to be moral or immoral, and what it is to live a moral life.

MORAL THEORY

If everyone knew in every case which course of action was the moral one, there would be no need for moral theory. People might still wonder whether they should act according to morality or not, but they would not need guidance concerning what morality required of them. In practice, there are many issues (such as abortion or the issues about life-saving drugs and used cars) about which most people are uncertain. Moral theory does not directly discuss such specific issues, but it does try to determine what it is to be moral in general. Moral theories try to state the basic principles or underlying ideas of morality. They seek the characteristics that make an action morally required, morally permitted (optional), or morally forbidden and that make a way of life morally good or bad.

If philosophers could succeed in finding the basic principles and underlying ideas of morality, there would be important results. People would have an explicit standard by which to judge difficult cases. They would not have to rely on an indefinite and implicit "sense" of what was moral and immoral. The explicit standard would tell them what characteristics make an action, a state of affairs, or a life moral, so that they would know what to look for. Moral theories tell people what the relevant facts are for deciding specific moral issues. People can then seek out these facts in each specific case. For example, if actions are immoral only if they cause unnecessary pain in conscious beings, you could investigate whether fetuses are conscious beings or whether they feel pain during abortions. This is what it is to apply the general principles and underlying ideas to specific issues. This application always requires good judgment, and there may not be a clear answer for some particularly hard issues. Nevertheless, knowing the characteristics that make something moral or immoral can only help moral judgment.

Another important result might be a change in a society's conception of the morality or immorality of specific types of behavior. In any society, many common practices are passed on from generation to generation without much thought about them. They may be assumed to be morally acceptable just because people in the society have always behaved that way. With the explicit standard provided by a moral theory, however, people are much more likely to reexamine what is commonly done. They are more likely to evaluate social practices in terms of the moral theory. For example, people are much more likely to consider whether it is moral to eat meat if they have a moral standard that says that good actions are those that produce the greatest amount of happiness for conscious beings. Realizing that meat usually comes from conscious beings, they are more likely to reevaluate the morality of killing and eating animals.

In the history of thought and culture, a large number of different moral theories have been proposed. The following sections consider some of the major moral theories that are most influential among contemporary philosophers.

ARISTOTLE AND VIRTUE

The ancient Greek philosopher Aristotle proposed a very influential moral theory. He claimed that the good life for humans (particularly for males in Aristotle's society) is to fulfill or realize their natural goals. To fulfill their natural goals, humans must develop a good character that expresses itself in good actions. Having a good character is having a set of virtues. Virtues are inner dispositions or tendencies to have the right emotions and desires and to engage in the right actions. Humans are essentially social beings, so that any person's right emotions, right desires, and right actions will include regarding and treating others in the right ways. Being moral toward other people follows from and contributes to personal excellence or having a good character. Individual well-being will promote the well-being of the community as well, because individuals always live in and are partly defined by their societies.

Happiness and Reason

In his *Nicomachean Ethics*, Aristotle first argues that happiness or "flourishing" is the main good for humans. Humans seek happiness as a final end or goal, not simply as a means to something else (for example, most people seek money only as a means to what they can purchase with it). Aristotle's term "happiness"—or "flourishing"—does not mean merely pleasure or the satisfaction of desires. Happiness is "activity of the soul in accordance with virtue." For a person, to be happy is to exercise her basic faculties in conformity with excellence or virtue. Happiness is the good or right exercise of those features that make a person what she is.

Humans are rational animals, according to Aristotle. Humans share with other animals the capacities of taking in nutrition, growing, perceiving, desiring, and moving their bodies. However, humans have the distinctive capacity to reason about things. The good life for humans is to exercise all of these capacities in a good way. It is particularly important to develop and to exercise in a good way your capacity to reason, since rationality is what makes humans what they are. There are two main areas in which the reasoning capacity can be exercised: in theoretical knowing and in practical living. There are virtues for each of these areas. Aristotle claimed that engaging in theoretical knowing is the best thing that humans can do. However, all humans must also engage in practical activity, and the exercise of reason in practical living is the field of morality.

Virtue

Humans should develop the virtues that lead them to rational practical action. These virtues, or good states of character, lead us to respond with the right emotions and right actions "at the right times, with reference to the right objects, toward the right people, with the right motive, and in the right way." The "right" ways of dealing with things are the ways that a wise, reasonable, and experienced person, a person with practical wisdom, deals with things. To fail to respond in all these right or reasonable ways is a defect, and to over-respond in various ways is an excess. The virtues, for Aristotle, are a mean or middle position between defect or under-responding, and excess or over-responding. Some traits of character, such as cowardice, lead a person to under-respond. A cowardly person does not face up to dangers or does too little to resist them. Other traits of character, such as recklessness or rashness, lead a person to over-respond. A reckless person is not careful enough in dealing with dangers, and a rash person may do far too much. The virtue of courage, which is the mean between these, leads a person to respond to dangers in the right ways. The courageous person recognizes how serious a danger is and deals with it appropriately.

Aristotle discussed a number of virtues for practical action. In addition to courage, he considered temperance or self-control (moderation in enjoying pleasures), generosity, magnificence, pride or high-mindedness, the right degree of ambition, good temper, friendliness, truthfulness, wittiness, the right sense of shame, and justice to be virtues. Many of these virtues are still thought to be character traits of a morally good person, but some of these virtues made more sense in ancient Athenian society than they do in contemporary society. Virtues lead to reasonable and appropriate emotions and actions in a societal context. Contemporary defenders of the "virtue approach" to morality frequently emphasize that some features of the morally good life may vary from society to society.

KANT AND RATIONAL RULES

Kant claimed that morality is based entirely upon rationality. Reason gives us moral requirements that all of our actions must meet. These are our moral duty, which everyone must obey. Acting according to moral duty does not always make you happy or serve your ordinary self-interest. Nevertheless, you are required by your essential nature, rationality, to follow the Categorical Imperative, which is the underlying principle of morality.

The Motive of Morality

Kant claimed that reason was the only source of moral behavior. He denied that actions done only to satisfy desires are morally good actions. He denied that actions which are only expressions of emotions or feelings, even kind feelings toward others, such as sympathy or generosity, are morally good actions. Although these actions may be in agreement with what morality requires, they do not have "moral worth" unless they are done from moral duty. To be morally good, an action must be done because it is the moral thing to do, not because you feel like doing it. From an external perspective, how you treat other people or yourself may be the same whether your action is motivated by moral duty or by desire or feeling. For example, a shopkeeper's outward behavior is the same whether he gives a child a fair deal out of a sense of moral duty or out of a sense of what will be good for business in the long run. It is better for society if all outward behavior is in agreement with moral behavior. However, actions are only morally good—have moral worth—if the internal intention is to do your moral duty.

Kant thought that this doctrine about moral goodness agrees with our ordinary moral thinking and that it is necessary for any morality that applies to all thinking beings. Morality is supposed to be universal. The same moral requirements are supposed to apply to all people, at all times, in all conditions. If being moral is to be the same for all rational beings, it cannot depend upon desires or emotions that might vary from person to person or from society to society. If being moral depended upon having kind feelings toward others, and if some person happened not to have those kind feelings, morality would not apply to him. If morality were based on desires or emotions, and if some society trained its members to have other desires or emotions, such as to want to take advantage of all outsiders, morality would not apply to that society. Since moral rules are universal, according to Kant, they must be based on what all people must have in common. Morality must be based on the rational or reasoning nature of people.

The Categorical Imperative

Kant claimed that all moral requirements are instances of one general moral requirement, which he called the Categorical Imperative. An imperative is a command or requirement, such as "you must do this." A categorical, or unconditioned, imperative would be a requirement that did not depend upon any conditions. Kant claimed that there is one command or requirement that is made of all rational beings without any conditions. It does not depend upon what a person wants, upon her emotions or sentiments, or upon what will make her happy. Rational beings are commanded to be moral without any of these conditions. All people are subject to the one general moral requirement, or Categorical Imperative.

The Categorical Imperative can be stated in several ways. Kant claimed that each of these formulas is ultimately equivalent to the other. Each emphasizes one feature of the Categorical Imperative, but they all express the same thing. The two most important statements of the Categorical Imperative are the Formula of Universal Law and the Formula of the End in Itself.

UNIVERSAL LAW

Act only according to that maxim whereby you can, at the same time, will that it should become a universal law.

END IN ITSELF

Act in such a way that you treat humanity, whether in your own person or in the person of another, always as an end in itself and never simply as a means.

The Formula of Universal Law says that morality consists of the requirement to do only those actions whose intention (maxim) can be willed to become a universal law. The basic idea here is that morality requires that the same standards for acting apply to all people. In immoral actions, a person wants to treat himself differently from other people. He wants special standards to apply to his action. The moral requirement is that before acting, you should always consider whether you could consistently will that everyone do what you are thinking of doing. As Kant explained, there are two tests that you should carry out. First, ask yourself if it is logically possible that everyone who is in these circumstances could do what you are thinking of doing. Most immoral actions will fail this test. For example, if you are considering telling someone a lie to gain some advantage for yourself, you have to ask yourself whether it is logically possible for everyone to lie in such circumstances. Since lying will help you only if people believe what you tell them, and people believe what someone tells them only because people generally tell the truth, if everyone regularly lied, no one would believe the lies. It is not logically possible for everyone to gain some advantage by lying, so that this proposed action does not pass the first test. The second test is necessary only if an action passes the first test. The second test is to ask yourself whether you could rationally want everyone who is in the circumstances to do what you are thinking of doing. Is it consistent with the nature of willing to will that everyone behave that way? For example, if you are considering being lazy and not developing your abilities, you have to ask yourself not only whether there could be a society in which no one developed her talents, but also whether it is rational to want this society to exist.

The Formula of the End in Itself says that morality consists of the requirement of treating people, including yourself, as intrinsically valuable. Morality requires that you respect people as rational actors who have their own goals and that you never treat them only as useful to accomplishing your goals. This does not mean that you cannot treat someone as a means to your goals, at all. It means that you cannot treat someone only as a means to your goals. You can treat a piece of lumber or any other thing that is not a rational agent solely in terms of its usefulness for what you want, but morality requires that you not treat people this way. People should be treated only in a way to which they could, in principle, consent.

Reason and Morality

Kant claimed that the Categorical Imperative comes from people's rational nature. The command to be moral does not come from an external source. Your fundamental rationality makes this requirement of you to be moral. You can refuse to act morally, but then you are going against your basic rationality.

The exact way in which the Categorical Imperative is supposed to follow from rationality itself is stated by Kant in a rather indirect way. The basic idea is that rationality requires that you treat similar things in similar ways. It is irrational to treat two things differently, unless there is a significant difference between them. Kant then applies this idea to a person's consideration of what to do. Rationality requires you to treat the action that you are considering as you would treat the action of any person in these circumstances. From the standpoint of rationality, it makes no difference that it is your action. You should do it only if you could will that everyone in these circumstances do it. This leads to the Formula of Universal Law.

UTILITARIANISM

Utilitarianism is the moral theory that claims that the amount of happiness is the basic moral factor. The moral goodness or badness of anything is a function of the amount of happiness, or utility, that it includes or produces. The morality of an action depends upon its consequences. In general, actions are right if they tend to promote happiness and actions are wrong if they tend to promote unhappiness. Happiness is pleasure and the absence of pain. Unhappiness is pain and the lack of pleasure. Utilitarianism is a moral theory because everyone's happiness is supposed to count equally. Right actions are concerned not just with the actor's happiness but with the general happiness. Right actions produce the greatest happiness for the greatest number of people.

Actions and General Rules

Utilitarians try to estimate or calculate how much happiness actions and types of actions produce. They take into account the intensity of pleasures and pains, their durations, how certain it is that they occur, how soon the pleasures or pains will occur, and how many people—or conscious beings who can feel pleasure or pain—will be affected. Some utilitarians have proposed that people should make this estimate every time they are considering any action. You should consider which action, from the range of possible actions that you might do, is likely to produce the greatest amount of happiness. This application of the utilitarian principle directly to individual actions is now called "act-utilitarianism." Act-utilitarianism would require people to be very self-sacrificing. If you always had to act so as to promote the general happiness, rather than your own happiness, you probably would have to sacrifice many benefits for yourself in order to provide them for others. In practically all cases, giving money for famine relief or for the desperately poor would produce more general happiness than spending it on yourself. Your action would have to be very charitable toward everyone, not just toward your family or friends.

Many utilitarians think that morality involves a two-step procedure. Actions should be evaluated according to general moral rules, and general moral rules should be evaluated according to how much happiness they are likely to produce. This position is called "rule-utilitarianism," because the utilitarian estimation of happiness is applied to general moral rules, not to each action. The two main advantages of rule-utilitarianism are that people would not have to think constantly about promoting the general happiness and that people could have rights that could not be violated to promote the general happiness.

Act-utilitarianism seems to require that everyone be a saint. Rule-utilitarianism does not require people to think about promoting the general happiness in all their actions. You should just follow the general moral rules, such as "do not steal" or "take care of your elderly parents," without trying to calculate the effect on the happiness of the world. The most famous utilitarian, John Stuart Mill (1806–1873), thought that the rule-utilitarian approach would not require people constantly to sacrifice their own happiness for the happiness of people or conscious beings in general. He thought that the moral rules that utilitarianism justifies would allow people to pursue their own individual happiness, most of the time. Only in those cases where your action will have a significant effect on the happiness of other people should the moral rules require you to do what will promote the general happiness.

Utilitarianism is sometimes criticized for not providing for human rights. It seems to endorse "scapegoating"—that is, treating some person or small group of persons horribly if this will produce more total happiness for people in general. An example might be forcing an innocent person into a painful or deadly medical experiment in order to improve or save many lives in the future. Rule-utilitarians try to justify individual rights that would prevent such things. They claim that people, in general, will be happier in the long run living in a society that has rules that give people rights. People will feel more secure with such rights. Human rights are justified as useful to promoting the greatest happiness for people.

Distribution and Quality

Utilitarianism claims that moral actions should promote the greatest amount of happiness for people, or conscious beings. However, there is a further moral question about how happiness should be distributed among people. As the case of "scapegoating" indicates, most people think that morality must include some principle of "fair distribution." It seems to make a moral difference in many cases whether the total amount of happiness to be produced by an action or a moral rule all goes to one person, goes to several people, or is divided into tiny amounts for every person, or conscious organism, alive. Utilitarianism does not include any obvious principle for distribution, but some utilitarians have tried to develop some guides based on the notion of the increased happiness of a person. They claim that the same benefit will make someone who is originally less happy happier than someone who is originally more happy. There would be a greater net increase in happiness by directing the benefit to someone who "needs it more" because he is originally less happy. In evaluating moral rules according to their production of happiness (rule-utilitarianism), some equality of distribution of the happiness can be taken into account, because this will produce the greatest total amount of happiness.

Mill attempted to introduce another distinction into utilitarianism. He claimed that pleasures can differ in quality, as well as in quantity or amount. Some pleasures are more valuable than other pleasures. The pleasures of humans' "higher faculties" are more valuable than the pleasures that humans share with other animals. The pleasures of thinking about and understanding the world and the arts are worth more than the pleasures of eating, drinking, sleeping, or sex. The basis for this difference in quality is that all who have experienced both types of pleasure consider the higher pleasures to be more desirable than the lower pleasures. Mill claimed that anyone who has experienced both qualities of pleasure would prefer to be a somewhat unsatisfied human being rather than be a totally satisfied pig. It is better to be "Socrates dissatisfied than a fool satisfied."

It is doubtful that all properly experienced people rank these qualities of pleasure in the way that Mill thought. Some experienced people seem to prefer lower pleasures. However, even if Mill was right about the ranking, the distinction between higher and lower pleasures changes the character of utilitarianism. It is no longer possible to evaluate things solely in terms of amounts of pleasure and pain. Mill's revised utilitarianism seems to consider happiness to be the satisfaction of people's wants. A method for comparing and adding up the amount of satisfaction of wants—satisfaction brings quantity and quality of pleasure—is necessary.

FEMINISM AND SPECIAL CARE

In recent years, some philosophers have claimed that the most important part of morality is not general rules for treating anybody in general, but rather the feelings and concern we have for people. Feminists are one subgroup of these philosophers. Feminism, in general, is the focus on women's distinctive experiences, interests, and viewpoints; as a social and political movement, feminism is concerned with equal rights and status for women. While different feminists have different views about morality, many feminists think that the major moral theories have been too focused on distinctively male experiences. The major moral theories have overemphasized "detached" reason and general principles that are universal in application. They have underemphasized care, compassion, and the desire not to hurt others.

Care

Many feminists think that moral emotions and personal relationships are the central area of morality. Moral theories should be more concerned about emotions such as compassion, sympathy, and identifying with another's feelings and interests. The relationship of caring for someone should be the core around which morality is formed. Caring is a personal relationship between someone who cares and someone who is cared for. The person who cares for the other is not self-centered. She is concerned for what the other feels and experiences, and she tries to nurture the other's growth and to help him or her fulfill his or her needs. A caring relationship exists only when the cared-for person responds to the care-giver. Ideally, the cared-for person responds by caring for the caregiver.

Caring is a personal relationship with people to whom you are close. The spreading of this caring relation to more remote others is the basis for a more generalized morality. A more generalized morality does not consist of rules for moral action, but rather of guidelines for being sensitive to others' needs and situations. Through sympathizing with others' situations, people should be emotionally committed to not hurting others in general. Where possible, they should be emotionally committed to helping others fulfill what the others themselves take to be their interests.

RELATIVISM AND CREATED VALUES

Some philosophers claim that there is and can be no morality that applies to everyone. They claim that there are no moral standards and rules that are objectively right or good. Morality is a human creation that serves different purposes for different individuals and societies. No one set of moral standards or rules can suit the interests of all individuals and all societies.

Arguments Against Objective Morality

Defenders of an objective morality recognize that not all people and not all societies have had the exact same moral standards. In spite of this diversity, they think that there are objective moral standards that everyone should seek out and adopt. Critics of objective morality think that all moral standards are only human creations. They argue for this claim in several ways. First, they think that the diversity of what has been taken to be objectively moral shows that everyone is not approaching the same ultimate standards. What is morally forbidden in one society, such as killing certain newborn infants or stealing from outsiders, may be permitted, or even required, in another. Second, they think that the moral standards and practices in any specific society can be entirely explained by natural factors, such as human needs, instincts, powers to act, the natural environment, and the surrounding peoples and cultures. Objective morals or intrinsic goodness are not needed in any way in order to explain the moral standards that people have had and why they have changed. Third, they claim that if objective moral standards did exist, they would be very strange parts of the world. Objective morals would have to be very different from ordinary natural things, such as rocks, plants, and animals and from the scientific laws that describe the behavior of natural things. Objective morals would have to be "super-natural" or non-natural, yet still have authority over how humans should act. Because objective morals would be such strange things, our ways of knowing about them would have to be different from our ways of knowing about the natural world. Defenders of the objectivity of morality respond that moral goodness is something other than a scientific fact, and that objective morality can be known in several ways. (See Justifications of Morality in chapter 9, p. 137.)

Relativism and Individualism

Different social groups have had different views about how people should live and how they should treat one another. Ethical relativism considers morality to be relative to different societies. There is no one morality that is intrinsically right. There are only different societal ideas about the right ways to act. Many ethical relativists want people to respect other cultures and to be tolerant of their values and morals. However, it is difficult to defend the value of tolerance toward outsiders without making tolerance itself objectively good. If tolerance is required of everyone, then there is at least one objective moral principle, and there may be others.

Some philosophers have criticized the major moral theories for accepting too much of the Judeo-Christian morality of equality and charity. They have proposed a more "natural" set of values in which some people are worth more than other people. Nietzsche claimed that much of Western morality is a "slave morality" or a "herd morality" that serves the interests of weak and less capable people and suppresses strong, capable, and creative people. He proposed that new values should be developed that would serve the interests of the elite in society. These elitist values would not be suitable for the average person. According to Nietzsche, creative activity was the highest form of the "will to power." This drive to be able to control things is the fundamental drive of living things. Hence, Nietzsche favored values that would promote creativity and other expressions of humans' natural drives and abilities.

Some twentieth-century philosophers propose that everyone should create his or her own values. Many existential philosophers think that all individuals, not just the elite, can create individualized conceptions of the good life. To develop your own values, you have to detach yourself from what society tells you to do. Some existentialists think that becoming free from inherited societal morality and creating your own values is required of you. If human existence does somehow require that people be free, there would be at least one objective value.

*M*oral theories try to state the basic principles or underlying ideas of morality. A successful moral theory would have important results. People would have an explicit standard by which to judge difficult moral cases. They would know what the relevant facts are for deciding moral issues, so that they could seek out these facts in each specific case. They would be more likely to reexamine traditionally accepted social practices in terms of the moral theory.

Aristotle claimed that the good life for humans was to fulfill or realize their natural goals. To fulfill their natural goals, humans must develop a good character that expresses itself in good actions. Having a good character is having a set of virtues. Virtues are inner dispositions or tendencies to have the right emotions and desires and to engage in the right actions. Happiness is "activity of the soul in accordance with virtue." Happiness is the right exercise of people's natural capacities, particularly of reason. Humans should develop the virtues that lead them to rational practical action. These virtues are a mean between the defect of under-responding in the right ways and the excess of over-responding. Aristotle considered the following to be virtues for practical action: courage, temperance or self-control, generosity, magnificence, pride or high-mindedness, the right degree of ambition, good temper, friendliness, truthfulness, wittiness, the right sense of shame, and justice.

Kant claimed that morality is based entirely upon rationality. Reason gives us moral requirements that all of our actions must meet. To be morally good, an action must be done because it is the moral thing to do, not because you feel like doing it. If being moral is to be the same for all rational beings, it cannot depend upon desires or emotions that might vary from person to person or from society to society. Since moral rules are universal, morality must be based on the rational or reasoning nature of people, which they all have in common.

Kant claimed that all moral requirements are instances of one general moral requirement, which he called the Categorical Imperative. The two most important statements of the Categorical Imperative are the Formula of Universal Law—act only according to that maxim whereby you can, at the same time, will that it should become a universal law—and the Formula of the End in Itself—act in such a way that you treat humanity, whether in your own person or in the person of another, always as an end in itself and never simply as a means. The basic idea of the first formula is that morality requires that the same standards for acting apply to all people. You should always consider whether you could consistently will that everyone do what you are thinking of doing. The basic idea of the second formula is that morality requires that you treat people, including yourself, as intrinsically valuable, not simply as useful to the satisfaction of your desires. Kant claimed that the Categorical Imperative comes from people's rational nature. Rationality requires that you treat similar things in similar ways.

Utilitarianism is the moral theory that claims that the amount of happiness is the basic moral factor. The morality of an action depends upon its consequences. In general, actions are right according to whether they tend to promote happiness. Happiness is pleasure and the absence of pain. Right actions produce the greatest happiness for the greatest number of people. Act-utilitarianism claims that people should estimate the effect on the general happiness every time they are considering any action. A person should consider which action, from the range of possible actions that he might do, is likely to produce the greatest amount of happiness. Rule-utilitarianism claims that morality involves a two-step procedure. Actions should be evaluated according to general moral rules, and general moral rules should be evaluated according to how much happiness they are likely to produce. Act-utilitarianism seems to require that everyone be very self-sacrificing. Rule-utilitarianism does not require people to think about promoting the general happiness in all their actions.

Rule-utilitarians try to justify individual rights as useful to the general happiness. People, in general, will be happier in the long run living in a society that has rules that give people rights. Utilitarianism does not include any obvious principle for distribution of happiness, but some utilitarians have tried to develop some guides based on the notion of the increased happiness of a person. Mill attempted to introduce into utilitarianism a distinction between higher and lower pleasures. The pleasures of humans' "higher faculties," such as thinking about and understanding the world and the arts, are more valuable than the pleasures that humans share with other animals. This requires some revisions in the method of estimating amounts of happiness.

Feminism, in general, is the focus on women's distinctive experiences, interests, and viewpoints. Feminists think that the major moral theories have overemphasized "detached" reason and general principles and have under-emphasized care, compassion, and the desire not to hurt others. Many feminists think that moral emotions and personal relationships are the central area of morality. Caring is a personal relationship in which one person is concerned for what the other feels and experiences, and tries to nurture the other's growth and help her fulfill her needs. The spreading of the caring relation to more remote others is the basis for a more generalized morality that is emotionally committed to not hurting others.

Some philosophers claim that there is and can be no morality that applies to everyone. They claim that there are no moral standards and rules that are objectively right or good. Morality is a human creation that serves different purposes for different individuals and societies. The main arguments against objective morality are that there are no signs that societies are approaching it, it is unnecessary to explain anything, and it would be a very strange type of existence. Ethical relativism considers morality to be relative to different societies. There are only different societal ideas about the right ways to act. Nietzsche claimed that much of Western morality is a "herd morality" that serves the interests of weak and less capable people and suppresses strong, capable, and creative people.

Selected Readings

Aristotle. *Nicomachean Ethics*. (Several good translations.)

Gilligan, Carol. *In a Different Voice*. Cambridge, MA: Harvard, 1982.

Kant, Immanuel. *Grounding for the Metaphysics of Morals* (also translated as "*Groundwork of. . .*" and "*Foundations of. . .*") (Several good translations).

Mackie, J.L. *Ethics: Inventing Right and Wrong*. New York: Penguin, 1977.

Mill, John S. *Utilitarianism*. (Several editions are available.)

Nietzsche, Friedrich. *On the Genealogy of Morals*. (Several good translations.)

11

Foundations of Government

Many people accept their form of government without much thought. They are accustomed to the way things have been done throughout their lifetime, so that they do not seriously consider the possibility of change. However, in many parts of the world and in earlier historical periods, the existing form of government has been strongly opposed by many people. Revolutions and reforms have taken place in order to improve the basis of rule in a society. Political philosophy is the study of the foundations of government. Political philosophy tries to determine what the basic purpose of government is, what justifies political authority, and who should rule.

WHAT IS A GOVERNMENT?

People do not live in isolation from one another. They have to be cared for as young children, and later on they interact with and are dependent upon other people in numerous ways. This is especially true of modern societies because there is so much specialization. Very few people grow their own food, make their own clothes, or create their own entertainment. The products that you use, the knowledge that you learn, and the jobs and activities in which you engage depend upon other people. Your complex interactions with other people are regulated in many ways. You cannot steal from, enslave, or physically assault other people. A church or a team to which you belong or a company for which you work is similarly regulated in various ways. It cannot steal from, enslave, or physically assault other churches, teams, companies, or other individuals. Everyday life depends upon these rules. Everyone has good reason to believe that other people will act according to laws and regulations, so that each can go about his own business. For example, you can, usually, safely walk down the sidewalk to your class, because there are restrictions on the behavior of individuals and organizations.

Government

A government is an organization that has the authority to make and enforce rules and laws about important parts of human life. A government has recognized official power over members of a society or a state. A government has to be legitimate in some way. Exactly what it is to have authority or to be legitimate is something on which philosophers, politicians, and political theorists disagree, but they do agree that authority and legitimacy are necessary. An organization which makes laws that no one follows is not a government. An organization which makes laws that no one accepts, but which can force people to obey its commands or laws is not a government. A ruling organization which is not in some way accepted by the people that it rules is not a government. A government has to be more than an "occupying army" that is constantly suppressing rebellion. It has to have authority to make and to enforce rules. Its laws and its enforcement of its laws have to be accepted by people. A government has to have the right to exercise control over people and organizations. The different views about the source of government authority will be explored in a later section.

Governments are not the only organizations that have some authority over people. In our society, people deal with many organizations that have some type of recognized official power over them. Companies, labor unions, churches, colleges, volunteer organizations, teams, and clubs all have their legitimate areas of power, their decision-making bodies, and their "chains of command." What distinguishes the state government from the "governments" of these organizations is the extent of its authority. The state government has authority over more areas of everyday life and, in some respects, over these other organizations themselves. The state government has authority over property, the exchange of property, the rules that dictate how people can treat each other without being punished for it (criminal law), what people must contribute to the goals of the state or to the common good (such as paying taxes and serving in the army), and who can stay in the territory of the state. The state government has some power to regulate all of the other organizations that exist within its domain. It can impose some restrictions on what a church or a company or a team can do. In some societies, there is not a sharp distinction between the state government and other organizations. The state government and the church (or political party) government may be the same or may be partners in regulating distinct parts of human life.

THE PURPOSE OF GOVERNMENT

The obvious purpose of government is to make and enforce laws and rules for a state. However, this is not a complete answer to the question about the purpose of government. The inquiry into the purpose of government is also an inquiry into the purpose of the laws and rules of a state. What are a government and its laws supposed to do? Why have any government at all? Some groups of people, such as the Mbuti pygmies of eastern Zaire, have lived without any government at all; they try to individually persuade people to act correctly, but no one is authorized to inflict penalties. Would anarchy, the absence of any government, be better than having a government? Most political thinkers claim that government serves an important purpose, or several purposes. The major theories about the purpose of government are the following.

TO PROMOTE GOD'S WILL

Probably the oldest theory is that government is the earthly representative of God or the gods. The purpose of government is to carry out the will of God or of the gods. The rules and laws in the state are supposed to be God's commands or, at least, to be useful for bringing about divinely ordained goals. What God wants for the people may not be what they want for themselves. Since God knows best, the government does not have to be concerned with promoting the general welfare, although it will be concerned with it if God commands so.

TO SERVE THE INTERESTS OF THE MOST POWERFUL

This is the cynical view about government. Government is just an organized form of domination. Moral considerations do not play any part. The individual, the group, or the class of people who has the most power to control others uses the government as an official means for carrying out their domination. The rules and laws that the government enforces are designed to promote the interests of the most powerful, not the interests of the people at large.

TO PROTECT PEOPLE FROM ONE ANOTHER

This is the most common theory about the purpose of government. It is the basic idea of most "social contract" theories. Without laws to restrict people's behavior and some way to enforce these laws, at least some people would treat other people very badly. They would take other people's property, sexually abuse them, make them work as slaves, and injure or kill any opponents. In such a lawless "state of nature," civilization could not develop or expand very much. Even if there was not a "war of all against all," everyone would have to be constantly concerned about those who were out to harm them. In Hobbes's words, human life would be "solitary, poor, nasty, brutish, and short." Any system of government that can protect people in general from being so badly treated is an improvement. The purpose of a government is to make and enforce laws that protect people and that require people to treat each other in at least a decent way. In this secure and lawful environment, people can develop agriculture, industry, and a civilized society.

TO PROMOTE THE GENERAL WELFARE

This theory gives government a more active role. Protecting people from physical harm and providing a lawful environment are good for people, but there are other good things that government should do as well. Government should make and enforce laws and take actions that contribute to the general happiness. Government may have to interfere with the otherwise lawful operation of individuals or businesses—for example, to prevent monopolies—in order to serve the interests of the general public. Government may itself have to provide services for people, such as education or medical care, that are important to their welfare.

TO CONSERVE A TRADITIONAL ORDER AND CULTURE

This theory is usually combined with some of the previous theories. It starts from the idea that people already live, or previously lived, in a lawful environment and already have a culture and a form of government. A main purpose of the government is to preserve the order, the culture, and the people's sense of themselves as a people or a nation. Government is supposed to preserve and improve people's sense of belonging to a cultural community and insure that this heritage survives.

TO DEVELOP AND CONTROL THE ECONOMY

This theory is also usually combined with other theories. In Marx's theory, government is under the control of blind economic forces throughout human history. The purpose of government is to promote the expansion of the forces of production. Government is supposed to aid the development of more and more effective ways of producing goods. In the final stage of human history, socialism and communism, people finally gain control over the economy. They are no longer subject to blind economic forces, such as a sudden drop in demand for their product. A government that is totally controlled by all of the workers can direct economic processes to promote the general welfare.

TO MAKE PEOPLE EQUAL

This recent theory is usually combined with the theory that government should promote the general welfare. It depends on the notion that it is good for people to be as equal with one another as possible. No one is intrinsically better or more valuable than anyone else, so that government should prevent "artificial" distinctions between people. Government should eliminate all inequalities of property, status, money, achievement, or power.

Conflicts Between Purposes

One government cannot serve all of these purposes at the same time. For example, there is a direct contradiction between serving the interests of the most powerful and making people equal. However, many governments attempt to carry out several of these purposes, such as protecting people from each other, promoting the general welfare, and controlling the economy. Governments can successfully serve several different purposes, but this requires a delicate balancing of the different goals. Even with a limited set of purposes, all of them cannot be served for all of the governed all of the time. For example, to promote the general welfare a government usually must intervene in people's lives. Some individual freedom is sacrificed for the sake of the happiness of others. Some people's rights to the produce of their labor or to property must be sacrificed to promote the general welfare. They must be forced to pay taxes, or to serve in the military, to support government services that they themselves do not need or want.

Political disputes arise over who should make what sacrifice for whose benefit. In our society, libertarians favor the greatest amount of individual liberty and the least amount of government service. They think that government should protect people's basic rights and liberties, but that people have to provide for their own welfare. Liberals favor a more extended set of rights and think that government should provide everyone with sufficient means to enjoy these rights. They favor more government service to provide for the needs, such as housing, education, food, and health care, of the population at large.

THE SOURCE OF AUTHORITY AND LEGITIMACY

A government is supposed to have the authority to make and to enforce rules and laws for the people who live within its territory. Not all ruling organizations have this authority. A criminal gang that can force people in an area to follow its commands has power but not authority and legitimacy. What gives a ruling organization authority? What makes its rule legitimate? There are several different theories about authority and legitimacy. As you will see, each of these theories considers authority and legitimacy to be connected with fulfilling the purpose of government. However, they differ about the purpose, or purposes, of government.

Divine Right

Throughout history, kings, queens, religious leaders, and other rulers have claimed that their authority comes from God or gods. God appoints or selects these rulers, and frequently their heirs. Since whatever God commands is the right thing, it is right for these rulers to rule. The Book of Samuel in the Bible, where God agrees to appoint a king for the Israelites after warning them that the king will have much power over them, has frequently been cited to support the "divine right of kings." Whatever the religious source for the authority of the rulers, a ruler whose authority comes from God need not serve the worldly interests of her subjects. Some hereditary rulers even seem to do little to promote God's will on earth or to further the practice of religion. However, a ruler who rebels against God's will is frequently thought to lose her authority.

Non-Resistance

The most minimal type of legitimacy that a ruling individual or organization can have is for people not to resist the rulers and to obey their rules and laws. According to this theory, the authority of a government is no more than the mere acceptance of it. Acceptance is no more than not resisting or rebelling against the government and its laws and rules. Since laws and rules are enforced by the threat of penalties, acceptance is not positive agreement with the government. Acceptance is just living under the government's enforced rules without actively opposing them or the government that makes and enforces them. Those who think that government is just an organized form of domination by the most powerful accept this theory of authority. Organized domination is "legitimate" when those who are dominated do not resist. Since morality is not involved in politics, this is the only relevant meaning that "authority" or "legitimacy" can have. An occupying army or criminal gang gains "legitimate authority" when people become resigned to its rule.

Consent of the Governed

This is by far the most common modern theory of the source of authority. A government receives from the people its authority to govern them. People give certain powers to an individual or an organization in order that it can fulfill the purpose of a government. In many versions, people also keep the power to remove their consent under certain conditions. In the words of the American Declaration of Independence, "That to secure these Rights, Governments are instituted among Men, deriving their just Powers from the

Consent of the Governed, that whenever any Form of Government becomes destructive of these Ends, it is the Right of the People to alter or to abolish it, and to institute new Government, . . . organizing its powers in such Form, as to them shall seem most likely to effect their Safety and Happiness."

The idea that a government's authority and legitimacy depends upon the consent of the governed has been connected with many different views about the purpose of government. The Declaration of Independence specifically refers to two purposes: the protection of natural rights, including the rights to life, liberty, and the pursuit of happiness; and the promotion of people's happiness.

HOBBES

Thomas Hobbes wrote one of the early political philosophies that traced the authority of government to the consent of the governed. In order to avoid a lawless "state of nature," in which their lives would be miserable, people form an agreement or "social contract." They agree to give to one man or group of men (the "sovereign") enough power to keep everyone in line and to provide a secure environment. The sole purpose of this government is to protect basically selfish people from one another and from outsiders and to provide a lawful environment for the production of goods. Hobbes thought that almost all power must be surrendered to the "sovereign" in order that the ruler or rulers could make and enforce the necessary laws and rules. Once they surrender this power to the ruler (Hobbes favored a king or a queen), the governed cannot change their mind. They have to continue to obey the sovereign, whatever he does, or risk a return of lawlessness. They cannot remove their consent or influence the sovereign in any way. Hence, the sovereign's laws and continued rule are not dependent upon continued consent of the governed.

ROUSSEAU

Jean Jacques Rousseau (1712–1778) provided a different account of the "social contract" that gives a government authority. Rousseau thought that the situation of people without a government, in a "state of nature," would be very different from Hobbes's "war of every man against every man." Humans are naturally good and would have some kindly feelings toward one another. However, they cannot reach their full potential without living in a society with others. The social contract is an agreement that is supposed to preserve what is valuable in the individual's freedom while also adding a new dimension, that of being moral. "Each of us puts his person and his power in common under the supreme direction of the general will, and, in our corporate capacity, we receive each member as an indivisible part of the whole." Each person surrenders all of his rights and powers to the whole community, the "general will." The "general will" is concerned with the good of the whole community, not with benefits for some particular part of it. Each person is an equal part of the community; therefore, each person's rights should be respected by everyone else. Everyone should act according to laws which he, as part of the general will, gives to himself. Everyone is called upon to defend any member against harm and to contribute to the common good. However, if any member refuses to obey the general will, the whole community should force him to obey. Large communities have to elect wise legislators to draw up laws and policies in agreement with the general will. They must also appoint executives to carry out the laws and the policies.

Promoting the General Welfare

Some political thinkers claim that a government has authority and legitimacy if it acts in the best interests of the governed. Its authority comes from acting rightly, whether or not the general population recognizes this. It would be good if the people also consented to the government, but this is not always possible. Even without this consent, the ruling organization is legitimate so long as it promotes the general welfare. The ruling organization may have to rule without popular consent either because it has knowledge, or because it has power that the people at large do not have.

The most frequent version of this paternalistic theory depends on people not knowing what is best for them. (Such a theory is called "paternalistic" because the ruler is compared to a father who is looking out for the interests of children over whom he has authority.) An individual person may act impulsively or may pursue his selfish interest even though this does not promote his ultimate self-interest (see chapter 9). Groups of people may similarly not realize what is in their ultimate interests. They may favor laws or policies that would ultimately harm them, or to which there are much better alternatives. Starting with Plato, many political theorists have thought that the wisest or most knowledgeable people should rule because they know best what is in everyone's interest. They may have a better understanding of moral goodness, or they may just be better at figuring out how to get the most satisfaction for different people's competing wants. In either case, their rule is legitimate if it improves people's lives or the people themselves.

An alternative version is that some organization must rule because only it has the power to overthrow or resist the domination of some self-interested group, class, or foreign state. If this self-interested group succeeded in dominating people, the welfare of the general population would be decreased. So long as the resisting party is acting to improve people's lives and to promote their interests, this party can legitimately rule even without popular support or consent. It can represent the interests of the general population without having their consent. Military rulers and revolutionary parties frequently justify their rule in this way. They claim that they must rule without popular consent because only they have the power to resist the return of the "bad old order."

THE BEST FORM OF GOVERNMENT

Forms of government are usually distinguished according to who has legitimate power to make laws and to decide and carry out government policies. Even if the authority of a government comes from the consent of the governed, it is not practical for any large group of people all to be involved in every activity of government. The general population has to delegate some authority to someone. Different forms of government result from differences in the giving of authority (permanent or removable consent), from differences in the authority given, and from different receivers of the authority.

Throughout history, political philosophers have argued over which form of government is best. They consider both moral and practical factors. Practical advantages frequently depend upon specific conditions that can vary over time and from country to country. Different views about the purpose of government and about the source of its authority are important factors in conceptions of the best form of government.

Religious Leadership

Direct rule by religious leaders has not been a popular form of government in Western cultures, but it has existed throughout history in some nations. For example, Iran was recently ruled by the Ayatollah Khomeini, and the ancient Israelites were ruled by the prophet Moses. The authority of religious leaders is supposed to come from God (divine right). The main purpose of their government is to promote God's will (God wants different things in different religions and even in different sects of one religion). Religious leadership can be considered the best form of government only if you accept the specific religion, if you think that God somehow selects the leaders, and if you think that religious goals should have priority over all non-religious goals.

Monarchy

Rule by hereditary kings or queens, or non-hereditary dictators, has been common throughout history. Monarchs have usually been thought to receive their authority from God (divine right), but some theorists have traced their authority to non-resistance, to consent of the governed (Hobbes), or to their promoting of the general welfare. There are some practical advantages to rule by kings or queens. A capable monarch can direct the state efficiently. One person is officially in charge, so that disputes between groups should not paralyze the government or threaten to divide the state. The king or the queen can rally the allegiance of the people. The people can identify with the monarch and so feel united with the community and the state. There should be less struggle for ruling power in a hereditary monarchy that has an automatic means for passing on authority to heirs.

However, there are also serious disadvantages. An incompetent or bad monarch can be very destructive. A monarch need not promote the general welfare or be popular with the people. An incompetent or bad monarch cannot be removed from power. There is no part of the government that can limit the monarch, so that there is a tendency toward abuse of power. These disadvantages have led to many forms of limited monarchy. Power may be shared between a monarch and a democratically elected legislature, and a bill of rights may further limit the power of the government.

Democracy

Democracy is the form of government in which the people governed or their elected representatives make laws and policies and carry them out. The authority to rule comes from the people governed, or from a subgroup of the governed who are citizens with the right to vote. They actively exercise control over the laws, decisions, and actions of the government. In a direct democracy, the citizens themselves publicly discuss issues, vote on them, and appoint officials to carry out policies. It is now impractical for any large group of people to do this, so that almost all democracies have elected representatives of the citizens. Elections and policies are usually determined by a majority vote, and those who lose a vote have to accept the decision. The vote of each citizen is supposed to count equally in a democracy, but throughout history there have been many different views about who should be allowed to vote. Those without land, those who do not pay taxes, women, those who do not believe in the right religion, those of another race, and immigrants have all been denied the vote at some time. Contemporary democracies have moved toward "universal suffrage," that all normal adult persons who satisfy certain residency requirements can vote.

Democracy is considered to be the best form of government for several reasons. If the authority of a government comes from the consent of the governed, democracy maintains the closest connection between the people governed and laws and policies. The people either directly make laws and policies or do so through their elected representatives. They can vote representatives and executives, those who carry out policies, out of office, so that leaders cannot abuse their power, at least not for long. If authority is thought to come from promoting the general welfare, democracy is still the best form if the people generally know best what is in their own interest and if their control over the government itself makes them more secure and happy. Although there are always groups with competing interests in any society, these competing interests have to win general support in order to set policies. The people's representatives decide which combination of interests is best for the whole society. Some theorists also claim that participating in the democratic process improves the citizens. It makes them more aware of important issues, of the different sides and perspectives on the issues, and of the importance of reaching agreements with others.

The three major arguments against democracy are that citizens do not know enough to decide important public issues, that democracy produces poor leaders, who are good only at getting elected, and that rule by vote of the majority suppresses different ideas and alternative life-styles. In order to deal with the problem of suppressing minority positions, some democracies have a bill of rights that limits the power of the government. The government is forbidden to interfere with certain basic rights of individuals, such as freedom of religion, freedom of speech, and privacy.

Meritocracy

A meritocracy is rule by those most knowledgeable and most capable. The leaders are supposed to attain their power based on merit. They are supposed to know more about what is good for the society and about how to attain it through effective management. A system of training and testing that is controlled by the current leaders is used to develop and select new leaders. Many nongovernment organizations, such as businesses, churches, sports teams, and college faculties, try to be meritocracies.

Rule by the most knowledgeable and most capable is considered to be the best form of government because the leaders are most likely to accomplish the purpose or purposes of government. They are selected for their ability to carry out these goals. Rule by an elite group is compatible with most of the different purposes of government. Even those who want government to make people equal sometimes support the temporary rule of an elite who will transform society. However, rule by a self-appointing elite is not compatible with continuing control of government by the people, although many democrats hope that the most knowledgeable and most capable people will be elected and appointed by the citizens.

The major arguments against meritocracy are that it does not rely upon the continuing consent of the governed, that it is very liable to abuse by factions who mistakenly think that they know what is good for society, and that it is unstable. There is no way to remove lazy, incompetent, or bad rulers who attain high positions. If some rulers who are bad at selecting new leaders ever get into power, the government will just get worse and worse.

Everyday life depends upon everyone following laws and rules. A government is an organization that has the authority to make and enforce rules and laws about important parts of human life. A government has to be legitimate in some way. What distinguishes the state government from the "governments" of other organizations is the extent of its authority. The state government has authority over property, the exchange of property, criminal law, the rules that dictate what people must contribute to the goals of the state or to the common good, and who can stay in the territory of the state.

What are a government and its laws supposed to do? Why have any government at all? The major theories about the purpose of government are that it: promotes God's will, serves the interests of the most powerful, protects people from one another, promotes the general welfare, conserves a traditional order and culture, develops and controls the economy, and makes people equal. Many governments attempt to carry out several of these purposes, but each of them cannot be served for all of the governed all of the time. Libertarians favor the greatest amount of individual liberty and the least amount of government service. Liberals favor a more extended set of rights and think that government should provide many services for the general population.

A government is supposed to have the authority to make and to enforce rules and laws for the people who live within its territory. There are several different theories about what gives a ruling organization authority and legitimacy. The divine right theory claims that God appoints rulers and gives them their authority to rule. The non-resistance theory claims that "might makes right." Government is just organized domination, and organized domination is "legitimate" when those who are dominated do not resist. The consent-of-the-governed theory claims that the people give certain powers to the government in order that it can fulfill the purpose or purposes of a government. In many versions, people also keep the power to remove their consent under certain conditions. Hobbes's social contract theory claims that people permanently surrender all power to a sovereign so that he can keep everyone in line and provide a lawful environment. Rousseau's social contract is an agreement that is supposed to preserve what is valuable in the individual's freedom while adding the new dimension of being moral. A person surrenders her power to the "general will" that is concerned with the good of the whole community. The promoting the general welfare theory claims that authority comes from acting rightly, whether or not the general population recognizes this. The government may have to rule without popular consent either because it knows better than the people what is in their ultimate interest, or because only it has the power to resist the domination of some self-interested group.

Forms of government are usually distinguished according to who has legitimate power to make laws and to decide and carry out government policies. Political philosophers consider both moral and practical factors in claiming that one form of government is best. Direct rule by religious leaders is favored by those who think that God selects the leaders and that religious goals should have priority over all non-religious goals. Rule by a monarch is considered to be best either because of divine right, or because a capable monarch unifies the people and the government. Democracy is *considered to be best because the citizens have the most control over laws and policies. They can vote representatives and executives out of office. They know best what is in their own interest, and participating in the democratic process may itself improve them. Meritocracy is considered to be best because the most knowledgeable and capable leaders are most likely to accomplish the purpose or purposes of government.*

Selected Readings

Diggs, B. J. *The State, Justice, and the Common Good.* Glenview, IL: Scott Foresman, 1974.

Feinberg, Joel. *Political Philosophy.* Englewood Cliffs, NJ: Prentice-Hall, 1971.

Marx, Karl. *The Communist Manifesto.* (Several good translations.)

Mill, John S. *Considerations on Representative Government.* (Several editions are available.)

Mill, John S. *On Liberty.* (Several editions are available.)

Plato. *The Republic.* (Several good translations.)

Rousseau, Jean J. *The Social Contract.* (Several good translations.)

Glossary

Act Utilitarianism	The moral theory that people should always do the action, from the available alternatives, that is most likely to produce the greatest amount of overall happiness.
Aesthetics	The study of the basic principles of the appreciation of art, including what makes something a work of art and how we interpret it.
Anarchy	The absence of any government.
Animism	The belief that all things are alive and have a mind or spirit.
A priori knowledge	Something that is known with certainty on some basis other than sense perception. Knowing mathematical truths is the most famous case of a priori knowledge.
Argument	A sequence of premises that leads to a conclusion.
Argument from Analogy	The theory that we know that other people have similar conscious experiences on the basis of the similarity of their bodily behavior to what our bodily behavior would be in their circumstances.
Argument from Design	*See* Teleological Argument.
Atheist	A person who does not believe in God.
Attributes	*See* Properties.
Auxiliary Hypotheses	Accepted theories that are presupposed in the testing of some other theory.
Behaviorism	The theory that what we think is mind is really only bodily behavior and dispositions to behave.

Big Bang The scientific theory that the physical universe started from an original explosion of matter-energy.

Bridge Laws Laws that connect theoretical entities with what can be directly observed.

Care A personal relationship that nurtures another's growth and helps her fulfill her needs, according to feminist moral theory.

Categorical Imperative The one general moral requirement that underlies all morality, according to Kant. One formulation of the Categorical Imperative is: Act only according to that maxim whereby you can at the same time will that it should become a universal law.

Causation The action of making a thing have some property or go through some change.

Certainty Without doubt. Absolute certainty of belief is necessary for knowledge, according to some theories.

Cogito, Sum Descartes's famous claim that since I think, I must exist, even if my thoughts are mistaken.

Coherence Theory of Truth The theory that truth is the "fitting together" or coherence of our beliefs with each other.

Communism The final stage of the development of human society, according to Marx, in which people finally gain control over the economy and share all that is produced in the society.

Compatibilism *See* Soft Determinism.

Compulsion Something that forces a person to act. Compulsion makes an action involuntary.

Consent of the Governed The claim that the authority of a government depends upon the people giving certain powers to it.

Contingent That which is not necessary and could have been otherwise.

Continuity Connected existence through space and time so that there are no gaps in the spatio-temporal path.

Correspondence Rules *See* Bridge Laws.

Correspondence Theory of Truth The theory that truth is a real agreement or correspondence between what is believed and an independent reality.

Cosmological Argument The argument that God must be the "first cause" of the universe.

Covering Law Model An account of how scientific theories explain and predict facts. The facts are deduced from the laws of the theory and a statement of the initial conditions.

Data What is given. What is perceived with the senses and the results of experiments are the most common types of data.

Deduction A type of argument in which the conclusion must be true if all of the premises are true. The premises prove the conclusion.

Democracy The form of government in which the people governed or their elected representatives make laws and policies and carry them out.

Determinism The theory that all events are completely caused or determined by antecedent conditions.

Deterrence The state of discouraging someone from doing something by threatening harm to them if they do it. That legal punishment deters law-breaking is one justification for it.

Diversity Argument The argument that a universal morality does not exist because the moral standards in different societies do not seem to converge toward one morality.

Divine Command The theory that God is the source of morality and that God requires people to be moral.

Divine Right The claim that God gives rulers their authority to rule.

Dualism The metaphysical theory that mind and matter are two distinct types of existing things. In traditional dualisms the mind can continue to exist without the body.

Emergent Properties The types of characteristics of a complex system that its component parts taken individually do not have. The existence of emergent properties is contrary to scientific reductionism.

Empirical Based on sense perception or on the observable results of an experiment.

Empirical Law Well-confirmed generalizations that employ only terms for what can be observed.

Empiricism The theory that all knowledge comes from sense perception and from inner observation of the mind itself. The most famous empiricists are Locke, Berkeley, and Hume.

End in Itself Something treated as intrinsically valuable. In Kant's ethics, morality requires that you treat all rational beings as ends in themselves, never only as means to your personal goals.

Epistemology The study of the nature of knowledge and of how it can be achieved. Epistemology is also called the "theory of knowledge."

Essence The defining nature or properties of a thing. A substance ceases to exist if any of its essential properties are lost.

Ethical Relativism The theory that there is no universal morality that is intrinsically right.

Ethics The study of how to live, of good and evil, of right and wrong, and of the principles of morality. Ethics is sometimes called "moral philosophy."

Existentialism A type of philosophy that focuses on questions about freedom, the meaning of life, and personal relationships.

Extension The defining feature of space, that it is spread out in three dimensions.

Evidence Something which supports or justifies what is believed.

Evolution A basic principle of biology that states that all organisms (plants and animals) change from earlier forms of life, over long periods of time, due to small changes in genetic transmission.

Faith Confident belief in God without the ordinary types of evidence.

Fallacy A deductive argument whose conclusion does not follow from its premises; an invalid argument.

Feminism The focus on women's distinctive experiences, interests, and viewpoints. As a social and political movement, feminism is concerned with equal rights and status for women.

Forms In the philosophy of Plato, forms are the eternal, unchanging, and perfect essences of things. Forms are more real than their imperfect instances in the ordinary world.

Freedom of Will Being able to choose whether to do something or not.

Free Will The theory that people have the power to detach themselves from any inner motivation and to choose any of several alternatives. The theory of free will denies that decisions are causally determined.

Functionalism The theory that psychological things, such as perceptions, desires, and feelings, are defined in terms of performing a function within a system of inner causes of bodily behavior.

Generalization A statement about all instances of a type of things. A major question about generalizations is how they can be justified by empirical evidence.

General Will In the political philosophy of Rousseau, the will of the whole community that determines the laws for everyone in the community.

Government An organization that has the authority to make and enforce rules and laws about important aspects of human life.

Hard Determinism The position that people are not responsible for their actions and decisions because these are causally determined.

Hedonism The view that the only good in life is pleasure, particularly one's own pleasure.

Higher Pleasures Pleasures that are more valuable than bodily pleasures and should be given more weight in calculations of utility, according to Mill's utilitarianism.

History of Philosophy The study of the major philosophies of different historical periods and of the influences on and effects of these philosophies.

Hypothesis An account of a situation that goes beyond any of the observed facts. A hypothesis explains the observed facts or data by fitting them into a larger picture.

Idea In some theories of the mind, an idea is an inner object of which we are directly aware. Through our direct awareness of an idea, we are indirectly aware of what it represents or pictures.

Idealism The metaphysical theory that only minds and their thoughts exist. Everything else is only an idea in some mind.

Induction The type of argument in which true premises provide support for the conclusion, but do not guarantee that the conclusion is true.

Infinite Regress A logical series that "goes back" without end; the relationship of terms in a series in which there cannot be a first term.

Innate Ideas Ideas that must exist as soon as the mind exists. Innate ideas are not learned from experience.

Instrumentalism The claim that scientific theories do not portray reality, so that theoretical entities are not real. Scientific theories are only useful instruments for predicting what will happen.

Intentionality The characteristic of minds and mental acts that they are about the objects of consciousness.

Intentional Object *See* Object of Consciousness.

Interactionism The theory that mind and body are distinct things and causally affect each other.

Invalid Characterizing deductive argument whose form does not guarantee that its conclusion is true when its premises are true.

Justification The basis or support for a belief that is supposed to show why the belief is true; sufficient reasons or evidence for a belief.

Legal Punishment The infliction of penalties by legal authorities on people who break the laws.

Liberalism A contemporary political philosophy that claims that government should provide everyone with sufficient means to enjoy their rights. Government should insure that people's needs, such as housing, education, food, and health care, are met.

Libertarianism A political philosophy that claims that government should protect people's basic rights and liberties, but that people have to provide for their own welfare.

Logic The study of the general structures of sound reasoning and good arguments.

Mental Act   A specific way of experiencing an object of consciousness, such as seeing, hearing, imagining, remembering, or desiring it.

Metaphysics   *See* Ontology.

Materialism   The metaphysical theory that only matter and the physical properties of matter exist.

Matter   The stuff of which material substances are made. Existing in matter is how many universals have instances.

Mean   The middle way between the extremes of defect and excess. In Aristotle's ethics, the virtues are a mean between tendencies to underrespond and tendencies to overrespond.

Meritocracy   A form of government in which a self-appointed elite of the most knowledgeable and most capable people rule.

Mind Substance   The enduring thing that underlies and has all of a person's experiences and mental properties.

Monotheism   The belief in only one God.

Moral Intuition   A special mental sense which can detect which actions and results of actions are objectively good or evil.

Morality   Rules for right behavior and for avoiding bad behavior. All specific moralities impose some restrictions on acting from selfish interests.

Moral Relativism   *See* Ethical Relativism.

Moral Theory   The attempt to state the basic principles and underlying ideas of morality.

Multiple Personalities   The existence in one body of more than one system of interacting desires, thoughts, memories, emotions, and other psychological features.

Mysticism   The belief that God can be encountered in special, non-ordinary types of experience.

Natural Law   Either the scientific generalizations for how things do in fact behave or the moral theory that there are naturally good ways for people to live.

Necessary Truths   True claims that cannot possibly be false.

Negligent   Guilty of failing to take the proper degree of care in doing something.

Nominalism   The Metaphysical position that our minds create universals by abstracting from particulars. Universals do not exist except as thoughts in our minds.

Non-resistance   The claim that the authority of a government is no more than the mere acceptance of or non-resistance to its rule.

Object of Consciousness	That which an experience portrays as it is portrayed. An object of consciousness need not exist independently of the mind and has only those characteristics that consciousness attributes to it.
Omnipotence	Being all-powerful. For example, God has the power to do anything that is not self-contradictory.
Omniscient	Being all-knowing. For example, God knows everything that ever has or will happen in any part of the universe.
Ontological Argument	The argument that God must exist because existence is one of the qualities of the most perfect being.
Ontology	The study of the basic categories and structures of what exists or of reality.
Pantheism	The belief that everything is part of God.
Paradigm	The accepted set of theories, instruments, agendas of problems to be solved, and ideas of successful scientific solutions that define a particular period in the history of a science.
Particulars	The individual instances of universals.
Passage of Time	The feature of time by which what is future becomes present and what is present becomes past.
Paternalism	A system of treating someone as a father treats his child; particularly, promoting what someone considers to be the interests of other people when the other people do not agree that these are their interests.
Person	A conscious, feeling being who has certain mental capacities and abilities, such as a sense of the past and the future, ideals, a complex self-conception, and the ability to reason and to use language.
Personal identity	The continuing to be the same individual person through time and change.
Philosophy of Art	*See* Aesthetics.
Philosophy of Language	The study of the basic structure of language and of how language connects with the world.
Philosophy of Mind	The study of the nature of mind, including what it is to be conscious, how we can know about our own and others' thoughts, and what the self and personal identity are.
Philosophy of Natural Science	The study of the basic categories of scientific reality (metaphysics) and of the methods for establishing scientific knowledge (epistemology).
Philosophy of Religion	The study of the nature of God, of how we can know about God, and of the significance of religious practices.
Philosophy of Social Science	The study of the basic categories of social scientific theories and of the methods for establishing social scientific knowledge.
Polytheism	The belief in multiple gods and goddesses.

Pragmatic Theory of Truth   The theory that truth is a matter of the usefulness of beliefs in practical action.

Premise   A statement that supports or is evidence for the conclusion of an argument.

Primary Qualities   Characteristics that atoms or matter really have.

Principle of Sufficient Reason   The claim that there is always a reason why something exists; nothing exists just arbitrarily.

Privacy   The way in which a person's thoughts are available only for him.

Privileged Access   The way in which our own thoughts are available to be known by us, but are not available for other people to observe.

Properties   The characteristics of a substance that depend upon the substance for their existence.

Psychological Determinism   The theory that all mental states and events are completely caused by antecedent mental states and events.

Psychological Hedonism   The theory that it is a fact that people pursue only what they think will bring them pleasure.

Qualities   *See* Properties.

Rational Intuition   The ability of the reasonable mind to "see" and know self-evident truths.

Rationalism   The theory that we attain knowledge only by a process of reasoning from self-evident first principles. Descartes, Spinoza, and Leibniz are the most famous rationalists.

Rationality   The ability to reason.

Relativism   The theory that knowledge is not the same for all people. Knowledge depends upon some structures that can vary from society to society, so that there is no single correct view.

Responsibility   The state of being rightfully subject to reward or punishment or praise or blame for something.

Retribution   Giving someone what they deserve. Retribution is one justification for legal punishment, because most people think that the law-breaker deserves to be punished.

Rule-Utilitarianism   The moral theory that people should follow moral rules that are likely to produce the greatest amount of overall happiness.

Scientific Reductionism   The view that scientific entities are all that exist. Everything else must be a complex arrangement of scientific entities or be only an appearance.

Secondary Qualities   Characteristics that atoms or matter cause us to perceive but which are not in the atoms or matter itself.

Self-conception A person's complex sense of who and what they are.

Self-interest The view that the good life consists of doing what will promote one's own interests, whether these interests are selfish or not.

Skepticism The theory that we do not and cannot know anything.

Slave Morality Nietzsche's term for any morality that primarily serves the interests of the weaker, suppressed, and less capable people in a society.

Social and Political Philosophy Study of the fundamental principles of society and the state, including what constitutes the best form of government.

Social Contract The theory that the authority of a government derives from an agreement or contract between people to give certain powers to the government in exchange for the benefits of law, order, and civilized society.

Social Role A socially defined way of behaving and interacting with people, such as being a good mother, an athlete, or a rock musician.

Soft Determinism The position that people are responsible for their actions and decisions even though these are causally determined by antecedent psychological factors. Soft determinism is also called "compatibilism" because it claims that freedom is compatible with determinism.

Sound Argument A valid deductive argument with true premises.

State of Nature The condition of human life before the development of government, according to social contract theories.

Strict Liability Being responsible in a moral or legal system for doing something whether the action is voluntary or not.

Substance That which underlies properties and endures through changes of properties.

Syllogism The most common type of valid deductive argument.

Teleological Argument The argument that God is necessary to explain the complex order of the universe. This is also called the "argument from design."

Theist A person who believes in God.

Theocracy Direct rule by religious leaders.

Theoretical Entities The non-ordinary things that scientific theories consider to exist. Theoretical entities cannot be observed with our unaided senses.

Theoretical Laws Laws that concern theoretical entities.

Theory of Knowledge *See* Epistemology.

Thing-in-itself Independently real things that we can never know because our minds structure everything that we perceive and think.

Transcendent Being above and beyond. For example, God is above and beyond the created world.

True Self An inner nature that is different from a person's everyday understanding of themselves. Many moral theories are based on the idea that people have a true self that should be developed.

Truth *See* Correspondence Theory, Coherence Theory, and Pragmatic Theory.

Unconscious Features of a person's mind that he does not experience or know but which affect his conscious experience and behavior.

Universal Morality Moral rules and requirements that are supposed to apply to all people at all times in all conditions.

Universals The general types of things, properties, or anything else.

Utilitarianism Moral theory that claims that the moral goodness or badness of anything is a function of the amount of happiness (or utility) that it includes or produces.

Valid Characterizing an argument whose form guarantees that its conclusion is true when its premises are true.

Virtue An inner disposition or tendency to have the right emotions and desires and to engage in the right actions.

Voluntary Action Behavior that is in a person's control; The person has some sense of what he or she is doing and consents to do it.

Will-to-power The drive to be able to control things that is the fundamental drive of living things, according to Nietzsche.

Worldview The general outlook that structures everything that a person perceives and thinks.

Index of Philosophers

Saint Anselm Archbishop of Canterbury, English, 1033-1109

Saint Thomas Aquinas Italian, Catholic philosopher and theologian, 1225-1274

Aristotle Ancient Greek, 384-322 B.C.

George Berkeley English, Anglican Bishop, 1685-1753

Gautama Buddha Indian, founder of Buddhism, 560-480 B.C.

Albert Camus French, philosopher and novelist, 1913-1960

René Descartes French, philosopher, mathematician, and scientist, 1596-1650

Ludwig Feuerbach German, 1804-1872

Sigmund Freud Austrian, psychoanalyst, 1856-1939

Galileo Galilei Italian, physicist and mathematician, 1564-1642

Gaunilo English monk, contemporary of Anselm

Martin Heidegger German, 1889-1976

Thomas Hobbes English, 1588-1679

David Hume English, 1711-1776.

Immanuel Kant German, philosopher and scientist, 1724-1804.

Sören Kierkegaard Danish, philosopher and religious thinker, 1813-1855.

Gottfried Leibniz	German, philosopher and mathematician, 1646-1716.
John Locke	English, philosopher and political theorist, 1632-1704.
Nicolas Malebranche	French, 1638-1715.
Karl Marx	German, philosopher, economist, and political activist, 1818-1883.
George Mead	American, philosopher and sociologist, 1863-1931.
John Stuart Mill	English, philosopher, economist, and political theorist, 1806-1873
Friedrich Nietzsche	German, philosopher, classicist, and psychologist, 1844-1900
Blaise Pascal	French, philosopher and mathematician, 1623-1662
Plato	Ancient Greek, 428-347 B.C.
Jean Jacques Rousseau	French, 1712-1778
Jean-Paul Sartre	French, philosopher, author, literary critic, and political theorist, 1905-1980
Benedict Spinoza	Dutch, 1632-1677
Benjamin Whorf	American, anthropologist and linguist, 1897-1941
Ludwig Wittgenstein	Austrian-English, 1889-1951

Selected Readings in Philosophy

Aristotle: Nicomachean Ethics

from BOOK I

Let us again revert to the good we are seeking, and consider what it can
be. For it seems different in different actions and arts; it is one thing in
medicine, another thing in strategy, and so on. What then is the good of each?
Surely that for whose sake everything else is done. In medicine this is health,
in strategy victory, in architecture a house. In every action and pursuit it is
the end, for it is for the sake of the end that all people do whatever else they
do. Therefore, if there is an end for all that we do, this will be the good
achievable by action, and if there are more than one, these will be the goods
achievable by action.

One argument has by a different course reached the same point; but we
must endeavor to state this even more clearly. Since there are evidently more
than one end, and we choose some of these—wealth, flutes, and in general
instruments—for the sake of something else, clearly not all ends are final
ends; but the highest good is evidently something final. Therefore, if there
is only one final end, this will be what we are seeking, and if there are more
than one, the most final of these will be what we are seeking. Now we call
that which is in itself worthy of pursuit more final than that which is worthy
of pursuit for the sake of something else, and that which is never desirable
for the sake of something else more final than the things that are desirable
both in themselves and for the sake of that other thing, and therefore we call

final that which is always desired for itself and never for the sake of something else.

Now happiness, more than all else, is held to be; for this we choose always for itself and never for the sake of something else, but honor, pleasure, reason, and every virtue we choose indeed for themselves (for if nothing resulted from them we should still choose each of them), but we choose them also for the sake of happiness, judging that by means of them we shall be happy. Happiness, on the other hand, no one chooses for the sake of these things, not indeed as a means to anything else at all.

From the point of view of self-sufficiency we reach the same conclusion; for the final good is thought to be self-sufficient. By self-sufficient we do not mean that which is sufficient for a man by himself, for one who lives a solitary life, but also for parents, children, wife, and in general for his friends and fellow citizens, since man is born for citizenship. But some limit must be set to this; for if we extend our requirement to ancestors and descendants and friends' friends we are in for an infinite series. Let us examine this question, however, on another occasion; the self-sufficient we now define as that which when isolated makes life desirable and lacking in nothing; and such we think happiness to be; and further we think it most desirable of all things, without being counted as one good thing among others—if it were so counted it would clearly be made more desirable by the addition of even the least of goods; for that which is added becomes an excess of goods, and of goods the greater is always more desirable. Happiness, then, is something final and self-sufficient, and is the end of action.

Perhaps, however, to say that happiness is the chief good seems a platitude, and a clearer account of what it is is still desired. This might perhaps be given, if we could first ascertain the function of man. For as with a flute player, a sculptor, or any artist, and, in general, for anyone that has a function or activity, one's good and excellence is thought to reside in his function, so would it seem to be for man, if he has a function. Have the carpenter and the tanner certain functions or activities, and has man none? Is he born without a function? Or as eye, hand, foot, and similarly each of the parts has a special function, so may one lay it down that man similarly has a function apart from all these? What then can this be? Life seems to be common even to plants, but we are seeking what is peculiar to man. We must exclude, therefore, the life of nutrition and growth. Next there would be called a life of perception, but *it* also seems to be common even to the horse, the ox, and every animal. There remains, then, what I may call an active life of the element that has a rational principle; of this, one part has such a principle in the sense of being obedient to one, the other in the sense of possessing one and exercising thought. And, as 'life of the rational element' also has two meanings, we must state that life in the sense of activity is what we mean; for this seems to be the more proper sense of the term.

The function of man is an activity of soul which follows or implies a rational principle. Now, the function of a man of a certain kind, and of a man who is good of that kind—a lyre- player and a good lyre-player, and so without qualification in all cases—eminence in respect of goodness being added to the name of the function; for the function of a lyre-player is to play the lyre, and the function of a good lyre-player is to do so well. If this is the case, (and we state the function of man to be a certain kind of life, and this to be an activity or actions of the soul implying a rational principle, and the function of a good man to be the good and noble performance of these, and if any action is well performed when it is performed in accordance with the appropriate excellence: if this is the case, human good turns out to be activity of soul in accordance with virtue, and if there are more than one virtue, in accordance with the best and most complete.

But we must add 'in a complete life.' For one swallow does not make a summer, nor does one day; and so too one day, or a short time, does not make a man blessed and happy.

from BOOK II

Virtue, then, is twofold, intellectual and moral, intellectual virtue in the main owes both its birth and its growth to teaching (for which reason it requires experience and time), while moral virtue comes about as a result of habit, whence also its name *ethike* is one that is formed by a slight variation from the word *ethos* (habit). From this it is also plain that none of the moral virtues arises in us by nature; for nothing that exists by nature can form a habit contrary to its nature. For instance the stone which by nature moves downwards cannot be habituated to move upwards, not even if one tries to train it by throwing it up ten thousand times; nor can fire be habituated to move downwards, nor can anything else that by nature behaves in one way be trained to behave in another. Neither by nature, then, nor contrary to nature do the virtues arise in us; rather we are adapted by nature to receive them, and are made perfect by habit.

Again, of all the things that come to us by nature we first acquire the potentiality and later exhibit the activity (this is plain in the case of the senses; for it was not by often seeing or often hearing that we got these senses, but on the contrary we had them before we used them, and did not come to have them by using them); but the virtues we get by first exercising them, as also happens in the case of the arts as well. For the things we have to learn before we can do them, we learn by doing them, e.g. men become builders by building and lyre-players by playing the lyre; so too we become just by doing just acts, temperate by doing temperate acts, brave by doing brave acts.

This is confirmed by what happens in states; for legislators make the citizens good by forming habits in them, and this is the wish of every legislator, and those who do not effect it miss their mark, and it is in this that a good constitution differs from a bad one.

Again, it is from the same causes and by the same means that every virtue is both produced and destroyed, and similarly every art; for it is from playing the lyre that both good and bad lyre- players are produced. And the corresponding statement is true of builders and of all the rest; men will be good or bad builders as a result of building well or badly. For if this were not so, there would have been no need of a teacher, but all men would have been born good or bad at their craft. This, then, is the case with the virtues also; by doing the acts that we do in our transactions with other men we become just or unjust, and by doing the acts that we do in the presence of danger, and being habituated to feel fear or confidence, we become brave or cowardly. The same is true of appetites and feelings of anger; some men become temperate and good-tempered, others self- indulgent and irascible, by behaving in one way or the other in the appropriate circumstances. Thus, in one word, states of character arise out of like activities. This is why the activities we exhibit must be of a certain kind; it is because the states of character correspond to the differences between these. It makes no small difference, then, whether we form habits of one kind or of another from our very youth; it makes a very great difference, or rather *all* the difference.

Since, then, the present inquiry does not aim at theoretical knowledge like the others (for we are inquiring not in order to know what virtue is, but in order to become good, since otherwise our inquiry would have been of no use), we must examine the nature of actions, namely how we ought to do them; for these determine also the nature of the states of character that are produced, as we have said.

That we must act according to the right rule is a common principle and must be assumed—it will be discussed later, i.e., both what the right rule is, and how it is related to the other virtues. But this must be agreed upon beforehand, that the whole account of matters of conduct must be given in outline and not precisely, as we said at the very beginning that the accounts we demand must be in accordance with the subject matter; matters concerned with conduct and questions of what is good for us have no fixity, any more than matters of health. The general account being of this nature, the account of particular cases is yet more lacking in exactness; for they do not fall under any art or precept but the agents themselves must in each case consider what is appropriate to the occasion, as happens also in the art of medicine or of navigation.

But though our present account is of this nature we must give what help we can. First, then, let us consider this, that it is the nature of such things to be destroyed by defect and excess, as we see in the case of strength and of health (for to gain light on things imperceptible we must use the evidence of sensible things); both excessive and defective exercise destroys the strength, and similarly drink or food which is above or below a certain amount destroys the health, while that which is proportionate both produces and increases and preserves it. So too is it, then, in the case of temperance and courage and the other moral virtues. For the man who flies from and fears everything and does not stand his ground against anything becomes a coward, and the man who fears nothing at all but goes to meet every danger becomes rash; and similarly the man who indulges in every pleasure and abstains from none becomes self-indulgent, while the man who shuns every pleasure, as boors do, becomes in a way insensible; temperance and courage, then, are destroyed by excess and defect, and preserved by the mean.

Again not only are the sources and causes of their origination and growth the same as those of their destruction, but also the sphere of their actualization will be the same; for this is also true of the things which are more evident to sense, e.g., of strength; it is produced by taking much food and undergoing much exertion, and it is the strong man that will be most able to do these things. So too is it with the virtues; by abstaining from pleasures we become temperate, and it is when we have become so that we are most able to abstain from them; and similarly too in the case of courage; for by being habituated to despise things that are terrible and to stand our ground against them we become brave, and it is when we have become so that we shall be most able to stand our ground against them.

We must take as a sign of states of character the pleasure or pain that ensues on acts; for the man who abstains from bodily pleasures and delights in this very fact is temperate, while the man who is annoyed at it is self-indulgent, and he who stands his ground against things that are terrible and delights in this or at least is not pained is brave, while the man who is pained is a coward. For moral excellence is concerned with pleasures and pains; it pleasure which makes us do bad things, and on account of the pain that we abstain from noble ones. Hence we ought to have been brought up in a particular way from our very youth, as Plato says, so as both to delight in and to be pained by the things that we ought; for this is the right education.

Again, if the virtues are concerned with actions and passions, and every passion and every action is accompanied by pleasure and pain, for this reason also virtue will be concerned with pleasures and pains. This is indicated also by the fact that punishment is inflicted by these means; for it is a kind of cure, and it is the nature of cures to be effected by contraries.

Again, as we said but lately, every state of soul has a nature relative to and concerned with the kind of things by which it tends to be made worse or better; but it is by reason of pleasures and pains that men become bad, by pursuing and avoiding these either—the pleasures and pains they ought not or when they ought not or as they ought not, or by going wrong in one of the other similar ways that may be distinguished. Hence men even define the virtues as certain states of impassivity and rest; not well, however, because they speak absolutely, and do not say 'as one ought' and 'as one ought not' and 'when one ought or ought not', and the other things that may be added. We assume, then, that this kind of excellence tends to do what is best with regard to pleasures and pains, and vice does the contrary.

The following facts also may show us that virtue and vice are concerned with these same things. There being three objects of choice and three of avoidance, the noble, the advantageous, the pleasant, and their contraries, the base, the injurious, the painful, about all of these the good man tends to go right and the bad man to go wrong, and especially about pleasure; for this is common to the animals, and also it accompanies all objects of choice; for even the noble and the advantageous appear pleasant.

Again, it has grown up with us all from our infancy; this is why it is difficult to rub off this passion, ingrained as it is in our life. And we measure even our actions, some of us more and others less, by the rule of pleasure and pain. For this reason, then, our whole inquiry must be about these; for to feel delight and pain rightly or wrongly has no small effect on our actions.

Again, it is harder to fight with pleasure than with anger, to use Heraclitus's phrase, but both art and virtue are always concerned with what is harder; for even the good is better when it is harder. Therefore for this reason also the whole concern both of virtue and of political science is with pleasures and pains; for the man who uses these well will be good, he who uses them badly bad.

That virtue, then, is concerned with pleasures and pains, and that by the acts from which it arises it is both increased and, if they are done differently, destroyed, and that the acts from which it arose are those in which it actualizes itself—let this be taken as said.

But the question might be asked, what do we mean by saying that people must become just by doing just acts, and temperate by doing temperate acts; for if people do just and temperate acts, they are already just and temperate, exactly as, if they do what is in accordance with the laws of grammar and of music, they are grammarians and musicians.

Or is this not true even of the arts? It is possible to do something that is in accordance with the laws of grammar, either by chance or at the suggestion of another. A man will be a grammarian, then, only when he has both done something grammatical and done it grammatically; and this means doing it in accordance with the grammatical knowledge in himself.

There is a difference also between the arts and the virtues. The products of the arts have their goodness in themselves, so that it is enough that they should have a certain character, but if the acts that are in accordance with the virtues have themselves a certain character it does not follow that they are done justly or temperately. The person also must satisfy certain conditions when he does them; in the first place he must know what he is doing, secondly he must choose the acts, and choose them for their own sakes, and thirdly his action must proceed from his own firm and unchangeable character. These are not considered as conditions of the possession of the arts, except the bare knowledge; but as a condition of the possession of the virtues has little or no weight, while the other conditions count not for a little but for everything.

Thus, deeds are called just and temperate when they are such as the just or the temperate man would do; but it is not the man who does these that is just and temperate, but the man who also does them *as* just and temperate men do them. It is fair to say, then, that it is by doing just deeds that the just man becomes just, and by doing temperate acts becomes the temperate man; without doing these, he would have not even have a prospect of becoming good.

But most people do not do these, but take refuge in theory and imagine they are being philosophers and that philosophy will make them good in this way, behaving somewhat like patients who listen attentively to their doctors, but do none of the things they are ordered to do. As the latter will not be made well in body by such a course of treatment, the former will not be made well in soul by such a course of philosophy.

We must next consider what virtue is. Since things that are found in the soul are of three kinds—passions, faculties, states of character virtue must be one of these. By passions I mean appetite, anger, fear, confidence, envy, joy, friendly feeling, hatred, longing, emulation, pity, and in general the feelings that are accompanied by pleasure or pain; by faculties the things in virtue of which we are said to be capable of feeling these, e.g., of becoming angry or being pained or feeling pity; by states of character the things in virtue of which we stand well or badly with reference to the passions, e. g., with reference to anger we stand badly if we feel it violently or too weakly, and well if we feel it moderately; and similarly with reference to the other passions.

Now neither the virtues nor the vices are *passions*, because we are not called good or bad on the ground of our passions, but are so called on the ground of our virtues and our vices, and because we are neither praised nor blamed for our passions; for the man who feels fear or anger is not praised, nor is the man who simply feels anger blamed, but the man who feels it in a certain way, but for our virtues and our vices we *are* praised or blamed.

Again, we feel anger and fear without choice, but the virtues are modes of choice or involve choice. Further, in respect of the passions we are said to be moved, but in respect of the virtues and the vices we are said not to be moved but to be disposed in a particular way.

For these reasons the virtues are not *faculties*; for we are neither called good nor bad, nor praised nor blamed, for the simple capacity of feeling the passions; again, we have the faculties by nature, but we are not made good or bad by nature; we have spoken of this before.

If, then, the virtues are neither passions nor faculties, all that remains is that they should be *states of character*.

Thus we have stated what virtue is in respect of its genus.

We must, however, not only describe virtue as a state of character, but also say what sort of state it is. We may remark, then, that every virtue or excellence both brings into good condition the thing of which it is the excellence and makes the work of that thing be done well; e.g., the excellence of the eye makes both the eye and its work good; for it is by the excellence of the eye that we see well. Similarly the excellence of the horse makes a horse both good in itself and good at running and at carrying its rider and at awaiting the attack of the enemy. Therefore, if this is true in every case, the virtue of man also will be the state of character which makes a man good and which makes him do his own work well.

How this is to happen we have stated already, but it will be made plain also by the following consideration of the specific nature of virtue. In everything that is continuous and divisible it is possible to take more, less, or an equal amount, and that either in terms of the thing itself or relatively to us; and the equal is an intermediate between excess and defect. By the intermediate in the object I mean that which is equidistant from each of the extremes, which is one and the same for all men; by the intermediate relatively to us that which is neither too much nor too little—and this is not one, nor the same for all. For instance, if ten is many and two is few, six is the intermediate, taken in terms of the object; for it exceeds and is exceeded by an equal amount; this is intermediate according to arithmetical proportion. But the intermediate relatively to us is not to be taken so; if ten pounds are too much for a particular person to eat and two too little, it does not follow that the trainer will order six pounds; for this also is perhaps too much for the person who is to take it, or too little—too little for Milo, too much for the beginner in athletic exercises. The same is true of running and wrestling. Thus a master of any art avoids excess and defect, but seeks the intermediate and chooses this—the intermediate not in the object but relatively to us.

If it is thus, then, that every art does its work well—by looking to the intermediate and judging its works by this standard (so that we often say of good works of art that it is not possible either to take away or to add anything, implying that excess and defect destroy the goodness of works of art, while the mean preserves it; and good artists, as we say, look to this in their work), and if, further, virtue is more exact and better than any art, as nature also is, then virtue must have the quality of aiming at the intermediate. I mean moral virtue; for it is this that is concerned with passions and actions, and in these there is excess, defect, and the intermediate. For instance, both fear and confidence and appetite and anger and pity and in general pleasure and pain may be felt both too much and too little, and in both cases not well; but to feel them at the right times, with reference to the right objects, towards the right people, with the right motive, and in the right way, is what is both intermediate and best, and this is characteristic of virtue. Similarly with regard to actions also there is excess, defect, and the intermediate. Now virtue is concerned with passions and actions, in which excess is a form of failure, and so is defect, while the intermediate is praised and is a form of success; and being praised and being successful are both characteristics of virtue. Therefore virtue is a kind of mean, since, as we have seen, it aims at what is intermediate.

On the other hand, it is possible to fail in many ways; for evil belongs to the class of the unlimited, as the Pythagoreans conjectured, and good to that of the limited, while to succeed is possible only in one way (for which reason also one is easy and the other difficult—to miss the mark easy, to hit it difficult); for these reasons also, then, excess and defect are characteristic of vice, and the mean of virtue;

For men are good in but one way, but evil in many.

Virtue, then, is a state of character concerned with choice, lying in a mean, i.e., the mean relative to us, this being determined by a rational principle, and by that principle by which the man of practical wisdom would determine it. Now it is a mean between two vices, that which depends on excess and that which depends on defect; and again it is a mean because the vices respectively fall short of or exceed what is right in both passions and actions, while virtue both finds and chooses that which is intermediate. Hence in respect of its substance and the definition which states its essence virtue is a mean, with regard to what is best and right an extreme.

But not every action nor every passion admits of a mean; for some have names that already imply badness, e.g., spite, shamelessness, envy, and in the case of actions adultery, theft, murder; for all of these and similar things imply by their names that they are themselves bad, and not the excesses or deficiencies of them. It is not possible, then, ever to be right with regard to them; one must always be wrong. Nor does goodness or badness with regard to such things depend on committing adultery with the right woman, at the right time, and in the right way, but simply to do any of them is to go wrong. It would be equally absurd, then, to expect that in unjust, cowardly, and voluptuous action there should be a mean, an excess, and a deficiency; for at that rate there would be a mean of excess and of deficiency, an excess of excess, and a deficiency of deficiency. But as there is no excess and deficiency of temperance and courage because what is intermediate is in a sense an extreme, so too of the actions we have mentioned there is no mean nor any excess and deficiency, but however they are done they are wrong; for in general there is neither a mean of excess and deficiency, nor excess and deficiency of a mean.

We must, however, not only make this general statement, but also apply it to the individual facts. For among statements about conduct those which are general apply more widely, but those which are particular are more genuine, since conduct has to do with individual cases, and our statements must harmonize with the facts in these cases. We may take these cases from our table. With regard to feelings of fear and confidence courage is the mean; of the people who exceed, he who exceeds in fearlessness has no name (many of the states have no name), while the man who exceeds in confidence is rash, and he who exceeds in fear and falls short in confidence is a coward. With regard to pleasures and pains—not all of them, and not so much with regard to the pains—the mean is temperance, the excess self-indulgence. Persons deficient with regard to the pleasures are not often found; hence such persons also have received no name. But let us call them 'insensible.'

With regard to giving and taking of money the mean is liberality, the excess and the defect prodigality and meanness. In these actions people exceed and fall short in contrary ways; the prodigal exceeds in spending and falls short in taking, while the mean man exceeds in taking and falls short in spending. (At present we are giving a mere outline or summary, and are satisfied with this; later these states will be more exactly determined.) With regard to money there are also other dispositions—a mean, magnificence (for the magnificent man differs from the liberal man; the former deals with large sums, the latter with small ones), an excess, tastelessness and vulgarity, and a deficiency, niggardliness; these differ from the states opposed to liberality, and the mode of their difference will be stated later.

With regard to honor and dishonor the mean is proper pride, the excess is known as a sort of 'empty vanity,' and the deficiency is undue humility; and as we said liberality was related to magnificence, differing from it by dealing with small sums, so there is a state similarly related to proper pride, being concerned with small honors while that is concerned with great. For it is possible to desire honor as one ought, and more than one ought, and less, and the man who exceeds in his desires is called ambitious, the man who falls short unambitious, while the intermediate person has no name. The dispositions also are nameless, except that of the ambitious man is called ambition. Hence the people who are at the extremes lay claim to the middle place; and we ourselves sometimes call the intermediate person ambitious and sometimes unambitious, and sometimes praise the ambitious man and sometimes the unambitious. The reason of our doing this will be stated in what follows; but now let us speak of the remaining states according to the method which has been indicated.

With regard to anger also there is an excess, a deficiency, and a mean. Although they can scarcely be said to have names, yet since we call the intermediate person good-tempered let us call the mean good temper; of the persons at the extremes let the one who exceeds be called irascible, and his vice irascibility, and the man who falls short an inirascible sort of person, and the deficiency in inirascibility.

Plato: The Republic

THREE PARTS OF THE SOUL

So far, then, we have a fact which is easily recognized. But here the difficulty begins. Are we using the same part of ourselves in all these three experiences, or a different part in each? Do we gain knowledge with one part, feel anger with another, and with yet a third desire the pleasures of food, sex, and so on? Or is the whole soul at work in every impulse and in all these forms of behavior? The difficulty is to answer that question satisfactorily.

I quite agree.

Let us approach the problem whether these elements are distinct or identical in this way. It is clear that the same thing cannot act in two opposite ways or be in two opposite states at the same time, with respect to the same part of itself, and in relation to the same object. So if we find such contradictory actions or states among the elements concerned, we shall know that more than one must have been involved.

Very well.

Consider this proposition of mine, then. Can the same thing, at the same time and with respect to the same part of itself, be at rest and in motion?

Certainly not.

We had better state this principle in still more precise terms, to guard against misunderstanding later on. Suppose a man is standing still, but moving his head and arms. We should not allow anyone to say that the same man was both at rest and in motion at the same time, but only that part of him was at rest, part in motion. Isn't that so?

Yes.

An ingenious objector might refine still further and argue that a peg-top, spinning with its peg fixed at the same spot, or indeed any body that revolves in the same place, is both at rest and in motion as a whole. But we should not agree, because the parts in respect of which such a body is moving and at rest are not the same. It contains an axis and a circumference; and in respect of the axis it is at rest inasmuch as the axis is not inclined in any direction, while in respect of the circumference it revolves; and if, while it is spinning, the axis does lean out of the perpendicular in all directions, then it is in no way at rest.

That is true.

No objection of that sort, then, will disconcert us or make us believe that the same thing can ever act or be acted upon in two opposite ways, or be two opposite things, at the same time, in respect of the same part of itself, and in relation to the same object.

I can answer for myself at any rate.

Well, anyhow, as we do not want to spend time in reviewing all such objections to make sure that they are unsound, let us proceed on this assumption, with the understanding that, if we ever come to think otherwise, all the consequences based upon it will fall to the ground.

Yes, that is a good plan.

Now, would you class such things as assent and dissent, striving after something and refusing it, attraction and repulsion, as pairs of opposite actions or states of mind—no matter which?

Yes, they are opposites.

And would you not class all appetites such as hunger and thirst, and again willing and wishing, with the affirmative members of those pairs I have just mentioned? For instance, you would say that the soul of a man who desires something is striving after it, or trying to draw to itself the thing it wishes to possess, or again, in so far as it is willing to have its want satisfied, it is giving its assent to its own longing, as if to an inward question.

Yes.

And, on the other hand, disinclination, unwillingness, and dislike, we should class on the negative side with acts of rejection or repulsion.

Of course.

That being so, shall we say that appetites form one class, the most conspicuous being those we call thirst and hunger?

Yes.

Thirst being desire for drink, hunger for food?

Yes.

Now, is thirst, just in so far as it is thirst, a desire in the soul for anything more than simply drink? Is it, for instance, thirst for hot drink or for cold, for much drink or for little, or in a word for drink of any particular kind? Is it not rather true that you will have a desire for cold drink only if you are feeling hot as well as thirsty, and for hot drink only if you are feeling cold; and if you want much drink or little, that will be because your thirst is a great thirst or a little one? But, just in itself, thirst or hunger is a desire for nothing more than its natural object, drink or food, pure and simple.

Yes, he agreed, each desire, just in itself, is simply for its own natural object. When the object is of such and such a particular kind, the desire will be correspondingly qualified.

We must be careful here, or we might be troubled by the objection that no one desires mere food and drink, but always wholesome food and drink. We shall be told that what we desire is always something that is good; so if thirst is a desire, its object must be, like that of any other desire, something—drink or whatever it may be—that will be good for one.

Yes, there might seem to be something in that objection.

But surely, wherever you have two correlative terms, if one is qualified, the other must always be qualified too; whereas if one is unqualified, so is the other.

I don't understand.

Well, 'greater' is a relative term; and the greater is greater than the less; if it is much greater, then the less is much less; if it is greater at some moment, past or future, then the less is less at that same moment. The same principle applies to all such correlatives, like 'more' and 'fewer,' 'double' and 'half'; and again to terms like 'heavier' and 'lighter,' 'quicker' and 'slower,' and to things like hot and cold.

Yes.

Take the various branches of knowledge: Is it not the same there? The object of knowledge pure and simple is the knowable—if that is the right word without any qualification; whereas a particular kind of knowledge has an object of a particular kind. For example, as soon as men learnt how to build houses, their craft was distinguished from others under the name of architecture, because it had a unique character, which was itself due to the character of its object; and all other branches of craft and knowledge were distinguished in the same way.

True.

This, then, if you understand me now, is what I meant by saying that, where there are two correlatives, the one is qualified if, and only if, the other is so. I am not saying that the one must have the same quality as the other—that the science of health and disease is itself healthy and diseased, or the knowledge of good and evil is itself good and evil—but only that, as soon as you have a knowledge that is restricted to a particular kind of object, namely health and disease, the knowledge itself becomes a particular kind of knowledge. Hence we no longer call it merely knowledge, which would have for its object whatever can be known, but we add the qualification and call it medical science.

I understand now and I agree.

Now, to go back to thirst: is not that one of these relative terms? It is essentially thirst for something.

Yes, for drink.

And if the drink desired is of a certain kind, the thirst will be correspondingly qualified. But thirst which is just simply thirst is not for drink of any particular sort—much or little, good or bad—but for drink pure and simple.

Quite so.

We conclude, then, that the soul of a thirsty man, just in so far as he is thirsty, has no other wish than to drink. That is the object of its craving, and towards that it is impelled.

That is clear.

Now if there is ever something which at the same time pulls it the opposite way, that something must be an element in the soul other than the one which is thirsting and driving it like a beast to drink; in accordance with our principle that the same thing cannot behave in two opposite ways at the same time and towards the same object with the same part of itself. It is like an archer drawing the bow: it is not accurate to say that his hands are at the same time both pushing and pulling it. One hand does the pushing, the other the pulling.

Exactly.

Now, is it sometimes true that people are thirsty and yet unwilling to drink?

Yes, often.

What, then, can one say of them, if not that their soul contains something which urges them to drink and something which holds them back, and that this latter is a distinct thing and overpowers the other?

I agree.

And is it not true that the intervention of this inhibiting principle in such cases always has its origin in reflection; whereas the impulses driving and dragging the soul are engendered by external influences and abnormal conditions?

Evidently.

We shall have good reason, then, to assert that they are two distinct principles. We may call that part of the soul whereby it reflects, rational; and the other, with which it feels hunger and thirst and is distracted by sexual passion and all the other desires, we will call irrational appetite, associated with pleasure in the replenishment of certain wants.

Yes, there is good ground for that view.

Let us take it, then, that we have now distinguished two elements in the soul. What of that passionate element which makes us feel angry and indignant? Is that a third, or identical in nature with one of those two?

It might perhaps be identified with appetite.

I am more inclined to put my faith in a story I once heard about Leontius, son of Aglaion. On his way up from the Piraeus outside the north wall, he noticed the bodies of some criminals lying on the ground, with the executioner standing by them. He wanted to go and look at them, but at the same time he was disgusted and tried to turn away. He struggled for some time and covered his eyes, but at last the desire was too much for him. Opening his eyes wide, he ran up to the bodies and cried, 'There you are, curse you; feast yourselves on this lovely sight!'

Yes, I have heard that story too.

The point of it surely is that anger is sometimes in conflict with appetite, as if they were two distinct principles. Do we not often find a man whose desires would force him to go against his reason, reviling himself and indignant with this part of his nature which is trying to put constraint on him? It is like a struggle between two factions, in which indignation takes the side of reason. But I believe you have never observed, in yourself or anyone else, indignation make common cause with appetite in behavior which reason decides to be wrong.

No, I am sure I have not.

Again, take a man who feels he is in the wrong. The more generous his nature, the less can he be indignant at any suffering, such as hunger and cold, inflicted by the man he has injured. He recognizes such treatment as just, and, as I say, his spirit refuses to be roused against it.

That is true.

But now contrast one who thinks it is he that is being wronged. His spirit boils with resentment and sides with the right as he conceives it. Persevering all the more for the hunger and cold and other pains he suffers, it triumphs and will not give in until its gallant struggle has ended in success or death; or until the restraining voice of reason, like a shepherd calling off his dog, makes it relent.

An apt comparison, he said; and in fact it fits the relation of our Auxiliaries to the Rulers: they were to be like watch-dogs obeying the shepherds of the commonwealth.

Yes, you understand very well what I have in mind. But do you see how we have changed our view? A moment ago we were supposing this spirited element to be something of the nature of appetite; but now it appears that, when the soul is divided into factions, it is far more ready to be up in arms on the side of reason.

Quite true.

Is it, then, distinct from the rational element or only a particular form of it, so that the soul will contain no more than two elements, reason and appetite? Or is the soul like the state, which had three orders to hold it together, traders, Auxiliaries, and counselors? Does the spirited element make a third, the natural auxiliary of reason, when not corrupted by bad upbringing?

It must be a third.

Yes, I said, provided it can be shown to be distinct from reason, as we saw it was from appetite.

That is easily proved. You can see that much in children: they are full of passionate feelings from their very birth; but some, I should say, never become rational, and most of them only late in life.

A very sound observation, said I, the truth of which may also be seen in animals. And besides, there is the witness of Homer in that line I quoted before: 'He smote his breast and spoke, chiding his heart.' The poet is plainly thinking of the two elements as distinct, when he makes the one which has chosen the better course after reflection rebuke the other for its unreasoning passion.

I entirely agree.

THE VIRTUES IN THE INDIVIDUAL

And so, after much tossing, we have reached the land. We are fairly agreed that the same three principles exist alike in the state and in the individual soul.

Exactly.

Does it not follow at once that state and individual will be wise or brave by virtue of the same element in each and in the same way? Both will possess in the same manner any quality that makes for excellence.

Certainly.

Then it applies to justice: we shall conclude that a man is just in the same way that a state was just. And we have surely not forgotten that justice in the state meant that each of the three orders in it was doing its own proper work. So we may henceforth bear in mind that each one of us likewise will be a just person, fulfilling his proper function, only if the several parts of our nature fulfill theirs.

Certainly.

And it will be the business of reason to rule with wisdom and forethought on behalf of the entire soul; while the spirited element ought to act as its subordinate and ally. The two will be brought into accord, as we said earlier, by that combination of mental and bodily training which will tune up one string of the instrument and relax the other, nourishing the reasoning part on the study of noble literature and allaying the other's wildness by harmony and rhythm. When both have been thus nurtured and trained to know their own true functions, they must be set in command over the appetites, which form the greater part of each man's soul and are by nature insatiably covetous. They must keep watch lest this part, by battening on the pleasures that are called bodily, should grow so great and powerful that it will no longer keep to its own work, but will try to enslave the others and usurp a dominion to which it has no right, thus turning the whole of life upside down. At the same time, those two together will be the best of guardians for the entire soul and for the body against all enemies from without: the one will take counsel, while the other will do battle, following its ruler's commands and by its own bravery giving effect to the ruler's designs.

Yes, that is all true.

And so we call an individual brave in virtue of this spirited part of his nature, when, in spite of pain or pleasure, it holds fast to the injunctions of reason about what he ought or ought not to be afraid of.

True.

And wise in virtue of that small part which rules and issues these injunctions, possessing as it does the knowledge of what is good for each of the three elements and for all of them in common.

Certainly.

And, again, temperate by reason of the unanimity and concord of all three, when there is no internal conflict between the ruling element and its two subjects, but all are agreed that reason should be ruler.

Yes, that is an exact account of temperance, whether in the state or in the individual.

Finally, a man will be just by observing the principle we have so often stated.

Necessarily.

Now is there any indistinctness in our vision of justice, that might make it seem somehow different from what we found it to be in the state?

There is no difference, in my opinion.

Because, if we have any lingering doubt, we might make sure by comparing it with some commonplace notions. Suppose, for instance, that a sum of money were entrusted to our state or to an individual of corresponding character and training, would anyone imagine that such a person would be specially likely to embezzle it?

No.

And would he not be incapable of sacrilege and theft, or of treachery to friend or country; never false to an oath or any other compact; the last to be guilty of adultery or of neglecting parents or the due service of the gods?

Yes.

And the reason for all this is that each part of his nature is exercising its proper function, of ruling or of being ruled.

Yes, exactly.

Are you satisfied, then, that justice is the power which produces states or individuals of whom that is true, or must we look further?

There is no need; I am quite satisfied.

And so our dream has come true—I mean the inkling we had that, by some happy chance, we had lighted upon a rudimentary form of justice from the very moment when we set about founding our commonwealth. Our principle that the born shoemaker or carpenter had better stick to his trade turns out to have been an adumbration of justice; and that is why it has helped us. But in reality justice, though evidently analogous to this principle, is not a matter of external behavior, but of the inward self and of attending to all that is, in the fullest sense, a man's proper concern. The just man does not allow the several elements in his soul to usurp one another's functions; he is indeed one who sets his house in order, by self-mastery and discipline coming to be at peace with himself, and bringing into tune those three parts, like the terms in the proportion of a musical scale, the highest and lowest notes and the mean between them, with all the intermediate intervals. Only when he has linked these parts together in well-tempered harmony and has made himself one man instead of many, will he be ready to go about whatever he may have to do, whether it be making money and satisfying bodily wants, or business transactions, or the affairs of state. In all these fields when he speaks of just and honorable conduct, he will mean the behavior that helps to produce and to preserve this habit of mind; and by wisdom he will mean the knowledge which presides over such conduct. Any action which tends to break down this habit will be for him unjust; and the notions governing it he will call ignorance and folly.

That is perfectly true, Socrates.

Good, said I. I believe we should not be thought altogether mistaken, if we claimed to have discovered the just man and the just state, and wherein their justice consists.

Indeed we should not.

Shall we make that claim, then?

Yes, we will.

So be it, said I. Next, I suppose, we have to consider injustice.

Evidently.

This must surely be a sort of civil strife among the three elements, whereby they usurp and encroach upon one another's functions and some one part of the soul rises up in rebellion against the whole, claiming a supremacy to which it has no right because its nature fits it only to be the servant of the ruling principle. Such turmoil and aberration we shall, I think, identify with injustice, intemperance, cowardice, ignorance, and in a word with all wickedness.

Exactly.

And now that we know the nature of justice and injustice, we can be equally clear about what is meant by acting justly and again by unjust action and wrongdoing.

How do you mean?

Plainly, they are exactly analogous to those wholesome and unwholesome activities which respectively produce a healthy or unhealthy condition in the body; in the same way just and unjust conduct produce a just or unjust character. Justice is produced in the soul, like health in the body, by establishing the elements concerned in their natural relations of control and subordination, whereas injustice is like disease and means that this natural order is inverted.

Quite so.

It appears, then, that virtue is as it were the health and comeliness and well-being of the soul, as wickedness is disease, deformity, and weakness.

True.

And also that virtue and wickedness are brought about by one's way of life, honorable or disgraceful.

That follows.

So now it only remains to consider which is the more profitable course: to do right and live honorably and be just, whether or not anyone knows what manner of man you are, or to do wrong and be unjust, provided that you can escape the chastisement which might make you a better man.

But really, Socrates, it seems to me ridiculous to ask that question now that the nature of justice and injustice has been brought to light. People think that all the luxury and wealth and power in the world cannot make life worth living when the bodily constitution is going to rack and ruin; and are we to believe that, when the very principle whereby we live is deranged and corrupted, life will be worth living so long as a man can do as he will, and wills to do anything rather than to free himself from vice and wrongdoing and to win justice and virtue?

Yes, I replied, it is a ridiculous question.

THE GOOD AND THE SUN

First we must come to an understanding. Let me remind you of the distinction we drew earlier and have often drawn on other occasions, between the multiplicity of things that we call good or beautiful or whatever it may be and, on the other hand, Goodness itself or Beauty itself and so on. Corresponding to each of these sets of many things, we postulate a single Form or real essence, as we call it.

Yes, that is so.

Further, the many things, we say, can be seen, but are not objects of rational thought; whereas the Forms are objects of thought, but invisible.

Yes, certainly.

And we see things with our eyesight, just as we hear sounds with our ears and, to speak generally, perceive any sensible thing with our sense-faculties.

Of course.

Have you noticed, then, that the artificer who designed the senses has been exceptionally lavish of his materials in making the eyes able to see and their objects visible?

That never occurred to me.

Well, look at it in this way. Hearing and sound do not stand in need of any third thing, without which the ear will not hear nor sound be heard; and I think the same is true of most, not to say all, of the other senses. Can you think of one that does require anything of the sort?

No, I cannot.

But there is this need in the case of sight and its objects. You may have the power of vision in your eyes and try to use it, and color may be there in the objects; but sight will see nothing and the colors will remain invisible in the absence of a third thing peculiarly constituted to serve this very purpose.

By which you mean——?

Naturally I mean what you call light; and if light is a thing of value, the sense of sight and the power of being visible are linked together by a very precious bond, such as unites no other sense with its object.

No one could say that light is not a precious thing.

And of all the divinities in the skies is there one whose light, above all the rest, is responsible for making our eyes see perfectly and making objects perfectly visible?

There can be no two opinions: of course you mean the Sun.

And how is sight related to this deity? Neither sight nor the eye which contains it is the Sun, but of all the sense-organs it is the most sun-like; and further, the power it possesses is dispensed by the Sun, like a stream flooding the eye. And again, the Sun is not vision, but it is the cause of vision and also is seen by the vision it causes.

Yes.

It was the Sun, then, that I meant when I spoke of that offspring which the Good has created in the visible world, to stand there in the same relation to vision and visible things as that which the Good itself bears in the intelligible world to intelligence and to intelligible objects.

How is that? You must explain further.

You know what happens when the colors of things are no longer irradiated by the daylight, but only by the fainter luminaries of the night: when you look at them, the eyes are dim and seem almost blind, as if there were no unclouded vision in them. But when you look at things on which the Sun is shining, the same eyes see distinctly and it becomes evident that they do contain the power of vision.

Certainly.

Apply this comparison, then, to the soul. When its gaze is fixed upon an object irradiated by truth and reality, the soul gains understanding and knowledge and is manifestly in possession of intelligence. But when it looks towards that twilight world of things that come into existence and pass away, its sight is dim and it has only opinions and beliefs which shift to and fro, and now it seems like a thing that has no intelligence.

This, then, which gives to the objects of knowledge their truth and to him who knows them his power of knowing, is the Form or essential nature of Goodness. It is the cause of knowledge and truth; and so, while you may think of it as an object of knowledge, you will do well to regard it as something beyond truth and knowledge and, precious as these both are, of still higher worth. And, just as in our analogy light and vision were to be thought of as like the Sun, but not identical with it, so here both knowledge and truth are to be regarded as like the Good, but to identify either with the Good is wrong. The Good must hold a yet higher place of honor.

You are giving it a position of extraordinary splendor, if it is the source of knowledge and truth and itself surpasses them in worth. You surely cannot mean that it is pleasure.

Heaven forbid, I exclaimed. But I want to follow up our analogy still further. You will agree that the Sun not only makes the things we see visible, but also brings them into existence and gives them growth and nourishment; yet he is not the same thing as existence. And so with the objects of knowledge: these derive from the Good not only their power of being known, but their very being and reality; and Goodness is not the same thing as being, but even beyond being, surpassing it in dignity and power.

Glaucon exclaimed with some amusement at my exalting Goodness in such extravagant terms.

It is your fault, I replied; you forced me to say what I think.

Yes, and you must not stop there. At any rate, complete your comparison with the Sun, if there is any more to be said.

There is a great deal more, I answered.

Let us hear it, then; don't leave anything out.

I am afraid much must be left unspoken. However, I will not, if I can help it, leave out anything that can be said on this occasion.

Please do not.

FOUR STAGES OF COGNITION: THE LINE

Conceive, then, that there are these two powers I speak of, the Good reigning over the domain of all that is intelligible, the Sun over the visible world—or the heaven as I might call it; only you would think I was showing off my skill in etymology. At any rate you have these two orders of things clearly before your mind: the visible and the intelligible?

I have.

Now take a line divided into two unequal parts, one to represent the visible order, the other the intelligible; and divide each part again in the same proportion, symbolizing degrees of comparative clearness or obscurity. Then (A) one of the two sections in the visible world will stand for images. By images I mean first shadows, and then reflections in water or in closegrained, polished surfaces, and everything of that kind, if you understand.

Yes, I understand.

Let the second section (B) stand for the actual things of which the first are likenesses, the living creatures about us and all the works of nature or of human hands.

So be it.

Will you also take the proportion in which the visible world has been divided as corresponding to degrees of reality and truth, so that the likeness shall stand to the original in the same ratio as the sphere of appearances and belief to the sphere of knowledge?

Certainly.

Now consider how we are to divide the part which stands for the intelligible world. There are two sections. In the first (C) the mind uses as images those actual things which themselves had images in the visible world; and it is compelled to pursue its inquiry by starting from assumptions and traveling, not up to a principle, but down to a conclusion. In the second (D) the mind moves in the other direction, from an assumption up towards a principle which is not hypothetical; and it makes no use of the images employed in the other section, but only of Forms, and conducts its inquiry solely by their means.

I don't quite understand what you mean.

Then we will try again; what I have just said will help you to understand. (C) You know, of course, how students of subjects like geometry and arithmetic begin by postulating odd and even numbers, or the various figures and the three kinds of angle, and other such data in each subject. These data they take as known; and, having adopted them as assumptions, they do not feel called upon to give any account of them to themselves or to anyone else, but treat them as self-evident. Then, starting from these assumptions, they go on until they arrive, by a series of consistent steps, at all the conclusions they set out to investigate.

Yes, I know that.

You also know how they make use of visible figures and discourse about them, though what they really have in mind is the originals of which these figures are images: they are not reasoning, for instance, about this particular square and diagonal which they have drawn, but about *the* Square and *the* Diagonal; and so in all cases. The diagrams they draw and the models they make are actual things, which may have their shadows or images in water; but now they serve in their turn as images, while the student is seeking to behold those realities which only thought can apprehend.

True.

This, then, is the class of things that I spoke of as intelligible, but with two qualifications: first, that the mind, in studying them, is compelled to employ assumptions, and, because it cannot rise above these, does not travel upwards to a first principle; and second, that it uses as images those actual things which have images of their own in the section below them and which, in comparison with those shadows and reflections, are reputed to be more palpable and valued accordingly.

I understand: you mean the subject matter of geometry and of the kindred arts.

(D) Then by the second section of the intelligible world you may understand me to mean all that unaided reasoning apprehends by the power of dialectic, when it treats its assumptions, not as first principles, but as *hypotheses* in the literal sense, things 'laid down' like a flight of steps up which it may mount all the way to something that is not hypothetical, the first principle of all; and having grasped this, may turn back and, holding on to the consequences which depend upon it, descend at last to a conclusion, never making use of any sensible object, but only of Forms, moving through Forms from one to another, and ending with Forms.

I understand, he said, though not perfectly; for the procedure you describe sounds like an enormous undertaking. But I see that you mean to distinguish the field of intelligible reality studied by dialectic as having a greater certainty and truth than the subject matter of the 'arts,' as they are called, which treat their assumptions as first principles. The students of these arts are, it is true, compelled to exercise thought in contemplating objects which the senses cannot perceive; but because they start from assumptions without going back to a first principle, you do not regard them as gaining true understanding about those objects, although the objects themselves, when connected with a first principle, are intelligible. And I think you would call the state of mind of the students of geometry and other such arts, not intelligence, but thinking, as being something between intelligence and mere acceptance of appearances.

You have understood me quite well enough, I replied. And now you may take, as corresponding to the four sections, these four states of mind: *intelligence* for the highest, *thinking* for the second, *belief* for the third, and for the last *imagining*. These you may arrange as the terms in a proportion, assigning to each a degree of clearness and certainty corresponding to the measure in which their objects possess truth and reality.

I understand and agree with you. I will arrange them as you say.

THE ALLEGORY OF THE CAVE

Next, said I, here is a parable to illustrate the degrees in which our nature may be enlightened or unenlightened. Imagine the condition of men living in a sort of cavernous chamber underground, with an entrance open to the light and a long passage all down the cave. Here they have been from childhood, chained by the leg and also by the neck, so that they cannot move and can see only what is in front of them, because the chains will not let them turn their heads. At some distance higher up is the light of a fire burning behind them; and between the prisoners and the fire is a track with a parapet built along it, like the screen at a puppet-show, which hides the performers while they show their puppets over the top.

I see, said he.

Now behind this parapet imagine persons carrying along various artificial objects, including figures of men and animals in wood or stone or other materials, which project above the parapet. Naturally, some of these persons will be talking, others silent.

It is a strange picture, he said, and a strange sort of prisoners.

Like ourselves, I replied; for in the first place prisoners so confined would have seen nothing of themselves or of one another, except the shadows thrown by the firelight on the wall of the Cave facing them, would they?

Not if all their lives they had been prevented from moving their heads.

And they would have seen as little of the objects carried past.

Of course.

Now, if they could talk to one another, would they not suppose that their words referred only to those passing shadows which they saw?

Necessarily.

And suppose their prison had an echo from the wall facing them? When one of the people crossing behind them spoke, they could only suppose that the sound came from the shadow passing before their eyes.

No doubt.

In every way, then, such prisoners would recognize as reality nothing but the shadows of those artificial objects.

Inevitably.

Now consider what would happen if their release from the chains and the healing of their unwisdom should come about in this way. Suppose one of them set free and forced suddenly to stand up, turn his head, and walk with eyes lifted to the light; all these movements would be painful, and he would be too dazzled to make out the objects whose shadows he had been used to see. What do you think he would say, if someone told him that what he had formerly seen was meaningless illusion, but now, being somewhat nearer to reality and turned towards more real objects, he was getting a truer view? Suppose further that he were shown the various objects being carried by and were made to say, in reply to questions, what each of them was. Would he not be perplexed and believe the objects now shown him to be not so real as what he formerly saw?

Yes, not nearly so real.

And if he were forced to look at the fire-light itself, would not his eyes ache, so that he would try to escape and turn back to the things which he could see distinctly, convinced that they really were clearer than these other objects now being shown to him?

Yes.

And suppose someone were to drag him away forcibly up the steep and rugged ascent and not let him go until he had hauled him out into the sunlight, would he not suffer pain and vexation at such treatment, and, when he had come out into the light, find his eyes so full of its radiance that he could not see a single one of the things that he was now told were real?

Certainly he would not see them all at once.

He would need, then, to grow accustomed before he could see things in that upper world. At first it would be easiest to make out shadows, and then the images of men and things reflected in water, and later on the things themselves. After that, it would be easier to watch the heavenly bodies and the sky itself by night, looking at the light of the moon and stars rather than the Sun and the Sun's light in the day-time.

Yes, surely.

Last of all, he would be able to look at the Sun and contemplate its nature, not as it appears when reflected in water or any alien medium, but as it is in itself in its own domain.

No doubt.

And now he would begin to draw the conclusion that it is the Sun that produces the seasons and the course of the year and controls everything in the visible world, and moreover is in a way the cause of all that he and his companions used to see.

Clearly he would come at last to that conclusion.

Then if he called to mind his fellow prisoners and what passed for wisdom in his former dwelling-place, he would surely think himself happy in the change and be sorry for them. They may have had a practice of honoring and commending one another, with prizes for the man who had the keenest eye for the passing shadows and the best memory for the order in which they followed or accompanied one another, so that he could make a good guess as to which was going to come next. Would our released prisoner be likely to covet those prizes or to envy the men exalted to honor and power in the Cave? Would he not feel like Homer's Achilles, that he would far sooner 'be on earth as a hired servant in the house of a landless man' or endure anything rather than go back to his old beliefs and live in the old way?

Yes, he would prefer any fate to such a life.

Now imagine what would happen if he went down again to take his former seat in the Cave. Coming suddenly out of the sunlight, his eyes would be filled with darkness. He might be required once more to deliver his opinion on those shadows, in competition with the prisoners who had never been released, while his eyesight was still dim and unsteady; and it might take some time to become used to the darkness. They would laugh at him and say that he had gone up only to come back with his sight ruined; it was worth no one's while even to attempt the ascent. If they could lay hands on the man who was trying to set them free and lead them up, they would kill him.

Yes, they would.

Every feature in this parable, my dear Glaucon, is meant to fit our earlier analysis. The prison dwelling corresponds to the region revealed to us through the sense of sight, and the fire-light within it to the power of the Sun. The ascent to see the things in the upper world you may take as standing for the upward journey of the soul into the region of the intelligible; then you will be in possession of what I surmise, since that is what you wish to be told. Heaven knows whether it is true; but this, at any rate, is how it appears to me. In the world of knowledge, the last thing to be perceived and only with great difficulty is the essential Form of Goodness. Once it is perceived, the conclusion must follow that, for all things, this is the cause of whatever is right and good; in the visible world it gives birth to light and to the lord of light, while it is itself sovereign in the intelligible world and the parent of intelligence and truth. Without having had a vision of this Form no one can act with wisdom, either in his own life or in matters of state.

So far as I can understand, I share your belief.

Then you may also agree that it is no wonder if those who have reached this height are reluctant to manage the affairs of men. Their souls long to spend all their time in that upper world—naturally enough, if here once more our parable holds true. Nor, again, is it at all strange that one who comes from the contemplation of divine things to the miseries of human life should appear awkward and ridiculous when, with eyes still dazed and not yet accustomed to the darkness, he is compelled, in a law-court or elsewhere, to dispute about the shadows of justice or the images that cast those shadows, and to wrangle over the notions of what is right in the minds of men who have never beheld Justice itself.

It is not at all strange.

No; a sensible man will remember that the eyes may be confused in two ways—by a change from light to darkness or from darkness to light; and he will recognize that the same thing happens to the soul. When he sees it troubled and unable to discern anything clearly, instead of laughing thoughtlessly, he will ask whether, coming from a brighter existence, its unaccustomed vision is obscured by the darkness, in which case he will think its condition enviable and its life a happy one; or whether, emerging from the depths of ignorance, it is dazzled by excess of light. If so, he will rather feel sorry for it; or, if he were inclined to laugh, that would be less ridiculous than to laugh at the soul which has come down from the light.

That is a fair statement.

If this is true, then, we must conclude that education is not what it is said to be by some, who profess to put knowledge into a soul which does not possess it, as if they could put sight into blind eyes. On the contrary, our own account signifies that the soul of every man does possess the power of learning the truth and the organ to see it with; and that, just as one might have to turn the whole body round in order that the eye should see light instead of darkness, so the entire soul must be turned away from this changing world, until its eye can bear to contemplate reality and that supreme splendor which we have called the Good. Hence there may well be an art whose aim would be to effect this very thing, the conversion of the soul, in the readiest way; not to put the power of sight into the soul's eye, which already has it, but to ensure that, instead of looking in the wrong direction, it is turned the way it ought to be.

Yes, it may well be so.

It looks, then, as though wisdom were different from those ordinary virtues, as they are called, which are not far removed from bodily qualities, in that they can be produced by habituation and exercise in a soul which has not possessed them from the first. Wisdom, it seems, is certainly the virtue of some diviner faculty, which never loses its power, though its use for good or harm depends on the direction towards which it is turned. You must have noticed in dishonest men with a reputation for sagacity the shrewd glance of a narrow intelligence piercing the objects to which it is directed. There is nothing wrong with their power of vision, but it has been forced into the service of evil, so that the keener its sight, the more harm it works.

Quite true.

And yet if the growth of a nature like this had been pruned from earliest childhood, cleared of those clinging overgrowths which come of gluttony and all luxurious pleasure and, like leaden weights charged with affinity to this mortal world, hang upon the soul, bending its vision downwards; if, freed from these, the soul were turned round towards true reality, then this same power in these very men would see the truth as keenly as the objects it is turned to now.

Yes, very likely.

Is it not also likely, or indeed certain after what has been said, that a state can never be properly governed either by the uneducated who know nothing of truth or by men who are allowed to spend all their days in the pursuit of culture? The ignorant have no single mark before their eyes at which they must aim in all the conduct of their own lives and of affairs of state; and the others will not engage in action if they can help it, dreaming that, while still alive, they have been translated to the Islands of the Blest.

Quite true.

It is for us, then, as founders of a commonwealth, to bring compulsion to bear on the noblest natures. They must be made to climb the ascent to the vision of Goodness, which we called the highest object of knowledge; and, when they have looked upon it long enough, they must not be allowed, as they now are, to remain on the heights, refusing to come down again to the prisoners or to take any part in their labors and rewards, however much or little these may be worth.

Shall we not be doing them an injustice, if we force on them a worse life than they might have?

You have forgotten again, my friend, that the law is not concerned to make any one class specially happy, but to ensure the welfare of the commonwealth as a whole. By persuasion or constraint it will unite the citizens in harmony, making them share whatever benefits each class can contribute to the common good; and its purpose in forming men of that spirit was not that each should be left to go his own way, but that they should be instrumental in binding the community into one.

True, I had forgotten.

You will see, then, Glaucon, that there will be no real injustice in compelling our philosophers to watch over and care for the other citizens. We can fairly tell them that their compeers in other states may quite reasonably refuse to collaborate: there they have sprung up, like a self-sown plant, in despite of their country's institutions; no one has fostered their growth, and they cannot be expected to show gratitude for a care they have never received. 'But,' we shall say, 'it is not so with you. We have brought you into existence for your country's sake as well as for your own, to be like leaders and king-bees in a hive; you have been better and more thoroughly educated than those others and hence you are more capable of playing your part both as men of thought and as men of action. You must go down, then, each in his turn, to live with the rest and let your eyes grow accustomed to the darkness. You will then see a thousand times better than those who live there always; you will recognize every image for what it is and know what it represents, because you have seen justice, beauty, and goodness in their reality; and so you and we shall find life in our commonwealth no mere dream, as it is in most existing states, where men live fighting one another about shadows and quarreling for power, as if that were a great prize; whereas in truth government can be at its best and free from dissension only where the destined rulers are least desirous of holding office.'

Quite true.

Then will our pupils refuse to listen and to take their turns at sharing in the work of the community, though they may live together for most of their time in a purer air?

No; it is a fair demand, and they are fair-minded men. No doubt, unlike any ruler of the present day, they will think of holding power as an unavoidable necessity.

Yes, my friend; for the truth is that you can have a well-governed society only if you can discover for your future rulers a better way of life than being in office; then only will power be in the hands of men who are rich, not in gold, but in the wealth that brings happiness, a good and wise life. All goes wrong when, starved for lack of anything good in their own lives, men turn to public affairs hoping to snatch from thence the happiness they hunger for. They set about fighting for power, and this internecine conflict ruins them and their country. The life of true philosophy is the only one that looks down upon offices of state; and access to power must be confined to men who are not in love with it; other wise rivals will start fighting. So whom else can you compel to undertake the guardianship of the commonwealth, if not those who, besides understanding best the principles of government, enjoy a nobler life than the politician's and look for rewards of a different kind?

There is indeed no other choice.

Hume: An Enquiry Concerning Human Understanding

PART I

I have frequently considered, what could possibly be the reason why all mankind, though they have ever, without hesitation, acknowledged the doctrine of necessity in their whole practice and reasoning, have yet discovered such a reluctance to acknowledge it in words, and have rather shown a propensity, in all ages, to profess the contrary opinion. The matter, I think, may be accounted for after the following manner. If we examine the operations of body, and the production of effects from their causes, we shall find that all our faculties can never carry us farther in our knowledge of this relation than barely to observe that particular objects are *constantly conjoined* together, and that the mind is carried, by a *customary transition*, from the appearance of one to the belief of the other. But though this conclusion concerning human ignorance be the result of the strictest scrutiny of this subject, men still entertain a strong propensity to believe that they penetrate farther into the powers of nature, and perceive something like a necessary connection between the cause and the effect. When again they turn their reflections towards the operations of their own minds, and *feel* no such connection of the motive and the action; they are thence apt to suppose, that there is a difference between the effects which result from material force, and those which arise from thought and intelligence. But being once convinced that we know nothing farther of causation of any kind than merely the *constant conjunction* of objects, and the consequent *inference* of the mind from one to another, and finding that these two circumstances are universally allowed to have place in voluntary actions; we may be more easily led to own the same necessity common to all causes. And though this reasoning may contradict the systems of many philosophers, in ascribing necessity to the determinations of the will, we shall find, upon reflection, that they dissent from it in words only, not in their real sentiment. Necessity, according to the sense in which it is here taken, has never yet been rejected, nor can ever, I think, be rejected by any philosopher. It may only, perhaps, be pretended that the mind can perceive, in the operations of matter, some farther connection between the cause and effect; and connection that has not place in voluntary actions of intelligent beings. Now whether it be so or not, can only appear upon examination; and it is incumbent on these philosophers to make good their assertion, by defining or describing that necessity, and pointing it out to us in the operations of material causes

It would seem, indeed, that men begin at the wrong end of this question concerning liberty and necessity, when they enter upon it by examining the faculties of the soul, the influence of the understanding, and the operations of the will. Let them first discuss a more simple question, namely, the operations of body and of brute unintelligent matter; and try whether they can there form any idea of causation and necessity, except that of a constant conjunction of objects, and subsequent inference of the mind from one to another. If these circumstances form, in reality, the whole of that necessity, which we conceive in matter, and if these circumstances be also universally acknowledged to take place in the operations of the mind, the dispute is at an end; at least, must be owned to be thenceforth merely verbal. But as long as we will rashly suppose, that we have some farther idea of necessity and causation in the operations of external objects; at the same time, that we can find nothing farther in the voluntary actions of the mind; there is no possibility of bringing the question to any determinate issue, while we proceed upon so erroneous a supposition. The only method of undeceiving us is to mount up higher; to examine the narrow extent of science when applied to material causes; and to convince ourselves that all we know of them is the constant conjunction and inference above mentioned. We may, perhaps, find that it is with difficulty we are induced to fix such narrow limits to human understanding: But we can afterwards find no difficulty when we come to apply this doctrine to the actions of the will. For as it is evident that these have a regular conjunction with motives and circumstances and characters, and as we always draw inferences from one to the other, we must be obliged to acknowledge in words that necessity, which we have already avowed, in every deliberation of our lives, and in every step of our conduct and behavior.

But to proceed in this reconciling project with regard to the question of liberty and necessity; the most contentious question of metaphysics, the most contentious science; it will not require many words to prove, that all mankind have ever agreed in the doctrine of liberty as well as in that of necessity, and that the whole dispute, in this respect also, has been hitherto merely verbal. For what is meant by liberty, when applied to voluntary actions? We cannot surely mean that actions have so little connection with motives, inclinations, and circumstances, that one does not follow with a certain degree of uniformity from the other, and that one affords no inference by which we can conclude the existence of the other. For these are plain and acknowledged matters of fact. By liberty, then, we can only mean *a power of acting or not acting, according to the determinations of the will*; that is, if we choose to remain at rest, we may; if we choose to move, we also may. Now this hypothetical liberty is universally allowed to belong to every one who is not a prisoner and in chains. Here, then, is no subject of dispute.

Whatever definition we may give of liberty, we should be careful to observe two requisite circumstances; *first*, that it be consistent with plain matter of fact; *secondly*, that it be consistent with itself. If we observe these circumstances, and render our definition intelligible, I am persuaded that all mankind will be found of one opinion with regard to it.

It is universally allowed that nothing exists without a cause of its existence, and that chance, when strictly examined, is a mere negative word, and means not any real power which has anywhere a being in nature. But it is pretended that some causes are necessary, some not necessary. Here then is the advantage of definitions. Let anyone *define* a cause, without comprehending, as a part of the definition, a *necessary connection* with its effect; and let him show distinctly the origin of the idea, expressed by the definition; and I shall readily give up the whole controversy. But if the foregoing explication of the matter be received, this must be absolutely impracticable. Had not objects a regular conjunction with each other, we should never have entertained any notion of cause and effect; and this regular conjunction produces that inference of the understanding, which is the only connection, that we can have any comprehension of. Whoever attempts a definition of cause, exclusive of these circumstances, will be obliged either to employ unintelligible terms or such as are synonymous to the term which he endeavors to define. And if the definition above mentioned be admitted; liberty, when opposed to necessity, not to constraint, is the same thing with chance; which is universally allowed to have no existence.

PART II

There is no method of reasoning more common, and yet none more blamable, than, in philosophical disputes, to endeavor the refutation of any hypothesis, by a pretense of its dangerous consequences to religion and morality. When any opinion leads to absurdities, it is certainly false; but it is not certain that an opinion is false, because it is of dangerous consequence. Such topics, therefore, ought entirely to be forborne; as serving nothing to the discovery of truth, but only to make the person of an antagonist odious. This I observe in general, without pretending to draw any advantage from it. I frankly submit to an examination of this kind, and shall venture to affirm that the doctrines, both of necessity and of liberty, as above explained, are not only consistent with morality, but are absolutely essential to its support.

Necessity may be defined two ways, conformably to the two definitions of *cause*, of which it makes an essential part. It consists either in the constant conjunction of like objects, or in the inference of the understanding from one object to another. Now necessity, in both these senses (which, indeed, are at bottom the same), has universally, though tacitly, in the schools, in the pulpit, and in common life, been allowed to belong to the will of man; and no one has ever pretended to deny that we can draw inferences concerning human actions, and that those inferences are founded on the experienced union of like actions, with like motives, inclinations, and circumstances. The only particular in which any one can differ, is, that either, perhaps, he will refuse to give the name of necessity to this property of human actions: But as long as the meaning is understood, I hope the word can do no harm: Or that he will maintain it possible to discover something farther in the operations of matter. But this, it must be acknowledged, can be of no consequence to morality or religion, whatever it may be to natural philosophy or metaphysics. We may here be mistaken in asserting that there is no idea of any other necessity or connection in the actions of body: But surely we ascribe nothing to the actions of the mind, but what everyone does, and must readily allow of. We change no circumstance in the received orthodox system with regard to the will, but only in that with regard to material objects and causes. Nothing, therefore, can be more innocent, at least, than this doctrine.

All laws being founded on rewards and punishments, it is supposed as a fundamental principle, that these motives have a regular and uniform influence on the mind, and both produce the good and prevent the evil actions. We may give to this influence what name we please; but, as it is usually conjoined with the action, it must be esteemed a *cause*, and be looked upon as an instance of that necessity, which we would here establish.

The only proper object of hatred or vengeance is a person or creature, endowed with thought and consciousness; and when any criminal or injurious actions excite that passion, it is only by their relation to the person, or connection with him. Actions are, by their very nature, temporary and perishing; and where they proceed not from some *cause* in the character and disposition of the person who performed them, they can neither redound to his honor, if good; nor infamy, if evil. The actions themselves may be blamable; they may be contrary to all the rules of morality and religion: But the person is not answerable for them; and as they proceeded from nothing in him that is durable and constant, and leave nothing of that nature behind them, it is impossible he can, upon their account, become the object of punishment or vengeance. According to the principle, therefore, which denies necessity, and consequently causes, a man is as pure and untainted, after having committed the most horrid crime, as at the first moment of his birth, nor is his character anywise concerned in his actions, since they are not derived from it, and the wickedness of the one can never be used as a proof of the depravity of the other.

Men are not blamed for such actions as they perform ignorantly and casually, whatever may be the consequences. Why? but because the principles of these actions are only momentary, and terminate in them alone. Men are less blamed for such actions as they perform hastily and unpremeditately than for such as proceed from deliberation. For what reason? but because a hasty temper, though a constant cause or principle in the mind, operates only by intervals, and infects not the whole character. Again, repentance wipes off every crime, if attended with a reformation of life and manners How is this to be accounted for? but by asserting that actions render a person criminal merely as they are proofs of criminal principles in the mind; and when, by an alteration of these principles, they cease to be just proofs, they likewise cease to be criminal. But, except upon the doctrine of necessity, they never were just proofs, and consequently never were criminal.

It will be equally easy to prove, and from the same arguments, that *liberty*, according to that definition above mentioned, in which all men agree, is also essential to morality, and that no human actions, where it is wanting, are susceptible of any moral qualities, or can be the objects either of approbation or dislike. For as actions are objects of our moral sentiment, so far only as they are indications of the internal character, passions, and affections; it is impossible that they can give rise either to praise or blame, where they proceed not from these principles, but are derived altogether from external violence.

Descartes: Meditations on First Philosophy

SYNOPSIS OF THE MEDITATIONS

In the first Meditation I set forth the reasons for which we may, generally speaking, doubt about all things and especially about material things, at least so long as we have no other foundations for the sciences than those which we have hitherto possessed. But although the utility of a Doubt which is so general does not at first appear, it is at the same time very great, inasmuch as it delivers us from every kind of prejudice, and sets out for us a very simple way by which the mind may detach itself from the senses; and finally, it makes it impossible for us ever to doubt those things which we have once discovered to be true.

In the second Meditation, mind, which making use of the liberty which pertains to it, takes for granted that all those things of whose existence it has the least doubt, are non-existent, recognizes that it is however absolutely impossible that it does not itself exist. This point is likewise of the greatest moment, inasmuch as by this means a distinction is easily drawn between the things which pertain to mind—that is to say to the intellectual nature—and those which pertain to body.

But because it may be that some expect from me in this place a statement of the reasons establishing the immortality of the soul, I feel that I should here make known to them that having aimed at writing nothing in all this Treatise of which I do not possess very exact demonstrations, I am obliged to follow a similar order to that made use of by the geometers, which is to begin by putting forward as premises all those things upon which the proposition that we seek depends, before coming to any conclusion regarding it. Now the first and principal matter which is requisite for thoroughly understanding the immortality of the soul is to form the clearest possible conception of it, and one which will be entirely distinct from all the conceptions which we may have of body; and in this Meditation this has been done. In addition to this it is requisite that we may be assured that all the things which we conceive clearly and distinctly are true in the very way in which we think them; and this could not be proved previously to the fourth Meditation. Further we must have a distinct conception of corporeal nature, which is given partly in this second, and partly in the fifth and sixth Meditations. And finally we should conclude from all this, that those things which we conceive clearly and distinctly as being diverse substances, as we regard mind and body to be, are really substances essentially distinct one from the other; and this is the conclusion of the sixth Meditation. This is further confirmed in this same Meditation by the fact that we cannot conceive of body excepting in so far as it is divisible, while the mind cannot be conceived of excepting as indivisible. For we are not able to conceive of the half of a mind as we can do of the smallest of all bodies; so that we see that not only are their natures different but even in some respects contrary to one another. I have not however dealt further with this matter in this treatise, both because what I have said is sufficient to show clearly enough that the extinction of the mind does not follow from the corruption of the body, and also to give men the hope of another life after death, as also because the premises from which the immortality of the soul may be deduced depend on an elucidation of a complete system of Physics. This would mean to establish in the first place that all substances generally—that is to say all things which cannot exist without being created by God—are in their nature incorruptible, and that they can never cease to exist unless God, in denying to them his concurrence, reduce them to nought; and secondly that body, regarded generally, is a substance, which is the reason why it also cannot perish, but that the human body, inasmuch as it differs from other bodies, is composed only of certain configuration of members and of other similar accidents, while the human mind is not similarly composed of any accidents, but is a pure substance. For although all the accidents of mind be changed, although, for instance, it think certain things, will others, perceive others, etc., despite all this it does not emerge from these changes another mind: the human body on the other hand becomes a different thing from the sole fact that the figure or form of any of its portions is found to be changed. From this it follows that the human body may indeed easily enough perish, but the mind (or soul of man [I make no distinction between them]) is owing to its nature immortal.

In the third Meditation it seems to me that I have explained at sufficient length the principal argument of which I make use in order to prove the existence of God. But none the less, because I did not wish in that place to make use of any comparisons derived from corporeal things, so as to withdraw as much as I could the minds of readers from the senses, there may perhaps have remained many obscurities which, however, will, I hope, be entirely removed by the Replies which I have made to the Objections which have been set before me. Amongst others there is, for example, this one, 'How the idea in us of a being supremely perfect possesses so much objective reality (that is to say participates by representation in so many degrees of being and perfection) that it necessarily proceeds from a cause which is absolutely perfect.' This is illustrated in these Replies by the comparison of a very perfect machine, the idea of which is found in the mind of some workman. For as the objective contrivance of this idea must have some cause, i.e., either the science of the workman or that of some other from whom he has received the idea, it is similarly impossible that the idea of God which is in us should not have God himself as its cause.

In the fourth Meditation it is shown that all these things which we very clearly and distinctly perceive are true, and at the same time it is explained in what the nature of error or falsity consists. This must of necessity be known both for the confirmation of the preceding truths and for the better comprehension of those that follow. (But it must meanwhile be rendered that I do not in any way there treat of sin—that is to say of the error which is committed in the pursuit of good and evil, but only of that which arises in the deciding between the true and the false. And I do not intend to speak of matters pertaining to the Faith or the conduct of life, but only of those which concern speculative truths, and which may be known by the sole aid of the light of nature.)

In the fifth Meditation corporeal nature generally is explained, and in addition to this the existence of God is demonstrated by a new proof in which there may possibly be certain difficulties also, but the solution of these will be seen in the Replies to the Objections. And further I show in what sense it is true to say that the certainty of geometrical demonstrations is itself dependent on the knowledge of God.

Finally in the sixth I distinguish the action of the understanding from that of the imagination; the marks by which this distinction is made are described. I here show that the mind of man is really distinct from the body, and at the same time that the two are so closely joined together that they form, so to speak, a single thing. All the errors which proceed from the senses are then surveyed, while the means of avoiding them are demonstrated, and finally all the reasons from which we may deduce the existence of material things are set forth. Not that I judge them to be very useful in establishing that which they prove, to wit, that there is in truth a world, that men possess bodies, and other such things which never have been doubted by anyone of sense; but because in these closely we come to see that they are neither so strong nor so evident as those arguments which lead us to the knowledge of our mind and of God; so that these last must be the most certain and most evident facts which can fall within the cognizance of the human mind. And this is the whole matter that I have tried to prove in these Meditations, for which reason I here omit to speak of many other questions with which I dealt incidentally in this discussion.

MEDITATION II

Of the Nature of the Human Mind; and that it is more easily known than the Body.

The Meditation of yesterday filled my mind with so many doubts that it is no longer in my power to forget them. And yet I do not see in what manner I can resolve them; and, just as if I had all of a sudden fallen into very deep water, I am so disconcerted that I can neither make certain of setting my feet on the bottom, nor can I swim and so support myself on the surface. I shall nevertheless make an effort and follow anew the same path as that on which I yesterday entered, i.e., I shall proceed by setting aside all that in which the least doubt could be supposed to exist, just as if I had discovered that it was absolutely false; and I shall ever follow in this road until I have met with something which is certain, or at least, if I can do nothing else, until I have learned for certain that there is nothing in the world that is certain. Archimedes, in order that he might draw the terrestrial globe out of its place, and transport it elsewhere, demanded only that one point should be fixed and immovable; in the same way I shall have the right to conceive high hopes if I am happy enough to discover one thing only which is certain and indubitable.

I suppose, then, that all the things that I see are false; I persuade myself that nothing has ever existed of all that my fallacious memory represents to me. I consider that I possess no senses; I imagine that body, figure, extension, movement and place are but the fictions of my mind. What, then, can be esteemed as true? Perhaps nothing at all, unless that there is nothing in the world that is certain.

But how can I know there is not something different from those things that I have just considered, of which one cannot have the slightest doubt? Is there not some God, or some other being by whatever name we call it, who puts these reflections into my mind? That is not necessary, for is it not possible that I am capable of producing them myself? I myself, am I not at least something? But I have already denied that I had senses and body. Yet I hesitate, for what follows from that? Am I so dependent on body and senses that I cannot exist without these? But I was persuaded that there was nothing in all the world, that there was no heaven, no earth, that there were no minds, nor any bodies: Was I not then likewise persuaded that I did not exist ? Not at all; of a surety I myself did exist since I persuaded myself of something (or merely because I thought of something). But there is some deceiver or other, very powerful and very cunning, who ever employs his ingenuity in deceiving me. Then without doubt I exist also if he deceives me, and let him deceive me as much as he will, he can never cause me to be nothing so long as I think that I am something. So that after having reflected well and carefully examined all things, we must come to the definite conclusion that this proposition: I am, I exist, is necessarily true each time that I pronounce it, or that I mentally conceive it.

But I do not yet know clearly enough what I am, I who am certain that I am; and hence I must be careful to see that I do not imprudently take some other object in place of myself, and thus that I do not go astray in respect of this knowledge that I hold to be the most certain and most evident of all that I have formerly learned. That is why I shall now consider anew what I believed myself to be before I embarked upon these last reflections; and of my former opinions I shall withdraw all that might even in a small degree be invalidated by the reasons which I have just brought forward, in order that there may be nothing at all left beyond what is absolutely certain and indubitable.

What then did I formerly believe myself to be? Undoubtedly I believed myself to be a man. But what is a man ? Shall I say a reasonable animal? Certainly not; for then I should have to inquire what an animal is, and what is reasonable; and thus from a single question I should insensibly fall into an infinitude of others more difficult; and I should not wish to waste the little time and leisure remaining to me in trying to unravel subtleties like these. But I shall rather stop here to consider the thoughts which of themselves spring up in my mind, and which were not inspired by anything beyond my own nature alone when I applied myself to the consideration of my being. In the first place, then, I considered myself as having a face, hands, arms, and all that system of members composed of bones and flesh as seen in a corpse which I designated by the name of body. In addition to this I considered that I was nourished, that I walked, that I felt, and that I thought, and I referred all these actions to the soul: but I did not stop to consider what the soul was, or if I did stop, I imagined that it was something extremely rare and subtle like a wind, a flame, or an ether, which was spread throughout my grosser parts. As to body I had no manner of doubt about its nature, but thought I had a very clear knowledge of it; and if I had desired to explain it according to the notions that I had then formed of it, I should have described it thus: By the body I understand all that which can be defined by a certain figure: something which can be confined in a certain place, and which can fill a given space in such a way that every other body will be excluded from it; which can be perceived either by touch, or by sight, or by hearing, or by taste, or by smell: which can be moved in many ways not, in truth, by itself, but by something which is foreign to it, by which it is touched (and from which it receives impressions): for to have the power of self-movement, as also of feeling or of thinking, I did not consider to appertain to the nature of body: on the contrary, I was rather astonished to find that faculties similar to them existed in some bodies.

But what am I, now that I suppose that there is a certain genius which is extremely powerful, and, if I may say so, malicious, who employs all his powers in deceiving me? Can I affirm that I possess the least of all those things which I have just said pertain to the nature of body? I pause to consider, I revolve all these things in my mind, and I find none of which I can say that it pertains to me. It would be tedious to stop to enumerate them. Let us pass to the attributes of soul and see if there is any one which is in me? What of nutrition or walking (the first mentioned)? But if it is so that I have no body it is also true that I can neither walk nor take nourishment. Another attribute is sensation. But one cannot feel without body, and besides I have thought I perceived many things during sleep that I recognized in my waking moments as not having been experienced at all. What of thinking? I find here that thought is an attribute that belongs to me; it alone cannot be separated from me. I am, I exist, that is certain. But how often? Just when I think; for it might possibly be the case if I ceased entirely to think, that I should likewise cease altogether to exist. I do not now admit anything which is not necessarily true: to speak accurately I am not more than a thing which thinks, that is to say a mind or a soul, or an understanding, or a reason, which are terms whose significance was formerly unknown to me. I am, however, a real thing and really exist; but what thing? I have answered: a thing which thinks.

And what more? I shall exercise my imagination (in order to see if I am not something more). I am not a collection of members which we call the human body: I am not a subtle air distributed through these members, I am not a wind, a fire, a vapour, a breath nor anything at all which I can imagine or conceive; because I have assumed that all these were nothing. Without changing that supposition I find that I only leave myself certain of the fact that I am somewhat. But perhaps it is true that these same things which I supposed were non-existent because they are unknown to me, are really not different from the self which I know. I am not sure about this, I shall not dispute about it now; I can only give judgment on things that are known to me. I know that I exist, and I inquire what I am, I whom I know to exist. But it is very certain that the knowledge of my existence taken in its precise significance does not depend on things whose existence is not yet known to me; consequently it does not depend on those which I can feign in imagination. And indeed the very term *feign* in imagination proves to me my error, for I really do this if I image myself a something, since to imagine is nothing else than to contemplate the figure or image of a corporeal thing. But I already know for certain that I am, and that it may be that all these images and, speaking generally, all things that relate to the nature of body are nothing but dreams (and chimeras). For this reason I see clearly that I have as little reason to say, 'I shall stimulate my imagination in order to know more distinctly what I am,' than if I were to say, 'I am now awake, and I perceive somewhat that is real and true: but because I do not yet perceive it distinctly enough, I shall go to sleep of express purpose, so that my dreams may represent the perception with greatest truth and evidence.' And, thus, I know for certain that nothing of all that I can understand by means of my imagination belongs to this knowledge which I have of myself, and that it is necessary to recall the mind from this mode of thought with the utmost diligence in order that it may be able to know its own nature with perfect distinctness.

But what then am I? A thing which thinks. What is a thing which thinks? It is a thing which doubts, understands, (conceives), affirms, denies, wills, refuses, which also imagines and feels.

Certainly it is no small matter if all these things pertain to my nature. But why should they not so pertain? Am I not that being who now doubts nearly everything, who nevertheless understands certain things, who affirms that one only is true, who denies all the others, who desires to know more, is averse from being deceived, who imagines many things, sometimes indeed despite his will, and who perceives many likewise, as by the intervention of the bodily organs? Is there nothing in all this which is as true as it is certain that I exist, even though I should always sleep and though he who has given me being employed all his ingenuity in deceiving me? Is there likewise any one of these attributes which can be distinguished from my thought, or which might be said to be separated from myself? For it is so evident of itself that it is I who doubts, who understands, and who desires, that there is no reason here to add anything to explain it. And I have certainly the power of imagining likewise; for although it may happen (as I formerly supposed) that none of the things which I imagine are true, nevertheless this power of imagining does not cease to be really in use, and it forms part of my thought. Finally, I am the same who feels, that is to say, who perceives certain things, as by the organs of sense, since in truth I see light, I hear noise, I feel heat. But it will be said that these phenomena are false and that I am dreaming. Let it be so; still it is at least quite certain that it seems to me that I see light, that I hear noise and that I feel heat. That cannot be false;

properly speaking it is what is in me called feeling; and used in this precise sense that is no other thing than thinking.

MEDITATION VI

Of the Existence of Material Things, and of the real distinction between the Soul and Body of man.

Nothing further now remains but to inquire whether material things exist. And certainly I at least know that these may exist in so far as they are considered as the objects of pure mathematics, since in this aspect I perceive them clearly and distinctly. For there is no doubt that God possesses the power to produce everything that I am capable of perceiving with distinctness, and I have never deemed that anything was impossible for Him, unless I found a contradiction in attempting to conceive it clearly. Further, the faculty of imagination which I possess, and of which, experience tells me, I make use when I apply myself to the consideration of material things, is capable of persuading me of their existence; for when I attentively consider what imagination is, I find that it is nothing but certain application of the faculty of knowledge to the body which is immediately present to it, and which therefore exists.

And to render this quite clear, I remark in the first place the difference that exists between the imagination and pure intellection (or conception). For example, when I imagine a triangle, I do not conceive it only as a figure comprehended by three lines, but I also apprehended these three lines as present by the power and inward vision of my mind, and this is what I call imagining. But if I desire to think of a chiliagon, I certainly conceive truly that it is a figure composed of a thousand sides, just as easily as I conceive of a triangle that it is a figure of three sides only; but I cannot in any way imagine the thousand sides of a chiliagon (as I do the three sides of a triangle), nor do I, so to speak, regard them as present (with the eyes of my mind). And although in accordance with the habit I have formed of always employing the aid of my imagination when I think of corporeal things, it may happen that in imagining a chiliagon I confusedly represent to myself some figure, yet it is very evident that this figure is not a chiliagon, since it in no way differs from that which I represent to myself when I think of a myriagon or any other many-sided figure; nor does it serve my purpose in discovering the properties which go to form the distinction between a chiliagon and other polygons. But if the question turns upon a pentagon, it is quite true that I can conceive its figure as well as that of a chiliagon without the help of my imagination; but I can also imagine it by applying the attention of my mind to each of its five sides, and at the same time to the space which they enclose. And thus I clearly recognize that I have need of a particular effort of mind in order to effect the act of imagination, such as I do not require in order to understand, and this particular effort of mind clearly manifests the difference which exists between imagination and pure intellection.

I remark besides that this power of imagination which is in one, inasmuch as it differs from the power of understanding, is in no wise a necessary element in my nature, or in (my essence, that is to say, in) the essence of my mind; for although I did not possess it I should doubtless ever remain the same as I now am, from which it appears that we might conclude that it depends on something which differs from me. And I easily conceive that if some body exists with which my mind is conjoined and united in such a way that it can apply itself to consider it when it pleases, it may be that by this means it can imagine corporeal objects; so that this mode of thinking differs from pure intellection only inasmuch as mind in its intellectual activity in some manner turns on itself, and considers some of the ideas which it possesses in itself; while in imagining it turns towards the body, and there beholds in it something conformable to the idea which it has either conceived of itself or perceived by the senses. I easily understand, I say, that the imagination could be thus constituted if it is true that body exists; and because I can discover no other convenient mode of explaining it, I conjecture with probability that body does exist; but this is only with probability, and although I examine all things with care, I nevertheless do not find that from this distinct idea of corporeal nature, which I have in my imagination, I can derive any argument from which there will necessarily be deduced the existence of body.

But I am in the habit of imagining many other things besides this corporeal nature which is the object of pure mathematics, to wit, the colors, sounds, scents, pain, and other such things, although less distinctly. And inasmuch as I perceive these things much better through the senses, by the medium of which, and by the memory, they seem to have reached my imagination, I believe that, in order to examine them more conveniently, it is right that I should at the same time investigate the nature of sense perception, and that I should see if from the ideas which I apprehend by this mode of thought, which I call feeling, I cannot derive some certain proof of the existence of corporeal objects.

And first of all I shall recall to my memory those matters which I hitherto held to be true, as having perceived them through the senses, and the foundations on which my belief has rested; in the next place I shall examine the reasons which have since obliged me to place them in doubt; in the last place I shall consider which of them I must now believe.

First of all, then, I perceived that I had a head, hands, feet, and all other members of which this body—which I considered as a part, or possibly even as the whole, of myself—is composed. Further I was sensible that this body was placed amidst many others, from which it was capable of being affected in many different ways, beneficial and hurtful, and I remarked that a certain feeling of pleasure accompanied those that were beneficial, and pain those which were harmful. And in addition to this pleasure and pain, I also experienced hunger, thirst, and other similar appetites, as also certain corporeal inclinations towards joy, sadness, anger, and other similar passions. And outside myself, in addition to extension, figure, and motions of bodies, I remarked in them hardness, heat, and all other tactile qualities, and, further, light and color, and scents and sounds, the variety of which gave me the means of distinguishing the sky, the earth, the sea, and generally all the other bodies, one from the other. And certainly, considering the ideas of all these qualities which presented themselves to my mind, and which alone I perceived properly or immediately, it was not without reason that I believed myself to perceive objects quite different from my thought, to wit, bodies from which those ideas proceeded; for I found by experience that these ideas presented themselves to me without my consent being requisite, so that I could not perceive any object, however desirous I might be, unless it were present to the organs of sense; and it was not in my power not to perceive it, when it was present. And because the ideas which I received through the senses were much more lively, more clear, and even, in their own way, more distinct than any of those which I could of myself frame in meditation, or than those I found impressed on my memory, it appeared as though they could not have proceeded from my mind, so that they must necessarily have been produced in me by some other things. And having no knowledge of those objects excepting the knowledge which the ideas themselves gave me, nothing was more likely to occur to my mind than that the objects were similar to the ideas which were caused. And because I likewise remembered that I had formerly made use of my senses rather than my reason, and recognized that the ideas which I formed of myself were not so distinct as those which I perceived through the senses, and that they were most frequently even composed of portions of these last, I persuaded myself easily that I had no idea in my mind which had not formerly come to me through the senses. Nor was it without some reason that I believed that this body (which by a certain special right I call my own) belonged to me more properly and more strictly than any other; for in fact I could never be separated from it as from other bodies; I experienced in it and on account of it all my appetites and affections, and finally I was touched by the feeling of pain and the titillation of pleasure in its parts, and not in the parts of other bodies which were separated from it. But when I inquired, why, from some, I know not what, painful sensation, there follows sadness of mind, and from the pleasurable sensation there arises joy, or why this mysterious pinching of the stomach which I call hunger causes me to desire to eat, and dryness of throat causes a desire to drink, and so on, I could give no reason excepting that nature taught me so; for there is certainly no affinity (that I at least can understand) between the craving of the stomach and the desire to eat, any more than between the perception of whatever causes pain and the thought of sadness which arises from this perception. And in the same way it appeared to me that I had learned from nature all the other judgments which I formed regarding the objects of my senses, since I remarked that these judgments were formed in me before I had the leisure to weigh and consider any reasons which might oblige me to make them.

But afterwards many experiences little by little destroyed all the faith which I had rested in my senses; for I from time to time observed that those towers which from afar appeared to me to be round, more closely observed seemed square, and that colossal statues raised on the summit of these towers, appeared as quite tiny statues when viewed from the bottom; and so in an infinitude of other cases I found error in judgments founded on the external senses. And not only in those founded on the external senses, but even in those founded on the internal as well; for is there anything more intimate or more internal than pain? And yet I have learned from some persons whose arms or legs have been cut off, that they sometimes seemed to feel pain in the part which had been amputated, which made me think that I could not be quite certain that it was a certain member which pained me, even although I felt pain in it. And to those grounds of doubt I have lately added two others, which are very general; the first is that I never have believed myself to feel anything in waking moments which I cannot also sometimes believe myself to feel when I sleep, and as I do not think that these things which I seem to feel in sleep, proceed from objects outside of me, I do not see any reason why I should have this belief regarding objects which I seem to perceive while awake. The other was that being still ignorant, or rather supposing myself to be ignorant, of the author of my being, I saw nothing to prevent me from having been so constituted by nature that I might be deceived even in matters which seemed to me to be most certain. And as to the grounds on which I was formerly persuaded of the truth of sensible objects, I had not much trouble in replying to them. For since nature seemed to cause me to lean towards many things from which reason repelled me, I did not believe that I should trust much to the teachings of nature. And although the ideas which I receive by the senses do not depend on my will, I did not think that one should for that reason conclude that they proceeded from things different from myself, since possibly some faculty might be discovered in me—though hitherto unknown to me—which produced them.

But now that I begin to know myself better, and to discover more clearly the author of my being, I do not in truth think that I should rashly admit all the matters which the senses seem to teach us, but, on the other hand. I do not think that I should doubt them all universally.

And first of all, because I know that all things which I apprehend clearly and distinctly can be created by God as I apprehend them, it suffices that I am able to apprehend one thing apart from another clearly and distinctly in order to be certain that the one is different from the other, since they may be made to exist in separation at least by the omnipotence of God; and it does not signify by what power this separation is made in order to compel me to judge them to be different: and, therefore, just because I know certainly that I exist, and that meanwhile I do not remark that any other thing necessarily pertains to my nature or essence, excepting that I am a thinking thing, I rightly conclude that my essence consists solely in the fact that I am a thinking thing (or a substance whose whole or nature is to think). And although possibly (or rather certainly, as I shall say in a moment) I possess a body with which I am very intimately conjoined, yet because, on the one side, I have a clear and distinct idea of myself inasmuch as I am only a thinking and unextended thing, and as, on the other, I possess a distinct idea of body, inasmuch as it is only an extended and unthinking thing, it is certain that this I (that is to say, my soul by which I am what I am), is entirely and absolutely distinct from my body, and can exist without it.

I further find in myself faculties employing modes of thinking peculiar to themselves, to wit, the faculties of imagination and feeling, without which I can easily conceive myself clearly and distinctly as a complete being; while, on the other hand, they cannot be so conceived apart from me, that is without an intelligent substance in which they reside, for)in the notion we have of these faculties, or, to use the language of the Schools) in their formal concept, some kind of intellection is comprised, from which I infer that they are distinct from me as its modes are from a thing. I observe also in me some other faculties such as that of change of position, the assumption of different figures and such like, which cannot be conceived, any more than can the preceding, apart from some substance to which they are attached, and consequently cannot exist without it; but it is very clear that these faculties, if it be true that they exist, must be attached to some corporeal or extended substance, and not to an intelligent substance, since in the clear and distinct conception of these there is sort of extension found to be present, but no intellection at all. There is certainly further in me a certain passive faculty of perception, that is, of receiving and recognizing the ideas of sensible things, but this would be useless to me (and I could in no way avail myself of it), if there were not either in me or in some other thing another active faculty capable of forming and producing these ideas. But this active faculty cannot exist in me (inasmuch as I am a thing that thinks) seeing that it does not presuppose thought, and also that those ideas are often produced in me without my contributing in any way to the same, and often even against my will; it is thus necessarily the case that the faculty resides in some substance different from me in which all the reality which is objectively in the ideas that are produced by this faculty is formally or eminently contained, as I remarked before. And this substance is either a body, that is, a corporeal nature in which there is contained formally (and really) all that which is objectively (and by representation) in those ideas, or it is God Himself, or some other creature more noble than body in which that same is contained eminently. But, since God is no deceiver, it is very manifest that He does not communicate to me these ideas immediately and by Himself, nor yet by the intervention of some creature in which their reality is not formally, but only eminently, contained. For since He has given me no faculty to recognize that this is the case, but, on the other hand, a very great inclination to believe (that they are sent to me or) that they are conveyed to me by corporeal objects, I do not see how He could be defended from the accusation of deceit if these ideas were produced by causes other than corporeal objects. Hence we must allow that corporeal things exist. However, they are perhaps not exactly what we perceive by the senses, since this comprehension by the senses is in many instances very obscure and confused; but we must at least admit that all things which I conceive in them clearly and distinctly, that is to say, all things which, speaking generally, are comprehended in the object of pure mathematics, are truly to be recognized as external objects.

As to other things, however, which are either particular only, as, for example, that the sun is of such and such a figure, etc., or which are less clearly and distinctly conceived, such as light, sound, pain and the like, it is certain that although they are very dubious and uncertain, yet on the sole ground that God is not a deceiver, and that consequently He has not permitted any falsity to exist in my opinion which He has not likewise given me the faculty of correcting, I may assuredly hope to conclude that I have within me the means of arriving at the truth even here. And first of all there is no doubt that in all things which nature teaches me there is some truth contained; for by nature, considered in general, I now understand no other thing than either God Himself or else the order and disposition which God has established in created things; and by my nature in particular I understand no other thing than the complexus of all the things which God has given me.

But there is nothing which this nature teaches me more expressly (nor more sensibly) than that I have a body which is adversely affected when I feel pain, which has need of food or drink when I experience the feelings of hunger and thirst, and so on; nor can I doubt there being some truth in all this.

Nature also teaches me by these sensations of pain, hunger, thirst, etc., that I am not only lodged in my body as a pilot in a vessel, but that I am very closely united to it, and so to speak so intermingled with it that I seem to compose with it one whole. For if that were not the case, when my body is hurt, I, who am merely a thinking thing, should not feel pain, for I should perceive this wound by the understanding only, just as the sailor perceives by sight when something is damaged in his vessel; and when my body has need of drink or food, I should clearly understand the fact without being warned of it by confused feelings of hunger and thirst. For all these sensations of hunger, thirst, pain, etc. are in truth none other than certain confused modes of thought which are produced by the union and apparent intermingling of mind and body.

Index

A

Abilities, sense of, 83–84
Abortion, 103
Absolute certainty, 39, 42–43
Acceptance, 163
Access, privileged, 84, 178
Action(s), 150–151
   freedom of, 122
   voluntary, 114–116, 180
Act-utilitarianism, 150–151, 171
Aesthetics, 4, 171
All-good, God as, 11, 138
Alternative realities, 31–32
American Declaration of Independence,
   164
Analogy, arguments from, 84–85, 171
Anarchy, 171
Animism, 171
Antecedent causation, 13–14, 15
A priori knowledge, 56–58, 171
   Kant on, 57–58
Argument(s), 5, 171
   from analogy, 84–85, 171
   deductive, 7
   from design, 11–13, 179
   diversity, 173
   form of, 5
   inductive, 7
   invalid, 5, 175
   against objective morality, 153–154
   sound, 6, 179
   valid, 5, 6, 180
Aristotle, 24, 27, 115, 181
   Nicomachean Ethics, 185–195
   and virtue, 145–147

Art, philosophy of, 4, 177
Atheist, 171
Atheistic existentialists, 21
Attributes, 24, 171
Authority, government as source of, 163–166
Auxiliary hypotheses, 68–69, 76, 171

B

Basic logic, 5
Behavior, inner causes of, 94–95
Behaviorism, 93–94, 171
Belief(s), 38–39
   building up justified, 45–48
   justification of, 41–43
   picture theory of, 38, 39, 50, 53
   truth of, 39–40
Berkeley, George, 33, 44–45, 50, 71, 181
Big-bang theory, 13, 15, 172
Bodily actions, 33
Body
   and mind, 91
   and same-body theory, 106–107
Brain, 50
   as a computer, 95
   and consciousness, 72–74
   and idealism, 34
   injury or deterioration, 104
   and same-brain theory, 108
Brain events, 91, 93
Bridge laws, 172
Buddha, Gautama, 134, 181
Buddhism, 11, 106

C

Camus, Albert, 21, 181
Care, 153, 172
Categorical imperative, 148–150, 172
Causation, 172
    antecedent, 13–14, 15
    doubts about, 55
Cause and effect, 25–26
Certainty, 172
    absolute, 39, 42–43
Character, continuity of, 110
Characteristics, identifying, 105
Choice, freedom of, 122
Choose, ability to, 117
Christianity, 9
Cogito, sum, 51, 172
Coherence theory of truth, 40, 172
Communism, 172
Compatibilism, 122–123, 172
Compulsion, 115–116, 172
    external, 118
    inner, 118
Computer, brain as, 95
Conclusion(s), 5
    deducing, 47
Confucianism, 11
Conscious experience, 81–86, 93
    features of, 82–84
    knowledge of own, 84
Consciousness
    and brain, 72–74
    objects of, 82, 177
    types of, 38
Consent of governed, 164–165, 172
Contingent, 172
Continuity, 172
    of character, 110
Core self, 105–106
Correspondence rules, 67, 172
Correspondence theory of truth, 39–40, 172
Cosmological argument for existence of God,
        13–16, 172
Covering law model, 172
Created values, and relativism, 153–155
Creationism versus evolution, 75–76
Creator, God as, 10
Culture, 60

D

Dalton, John, 77
Darwin, Charles, 74

Data, 172
Death, life after, 28
Deception, 51
Deduction, 47, 173
Deductive arguments, 7
Deductive logic, 5–7, 42, 47
Deductive-nomological model, 68
Deductive proof, 43
Deep self, 139
Democracy, 167–168, 173
Dependence, problem of, 92
Descartes, René, 181
    on absolute certainty, 39, 42–43
    argument against skepticism, 50, 51–53
    and dualism, 91
    Meditations on First Philosophy, 220–233
    and mind versus matter, 86–87
    on objects of consciousness, 84
    on ontological argument, 16
    on primary qualities, 71
    on rationality, 90
Description, levels of, 95–96
Design, arguments from, 11–13, 171
Desire, 90
Determinism, 119, 173
    hard, 121–122, 174
    objections to, 119–120
    physical, 119–120
    psychological, 120–121, 178
    and responsibility, 121–123
    soft, 122–123, 179
Deterrence, 125, 126, 173
Dialectic, existential, 21
Disputed issues, and philosophy, 2–3
Diversity argument, 173
Divine command, 137–138, 173
Divine idealism, 32–33
Divine right, 163, 167, 173
Dreams, 49–50
Dualism, 91–93, 173
    of properties, 92–93

E

Effect, cause and, 25–26
Einstein, Albert, 69
Emergent properties, 72, 74, 92–93, 173
Empirical, 173
Empirical laws, 66–67, 173
Empiricism, 44–45, 55, 56–57
End in itself, 173
    formula of, 148, 149

*Enquiry Concerning Human Understanding,
An* (Hume), 215–219
Entities
 psychological, 107
 scientific, 30–31
 theoretical, 179
Epiphenomenalism, 93
Epistemology, 4, 173
Error, generalization as form of, 46
Essence, 173
Ethical relativism, 154, 173
Ethics, 4, 173
Euclidean geometry, 26, 57
Everyday reality, versus scientific reality, 70–74
Evidence, 174
Evil, problem of, 17–18
Evolution, 12, 74–75, 174
 as corresponding guarantee, 53–54
 as scientific, 75–76
Existential dialectic, 21
Existentialism, 21, 174
Experience, conscious, 81–86, 93
Extension, 174
External compulsion, 118
External reality, 33, 54
External world, God and, 52–53

F

Faith, 20, 174
Fallacies, 6–7, 174
Feelings, 82
Feminism, 152–153, 174
Fetus, status of unborn, 103
Feuerbach, Ludwig, 18, 181
First-cause argument for existence of God, 13–16
Forms, 28–29, 174
Free action, 114–116
Freedom and responsibility
 commonsense and legal conceptions,
  114–119
 and determinism, 119–123
 and free will, 123–124
 and legal punishment, 125–127
 responsibility, 116–117
 voluntary action, 114–116
Freedom of action, 122
Freedom of choice, 122
Freedom of will, 174
Free will, 17, 120, 123–124, 174
 defenders of, 120, 124
Freud, Sigmund, 106, 181

Friendship, 141
Functionalism, 96, 174

G

Galilei, Galileo, 66, 70, 181
Gaunilo, 16–17, 181
Generalizations, 174
 forming, 46
General will, 174
Geometry, 43
God, 9
 arguments against existence of, 17–19
 arguments for existence of, 11–17
 existence of, 52
 and external world, 52–53
 as human creation, 18–19
 and meaning of life, 20–21
 nature of, 9–11
 or oneness, 29
 promoting will of, 160
 as source of morality, 137–138
Good life
 and close personal relations, 140–141
 maximum satisfaction of wants theory of,
  134–135
 and morality, 137–139
 and religion, 139–140
 and self-interest, 133–136
 and selfishness, 131–133
Governed, consent of, 164–165, 172
Government
 best form of, 166–169
 conflicts between purposes of, 162
 defining, 158–160, 174
 purpose of, 160–162
 as source of authority and legitimacy, 163–166

H

Happiness, 146
Hard determinism, 121–122, 174
Hedonism, 131–132, 174
 psychological, 132, 178
Heidegger, Martin, 86, 106, 181
Herd morality, 154
Higher pleasures, 174
Hinduism, 11
History of philosophy, 5, 174
Hobbes, Thomas, 86, 161, 164, 167, 181
Holy, God as, 11
Human creation theory, 18–19

Hume, David, 12, 44, 45, 55, 181
  Enquiry Concerning Human Understanding,
    An, 215–219
Hypothesis, 46–47, 66, 67, 175
  auxiliary, 68–69, 76, 171

I

Idea, 38, 39–40, 175
  innate, 44, 175
Idealism, 31, 32–33, 175
  arguments against, 33–34
  divine, 32–33
  social, 32, 34
Ideals, 102
Identifying characteristics, 105
Ignorance, 115, 116
Illusions, perceptual, 23
Imperative, categorical, 148–150, 172
Independent reality, 58
Individualism, and relativism, 154–155
Induction, 175
  doubts about, 55–56
Inductive arguments, 7
Inductive logic, 7
Infinite regress, 175
Innate ideas, 44, 175
Inner compulsion, 118
Instrumentalism, 69–70, 73, 175
Intentionality, 88–89, 175
Intentional object, 88–89, 175
Interaction, 91, 92
  questions about, 91–92
Interactionism, 175
Intuition
  moral, 138, 176
  of objective goodness, 138
  rational, 178
Invalid arguments, 5, 175
Islam, 9

J

Judaism, 9
Justification, 41–43, 175
  of morality, 137–139

K

Kant, Immanuel, 16, 30, 181
  on a priori knowledge, 57–58
  and rational rules, 147–150

Khomeini, Ayatollah, 166
Kierkegaard, Sören, 20, 21, 181
Knowledge, 37
  a priori, 56–58, 171
  and belief, 38–39
  and building up justified belief, 45–48
  commonsense conceptions of, 37–43
  and empiricism, 44–45
  and justification, 41–43
  of other minds, 84–85
  of own conscious experience, 84
  and rationalism, 43–44
  relativism about, 58–61
  scientific, 65–70
  and skepticism, 48–56
  theory of, 4, 179
  and truth, 39–41

L

Language, 59–60
  ability to communicate through, 102
  philosophy of, 5, 177
  understanding of, 34
Law(s)
  empirical, 66–67, 173
  natural, 138–139, 176
  of non-contradiction, 32
  scientific, 12, 94
  theoretical, 67, 179
  universal, 148, 149
Legal punishment, 125–127, 175
Legitimacy, government as source of,
    163–166
Leibniz, Gottfried, 43, 92, 182
Liability, strict, 116–117, 179
Liberalism, 175
Libertarianism, 124, 162, 175
Life
  after death, 28
  meaning of, 20–21
Locke, John, 27, 39, 43, 44, 102, 107, 109, 110
Logic, 4, 175
  basic, 5
  deductive, 5–7, 42, 47
  inductive, 7
Love, 140–141

M

Malebranche, Nicolas, 92, 182
Marx, Karl, 18, 161, 182

Marxism, 59
Materialism, 93–96, 101, 176
Mathematical truths, 56
Matter, 25, 176
 versus mind, 86–90
Maximum satisfaction of wants theory of
  good life, 134–135
 and self-development, 135–136
Mead, George, 86, 182
Mean, 176
Meditations on First Philosophy, 220–233
Memory, 110
Mental acts, 82–83, 88, 176
Mental causes, 93
Mental connections, 110
Mental connections theory, 109–111
 problems for, 111
Mental decisions, 120
Mental deficiencies, 118–119
Mental events, 91
Mentally defective humans, 102–103
Mental properties, 87, 92–93
Mental separation, 107
Meritocracy, 168–169, 176
Metaphysics, 4, 24, 176
 of ordinary world, 27
Mill, John Stuart, 151–152, 182
Mind, 81
 and body, 91
 conscious experience, 81–86
 and dualism, 91–93
 and materialism, 93–96
 versus matter, 86–90
 philosophy of, 4, 177
 and same-mind theory, 108–109
Mind substance, 176
Monarchy, 167
Monotheism, 9, 176
Moral intuition, 138, 176
Morality, 137, 176
 arguments against objective, 153–154
 justifications of, 137–139
 motive of, 147–148
 and reason, 149–150
 and self-interest, 136
 universal, 148, 180
Moral philosophy, 4
Moral relativism, 176
Moral theory, 144–145, 176
 and feminism, 152–153
 rational rules in, 147–150
 and relativism, 153–155

Moral theory (*cont'd*)
 and special care, 153
 and utilitarianism, 150–152
 virtue in, 145–147
Motive of morality, 147–148
Multiple personalities, 176
Mystical experiences, 19
Mysticism, 176

N

Natural law, 138–139, 176
Natural science, philosophy of, 4, 177
Natural selection, 12, 75
Nature
 of God, 9–11
 state of, 179
Necessary truths, 176
Negligence, 116, 176
Neuroscience, 107
Newton, Sir Isaac, 69
Nicomachean Ethics (Aristotle), 185–195
Nietzsche, Friedrich, 18, 21, 154, 182
Nominalism, 25, 176
Non-contradiction, law of, 32
Non-resistance, 163, 176

O

Objective goodness, intuition of, 138
Objective morality, arguments against, 153–154
Objectivity, scientific, 76–77
Object of consciousness, 82, 177
Observation, sensory, 66–67
Omnipotence, 10, 177
Omniscience, 10, 177
Oneness, or God, 29
Ontological argument for existence of God, 16–17,
  52, 177
Ontology, 4, 177
Ordinary reality, 23–27
Ordinary world, metaphysics of, 27
Organized domination, 163

P

Pantheism, 29, 177
Paradigm, 76–77, 177
Particulars, 25, 177
Pascal, Blaise, 20, 182
Passage of time, 26–27, 177
Paternalism, 165, 177

Perceiving, conscious, 81
Perception, 33, 95
    sense, 33–34, 38, 43, 44, 45–46, 49, 56
Perceptual illusions, 23
Person(s), 177
    becoming, 103–114
    ceasing to be, 104
    characteristics of, 101–102
    core self of, 105–106
    definition of, 100–101
    identifying characteristics of, 105
    and mental deficiencies, 102–103
    and sense of self, 104–106
    social role of, 105
Personal, God as, 10
Personal identity, 177
    through time, 106–111
Personal relations, close, 140–141
Person-stage, 110
Philosophy
    activity and results, 3
    areas of, 4–5
    of art, 4, 177
    definition of, 1–2
    disputed issues, 2–3
    history of, 5, 174
    of language, 5, 177
    of mind, 4, 177
    moral, 4
    of natural science, 4, 177
    political, 4, 179
    of religion, 4, 177
    social, 4, 179
    of social science, 5, 177
Physical determinism, 119
Physical things, properties of, 70
Picture theory of belief, 38, 39, 50, 53
Plato, 24, 28–29, 37, 136, 165, 182
    Republic, The, 196–214
Political philosophy, 4, 179
Polytheism, 9, 177
Pragmatic theory of truth, 40–41, 178
Premises, 5, 178
Primary qualities, 71, 178
Principle of sufficient reason, 41–42, 178
Privacy, 89, 178
Privileged access, 84, 178
Processes, 83
Properties, 24, 178
    dualism of, 92–93
    emergent, 72, 74, 92–93, 173
    mental, 87, 92–93

Properties (*cont'd*)
    secondary, 88
Protection, 126–127
Psychoanalysts, 106
Psychological determinism, 120–121, 178
Psychological entities, 107
Psychological hedonism, 132, 178
Psychology, 95–96
Punishment, legal, 125–127, 175

Q

Qualities, 24, 178
    primary, 71, 178
    secondary, 71, 72, 178

R

Rational intuition, 178
Rationalism, 42, 43–44, 56, 178
Rationality, 90, 178
Rational rules, 147–150
Reality, 23
    alternative, 31–32
    characteristics of, 24
    external, 33, 54
    and idealism, 32–34
    independent, 58
    ordinary, 23–27
    scientific versus everyday, 70–74
    ultimate, 28–31
Reason, 146
    ability to, 102
    and morality, 149–150
    sufficient, 41–42, 178
Reductionism, scientific, 71–72, 73, 178
Reflex movements, 115
Reform, 126
Relativism, 58, 178
    arguments against, 60–61
    and created values, 153–155
    ethical, 154, 173
    evidence for, 59–60
    extreme and moderate, 58–59
    and individualism, 154–155
    moral, 138, 176
Religion, 139–140
    faith in, 20
    philosophy of, 4, 177
    religious experiences, 19–20
Religious experiences, 19–20
Religious leadership, 166

Representation, 38, 39–40
Republic, The (Plato), 196–214
Responsibility, 116–117, 178
   and determinism, 121–123
Retribution, 125, 178
Romantic love, 140–141
Rousseau, Jean Jacques, 164–165, 182
Rule-utilitarianism, 151, 178

S

Saint Anselm, 16–17, 181
Saint Thomas Aquinas, 11, 14, 181
Same-body theory, 106–107
   problems for, 107
Same-brain theory, 108
   problems for, 108
Same-mind substance theory, 108–109
   problems for, 109
Sartre, Jean-Paul, 21, 106, 182
Scapegoating, 151
Science, 65
   and evolution versus creationism, 74–76
Scientific entities, 30–31
Scientific knowledge, 65–70
Scientific laws, 12, 94
Scientific objectivity, 76–77
Scientific reality, versus everyday reality, 70–74
Scientific reductionism, 71–72, 73, 178
Scientific theories, 67
   testing, 68–69
Secondary properties, location of, 88
Secondary qualities, 71, 72, 178
Self, 105
   core, 105–106
   deep, 139
   sense of, 104–106
   true, 139, 180
Self-conception, 102, 179
Self-development, 133
   and maximum satisfaction of informed wants
      theory, 135–136
Self-existent, God as, 10
Self-interest, 133–136, 179
   and morality, 136
Selfishness, 131–133
Sense perception, 33–34, 38, 43, 44, 45–46, 49, 56
Sensory observation, 66–67
Skepticism, 48–49, 179
   arguments against, 51–54
   arguments for, 49–50
   Hume's, 55–56

Slave morality, 154, 179
Social contract, 136, 164, 179
Social idealism, 32, 34
Social philosophy, 4, 179
Social roles, 105, 179
Social science, philosophy of, 5, 177
Socrates, 152
Soft determinism, 122–123, 179
Solipsism, 32, 34
Soul, 104
Sound argument, 6, 179
Space, 26–27
Spatial-temporal location, 26
Spinoza, Benedict, 29, 43, 182
State of nature, 179
Strict liability, 116–117, 179
Substance, 24–25, 179
Sufficient reason, principle of, 14, 15–16
Syllogism, 6, 47, 179

T

Taoism, 11
Teleological argument for existence of God,
      11–13, 179
Theists, 13, 179
Theocracy, 179
Theoretical entities, 179
Theoretical laws, 67, 179
Theoretical terms, 67
Theory of knowledge, 4, 179
Thing-in-itself, 30, 58, 179
Time, 26–27
   passage of, 177
Transcendent, God as, 10, 180
True self, 139, 180
Truth, 39–41, 180
   coherence theory of, 40, 172
   correspondence theory of, 39–40, 172
   mathematical, 56
   necessary, 176
   pragmatic theory of, 40–41, 178

U

Ultimate reality, 28–31
Unconscious, 180
Universal law, formula of, 148, 149
Universal morality, 148, 180
Universals, 25, 180
Unknowable, 29–30, 57
Utilitarianism, 150–152, 180

V

Valid argument, 5, 6, 180
Value, 90
　relativism and created, 153–155
Variables, 5
Vengeance, 125
Virtue, 146–147, 180
　and Aristotle, 145–147
Voluntary action, 114–116, 180
　responsibility for, 116

W

Wants, satisfying, 133–135
Welfare, general role of government in
　promoting, 165
Whorf, Benjamin, 60, 182
Will, freedom of, 174
Will-to-power, 180
Wittgenstein, Ludwig, 34, 182
Worldview, 180

OTHER BOOKS IN THE HARPERCOLLINS COLLEGE OUTLINE SERIES

ART
History of Art 0-06-467131-3
Introduction to Art 0-06-467122-4

BUSINESS
Business Calculus 0-06-467136-4
Business Communications 0-06-467155-0
Introduction to Business 0-06-467104-6
Introduction to Management 0-06-467127-5
Introduction to Marketing 0-06-467130-5

CHEMISTRY
College Chemistry 0-06-467120-8
Organic Chemistry 0-06-467126-7

COMPUTERS
Computers and Information Processing 0-06-467176-3
Introduction to Computer Science and Programming
    0-06-467145-3
Understanding Computers 0-06-467163-1

ECONOMICS
Introduction to Economics 0-06-467113-5
Managerial Economics 0-06-467172-0

ENGLISH LANGUAGE AND LITERATURE
English Grammar 0-06-467109-7
English Literature From 1785 0-06-467150-X
English Literature To 1785 0-06-467114-3
Persuasive Writing 0-06-467175-5

FOREIGN LANGUAGE
French Grammar 0-06-467128-3
German Grammar 0-06-467159-3
Spanish Grammar 0-06-467129-1
Wheelock's Latin Grammar 0-06-467177-1
Workbook for Wheelock's Latin Grammar
    0-06-467171-2

HISTORY
Ancient History 0-06-467119-4
British History 0-06-467110-0
Modern European History 0-06-467112-7
Russian History 0-06-467117-8
20th Century United States History 0-06-467132-1
United States History From 1865 0-06-467100-3
United States History to 1877 0-06-467111-9
Western Civilization From 1500 0-06-467102-X

Western Civilization To 1500 0-06-467101-1
World History From 1500 0-06-467138-0
World History to 1648 0-06-467123-2

MATHEMATICS
Advanced Calculus 0-06-467139-9
Advanced Math for Engineers and Scientists
    0-06-467151-8
Applied Complex Variables 0-06-467152-6
Basic Mathematics 0-06-467143-7
Calculus with Analytic Geometry 0-06-467161-5
College Algebra 0-06-467140-2
Elementary Algebra 0-06-467118-6
Finite Mathematics with Calculus 0-06-467164-X
Intermediate Algebra 0-06-467137-2
Introduction to Calculus 0-06-467125-9
Introduction to Statistics 0-06-467134-8
Ordinary Differential Equations 0-06-467133-X
Precalculus Mathematics: Functions & Graphs
    0-06-467165-8
Survey of Mathematics 0-06-467135-6

MUSIC
Harmony and Voice Leading 0-06-467148-8
History of Western Music 0-06-467107-7
Introduction to Music 0-06-467108-9
Music Theory 0-06-467168-2

PHILOSOPHY
Ethics 0-06-467166-6
History of Philosophy 0-06-467142-9
Introduction to Philosophy 0-06-467124-0

POLITICAL SCIENCE
The Constitution of the United States 0-06-467105-4
Introduction to Government 0-06-467156-9

PSYCHOLOGY
Abnormal Psychology 0-06-467121-6
Child Development 0-06-467149-6
Introduction to Psychology 0-06-467103-8
Personality: Theories and Processes 0-06-467115-1
Social Psychology 0-06-467157-7

SOCIOLOGY
Introduction to Sociology 0-06-467106-2
Marriage and the Family 0-06-467147-X

Available at your local bookstore or directly from HarperCollins at 1-800-331-3761.